MULTINATIONALS AS MUTUAL INVADERS

MULTINATIONALS AS MUTUAL INVADERS:

INTRA-INDUSTRY DIRECT FORIEGN INVESTMENT

Edited by
ASIM ERDILEK

CROOM HELM
London & Sydney

© 1985 Asim Erdilek

Croom Helm Ltd, Provident House, Burrell Row,
Beckenham, Kent BR3 1AT

Croom Helm Australia Pty Ltd, First Floor, 139 King Street,
Sydney, NSW 2001, Australia

British Library Cataloguing in Publication Data

Multinationals as mutual invaders.
    1. Commerce
    2. International business enterprises
    I. Erdilek, Asim
    382   HF1008

ISBN 0-7099-0935-7

Typeset by Mayhew Typesetting, Bristol, UK
Printed and bound in Great Britain
by Billing & Sons Limited, Worcester.

CONTENTS

Contents

FIGURES AND TABLES

Figures

Tables

To Rolf R. Piekarz

ACKNOWLEDGEMENTS

This volume owes its existence directly to the 22 contributors, whose papers and comments it includes, and indirectly but crucially to the support of two institutions and several persons. I would like to express my thanks to all the contributors as well as to:

(1) Case Western Reserve University (CWRU) for granting me a two-year leave of absence (1981–3) at the US National Science Foundation (NSF), during which I monitored the NSF's Research Programme in International Economic Policy,

(2) the NSF for providing the indispensable financial and organisational assistance for much of the research underlying this volume,

(3) Dr Rolf R. Piekarz of the NSF's Policy Research and Analysis (PRA) Division for sharing, encouraging and guiding my interest in the research on intra-industry direct foreign investment (IDFI), and Drs Eileen L. Collins, Susan Cozzens, Carole E. Kitti, Alan I. Rapoport and Eleanor Thomas of his staff for their generous support.

(4) Minnie H. Mills and Carole Grider of the NSF, Charmion Getter, Carolyne Jones, Cheryl Kominek and Carol Thomas of CWRU for their typing and administrative aid, and Atif Cezairli of CWRU for his research assistance.

MULTINATIONALS AS MUTUAL INVADERS

INTRODUCTION

Asim Erdilek

This volume contains the six papers and twelve comments that were commissioned for and presented at a US National Science Foundation workshop on intra-industry direct foreign investment (IDFI), on 21 April 1983, in Washington, DC. The workshop, which I organised and chaired, was attended by about 70 persons, consisting of academicians, US policy-makers and officials of international organisations. The purpose of the workshop was to examine the analytical, policy-relevant and empirical aspects of IDFI, some of which had been explored earlier by Dunning (1981b), Erdilek (1976, 1982a, 1983), Flowers (1976), Graham (1974, 1978), Hymer and Rowthorn (1970) as well as a few others.

IDFI can be defined as the two-way DFI by multinational enterprises (MNEs), based in different countries, in each other's home markets, to produce goods and services that are close substitutes in either consumption or production, and thus can be classified in the same industry. IDFI is a subset of cross-DFI (CDFI), which can be defined as *total* two-way DFI, with its constituent one-way DFIs occurring in either the same industry or different industries.[1] Clearly, like intra-industry trade, which is an alternative form of market interpenetration across national boundaries, IDFI depends on the 'industry' definition of the statistical classification used. Its empirical significance, when measured in the same way as intra-industry trade, is expected to be inversely proportional to the level of industry disaggregation or the degree of industry homogeneity. This definitional and statistical relativity of IDFI is actually not much more bothersome than that of DFI in general when, for example, we try to distinguish DFI from portfolio foreign investment. Unfortunately, a certain amount of arbitrariness is unavoidable.

IDFI, like intra-industry trade, between the United States and other Western industrialised countries has increased substantially since the early 1970s (Dunning, 1981b). It has become a much more important part of CDFI, which has also risen significantly (OECD, 1981; Erdilek, 1982a).[2] Therefore, IDFI now calls for further theoretical and empirical research which should be assisted by the pioneering studies in this volume.

Both the determinants and effects of IDFI have raised important policy-issues in (1) market structure, competition and antitrust, (2) research (R) and development (D), innovation, technology transfer and diffusion, and (3) foreign trade and DFI, all of which pertain to the current debate on national industrial policies (NIPs).[3] Indeed, some individual developed countries' independently formulated and competitively pursued NIPs may well be checked and frustrated by the global orientation of MNEs that are 'mutual invaders' in those countries. IDFI can not only have a significant influence on the outcomes of NIPs, but also can itself be affected by them. Some countries may well try to exploit IDFI as a means of undermining each others' NIPs, for example, via violations of the national-treatment principle, coupled with claims of extraterritoriality. IDFI can, therefore, be viewed as yet a higher level of economic (as well as political and social) interdependence among Western industrial nations in our time, which seriously complicates the meaning of their individual 'international competitiveness' *vis-à-vis* one another.

Focusing on the possible *effects* of IDFI, we can elaborate the three major areas of public-policy concern mentioned above, in terms of the following questions:

(1) What are the likely effects of IDFI on competition among firms, especially MNEs, and on the implementation of antitrust policies? For example,

   (i) Is IDFI a likely substitute for international cartelisation?

  (ii) Does IDFI reduce industrial market concentration?

 (iii) Do mutual acquisitions (via IDFI) of weak firms (in contrast to green-field investments) by strong ones improve productive efficiency and financial viability of the former or do they increase concentration and reduce competition?

 (iv) What are the problems of reciprocal extraterritoriality created by IDFI with regard to different national antitrust regulations?

(2) What are the likely effects of IDFI on technological positions of firms and industries? For example,

   (i) Does IDFI stimulate or does it hinder world-wide R and D, innovation, technology transfer and diffusion?

  (ii) Under what circumstances does one country gain or lose in industrial development relative to other countries as a result of the IDFI activities of its own MNEs and the foreign-based MNEs?

(3) What are the likely effects of IDFI on the volume, pattern and balance of foreign trade? For example,

(i) If IDFI leads to greater volume of intra-firm (as opposed to inter-firm) trade, does it also reduce the effectiveness of individual DFI-partner countries' trade policies in achieving national (either micro or macro) economic objectives, for example, increases in output, employment and exports?

(ii) Does IDFI, by substituting local production for trade mutually (often under either actual or threatened import restrictions) alleviate either inter-industry or intra-industry (but inter-firm) trade frictions between DFI-partner countries?

(iii) Does IDFI itself distort global production and trade patterns under either market imperfections or government-imposed performance requirements?

I should note, however, that not all serious students of DFI yet agree that IDFI is a particularly significant economic phenomenon deserving of special attention, apart from that accorded seperately and independently to its constituent one-way DFIs. Even a few of the twelve comments included in this volume express a certain degree of scepticism about the theoretical and/or empirical content of IDFI. They tend to view IDFI merely as a corollary to the existing models of DFI in general. They also doubt that it can be easily identified and measured. (Of course, the same could have been said of intra-industry *trade* before it began to receive a decade or so ago what is by now widespread attention. Furthermore, although one-way DFI can be analysed by a firm-level theory only, IDFI by definition involves at least two parent-firms and thus would seem to require an *industry*-level theory as well.) None the less, during the workshop, a consensus emerged that IDFI, like intra-industry trade, especially intra-firm trade, needs to be researched for both academic and public-policy purposes. Of course, the reader should decide this issue for himself or herself on the basis of the analysis and evidence presented here. In any case, this volume should benefit its readers by providing them with greater insight into the still increasing globalisation of industries and interdependence of national industrial policies.

The first two chapters in the volume, by Dunning and Norman and by Rugman, are both primarily concerned with the *determinants* of IDFI in the general analytical framework of international economic involvement. Dunning and Norman offer an elaborate two-dimensional taxonomy of such involvement, following a general-equilibrium approach and utilising Dunning's 'eclectic', that is, ownership-location-internalisation (OLI) theory of DFI as a unifying paradigm. After discussing the analytical relationships between IDFI and other forms of international economic involvement, for example, inter-industry DFI and intra-industry trade, Dunning and Norman speculate that IDFI may be 'the final stage in the evolvement of international economic transactions' and that it, together with its complement intra-firm trade, may 'continue to flourish and grow in significance'.

The two comments, by Vernon and by Krugman, on Dunning and Norman's chapter both articulate fundamental criticisms of the mainly static taxonomic approach. Vernon is critical of that approach for neglecting the dynamic, strategic and oligopolistic aspect of IDFI, that is, the 'sequential behavior of the firm interacting with other firms'. In particular, he stresses the major importance of uncertainty as a motive for IDFI. He also draws attention to significant intra-firm learning-by-doing in the dynamics of inter-firm rivalry. Krugman, on the other hand, criticises the Dunning–Norman approach, first, for deriving the causes of IDFI from its effects (instead of the other way around), and second, for defining IDFI as two-way investment in industries whose products are close substitutes in either consumption or production. Krugman prefers to define IDFI as 'an extension of control' via 'two-way exportation of technological know-how' due primarily to economies of scale and economies of scope. But his definition may be considerably more difficult to operationalise in measuring and modelling IDFI.

Rugman follows, in his chapter, a less general-equilibrium-oriented and more micro (firm-level) approach than that of Dunning and Norman. He treats their location (L) component of the OLI theory as an exogenous country-specific advantage (CSA) and combines the ownership (O) and internalisation (I) components into his firm-specific advantage (FSA). Rugman traces the emergence of both one-way DFI and IDFI, as well as their 'natural companion' intra-industry trade (which, for simplification, he prefers to identify entirely with intra-firm trade), to either natural or government-induced market-imperfections that increase firms' transaction-costs. He presents recent empirical evidence from several industries and countries, for example, MNEs producing pharmaceuticals in Canada, in support of his theoretical analysis.

The first comment on Rugman's chapter is by Kravis who finds neither Rugman's internalisation-based theory nor the dynamic oligopolistic-rivalry theory of IDFI general enough. He argues that a more general theory must explain: (i) the country-location of parent firms, (ii) why parents establish or acquire affiliates, that is, why some firms become MNEs, and (iii) the interactions between home- and host-country characteristics. From these three components (only the second of which Rugman emphasises), he derives four interesting hypotheses — waiting to be empirically tested — about IDFI determinants. In the second comment, Rousslang, too, is critical of Rugman's exogenous treatment of the CSAs and the FSAs. Furthermore, he takes issue with some of Rugman's favourable conclusions on the efficiency and welfare implications of IDFI.

Graham's chapter is concerned primarily with the *effects* of IDFI on market structure and inter-firm rivalry, in terms of the dynamic criterion of product innovation, that is, introduction of new products by rival firms as a time-dependent corporate strategy. He adapts a model previously developed by Scherer (1967, 1980) to an essentially game-theoretic analysis of inter-firm rivalry and IDFI in globally oligopolistic industries. One of them is the tyre industry, which Graham examines in some detail. He also discusses three major public-policy issues of IDFI from the viewpoint of the United States both as a home- and as a host-country.

Hennart's comment focuses on the lack of generality of Graham's game-theoretic analysis of IDFI in terms of oligopolistic rivalry (through 'exchange of threats'). He provides interesting evidence from the history of international business for his criticism. His conclusion that IDFI is 'the sign of increased world-wide rivalry in most industries', is, however, in broad agreement with Graham's analysis. Finan, in his comment, on the other hand, argues that Graham's analysis needs to be sharpened (especially by distinguishing more clearly among alternative modes of overseas market-entry) and qualified in order to deal with the specific issues raised by the IDFI. He emphasises that there can be significant exceptions to Graham's general conclusions, especially as regards the pro-competitive effects of IDFI.

The Nelson and Silvia chapter surveys the largely uncharted and somewhat forbidding territory of the interactions between US *anti-trust* policy and IDFI. Naturally, and perhaps frustratingly, it raises more questions than those it answers. But as such, it provides plenty of potentially rewarding research directions and ideas to those who wish to explore and exploit the territory further.

Hawkin's comment reflects the 'frustrating' nature of Nelson and Silvia's chapter. Hawkins does recognise, however, that Nelson and Silvia are attempting a 'complex and burdensome' analysis in order to shed some light on 'one of the more important unresolved economic policy issues facing the United States'. Nye, on the other hand, directs his comment at elaborating several of the many issues raised by Nelson and Silvia, instead of bemoaning the present lack of definite conclusions. Furthermore, Nye, like Hawkins but in greater detail, emphasises the differences in national antitrust policies across countries as an important element in the analysis of antitrust and IDFI interactions.

McCulloch, in Chapter 5, examines the relationship of IDFI with *foreign trade*. She begins with a critical review of the theoretical frameworks underlying the Dunning–Norman and Rugman chapters. She endorses Rugman's emphasis on internalisation as the primary explanation of IDFI but disagrees with his interpretation of that concept. Her interpretation, treating internalisation as a risk-management strategy, is based more directly on the seminal contribution by Coase (1937). Then, after noting the primarily positive, that is, descriptive approach of the 'eclectic' (OLI) theory which underlies the Dunning–Norman taxonomy, McCulloch offers an alternative taxonomy of her own. She argues that her five-category classification of the stimuli for DFI is more suitable for *normative*, that is, prescriptive analysis. Indeed, she devotes a greater part of her attention to analysis of public-policy issues, especially those pertaining to linkages between DFI and trade (for example, substitutability versus complementarity between them). Her suggestions for future research, however, cover both normative and positive unanswered questions.

Balassa, in his comment, registers his several, primarily empirical disagreements with McCulloch's analysis of DFI and IDFI stimuli. He focuses on IDFI between the United States and the European Economic Community, drawing heavily from his earlier ideas in Balassa (1966), within the framework of dynamic oligopolistic rivalry across national boundaries. Grossman, in his comment, supports McCulloch's analysis on the whole and elaborates further some of her ideas, regarding especially diversification and reduction of uncertainty (via internalisation) as DFI motives. Moreover, he emphasises '. . . the extent to which formal model-building and hypothesis-testing on aspects of DFI have fallen behind more casual modes of theoretical and empirical analysis'.

In the final chapter of the volume, Vukmanic, Czinkota and Ricks take up the problems of *empirical* IDFI analysis, focusing primarily on the imperfections in national and international data. Although their concern is mainly with the US data, they also present a comprehensive survey of non-US data sources. They conclude with several suggestions to improve the collecting and processing of DFI data and to provide researchers with better access to those data.

Lipsey, in his comment, points to several shortcomings, especially omissions of the Vukmanic–Czinkota–Ricks chapter (for example, in the survey of DFI-data sources). Moreover, he is critical of what he considers to be an overemphasis on US-data issues and an unwarranted pessimism about obtaining internationally comparable DFI data. He is also sceptical about some of the recommendations of Vukmanic, Czinkota and Ricks for generating more and better data. Overall, he advocates a much more selective approach to collecting data for studying IDFI. Bale, in his comment, besides repeating some of Lipsey's criticisms, emphasises the administrative and financial constraints that the US Government faces in offering researchers more and better DFI data. He acknowledges that both private researchers and public-policy makers are often frustrated with the imperfections in the official data on DFI. However, he suggests that private-sector (business and labour) resources can make a better contribution to alleviating that frustration.

In conclusion to this introduction, let me again stress the largely *exploratory* nature of the chapters and comments contained in this book. Thus, it is not surprising that there is much on which the 22 contributors disagree with each other. The reader may find this somewhat disconcerting but also rather stimulating. After all, what better evidence could he or she be offered for the existence of a theoretical as well as an empirical research agenda that is worth his or her serious consideration?

Notes

1. Whether CDFI and IDFI are defined as occurring between a given country and the rest of the world (that is, all its DFI-partner countries combined) or between that country and its individual DFI-partners separately does make a difference. Although the former (and broader) definition is symmetrical with the more common definitions used in international trade analysis, much of the discussion in this volume indicates that the latter (that is, bilateral) definition may be more appropriate in many cases for either theoretical or empirical analysis. Whether we like it or not, bilateralism ('reciprocity') in international economic transactions, especially DFI, has increased in importance since the late 1970s.

2. The ratio of the stock of US total inward DFI to the stock of US total outward DFI rose from 18 per cent in 1970 to 45 per cent in 1982. With increased (broadly defined) CDFI, the United States has become the most important

host- as well as home-country in the world, in terms of the absolute sizes of its total inward and outward DFI stocks, respectively.

3. National industrial policy (NIP) is essentially a microeconomic but amorphous concept. It implies less than full confidence in the efficacy of free markets to allocate resources efficiently. It refers to any form of national co-ordination or central allocation of industrial resources under government guidance (incentives or directives) as a means to increasing a country's international competitiveness. NIP is supposed to refurbish ailing old ('sunset') industries ('losers') and nurture ('target') healthy young ('sunrise') industries ('winners'). Thus, it is expected to facilitate an economy's transition from 'low-techology' industrialisation to 'high-technology' industrialisation (that is, to achieve 'reindustrialisation' by 'restructuring').

The interest in NIP is often tied with the concern about the global 'high-technology' race among the United States, the European Economic Community and Japan (*Wall Street Journal*, 1 February 1984, p. 26). NIP connotes a more active and direct government involvement than 'positive adjustment policy' which has been advocated for its members by the Organisation for Economic Cooperation and Development (OECD). In the final analysis, it could be argued that *every* country actually has had either a formal or informal NIP, that is, a set of all the industry-specific actions or *non*-actions in areas such as taxation and subsidisation, antitrust, R and D, trade and DFI.

1 INTRA-INDUSTRY PRODUCTION AS A FORM OF INTERNATIONAL ECONOMIC INVOLVEMENT: AN EXPLORATORY ANALYSIS

John H. Dunning and George Norman

Introduction

This chapter examines some of the determinants of intra-industry international production[1] within the broader context of a unified (or eclectic) paradigm of international economic involvement.[2] First, it presents a typology of inter-country economic transactions. Second, it suggests an analytical framework by which the extent and character of these transactions can be identified and explained. Third, in arguing that intra-industry production has common features with other forms of international commerce — and particularly those of *intra*-industry trade and inter-industry production — it uses a building-block approach to hypothesising about recent trends in this kind of multinational enterprise (MNE) activity (Erdilek, 1982a).

A Taxonomy of International Economic Involvement

To some extent, all typologies reflect the purposes for which they are designed. Our classification of international transactions is no exception. In particular, we shall focus attention on two sets of variables most germane to our interests.

The first is the similarity or difference in the nature of outward and inward transactions of a country. In practice, these range on a continuum from those which are completely independent of each other to those which are completely substitutable for each other.[3] In our analysis, we shall adopt a threefold classification. Inter-industry economic involvement embraces cross-border transactions in different goods,[4] and is substantially, if not solely, based on the unequal distribution of immobile factor endowments. Intra-industry transactions incorporate those in identical or *closely* similar goods, and are based, not on the above criteria, but on the extent to which different locations enable the gains of plant concentration and specialisation, and those arising from the common ownership of multiple activities, to be exploited. Inter-intra industry involvement embraces trade in *broadly* similar goods and reflects some of the characteristics of each of the two other kinds.

The second group of variables relate to the mode or organisation of the transactions used by economic agents.[5] These also vary along a continuum ranging from arm's-length transactions conducted in the spot market to internal transactions within the same organisation. Again, we shall illustrate the two extremes and one intermediate mode, namely, contract or co-operative transactions. These latter embrace such arrangements as subcontracting, management agreements, franchising, licensing, etc. They incorporate some of the features of the market, for example, they are conducted between independent parties; and some of those of hierarchies, for example, there may be some influence or control exerted by one of the parties over the other. The above classification suggests a 3 × 3 matrix and this is set out in Table 1.1.

Each of the nine cells illustrated may be further divided into subcells. In Table 1.1 we have identified two additional criteria. One measured vertically, relates to *what* is traded. Here, we make the distinction between assets, and/or asset rights and products (which may range from intermediate to final commodities and services). For example, foreign production involves the intra-firm transfer of assets (capital) and asset rights (technology),[6] while spot market trade embraces off-the-shelf transactions in products between independent firms at arm's-length prices. The second criterion — measured horizontally — is the trading environment. This consists both of the market structure in which goods and assets are internationally transacted (for example, number of firms, product differentiation, barriers to entry, etc.); and the extent and form of non-market (for example, government) intervention. While we shall acknowledge that these market imperfections may influence the transactions classified to any one of our nine cells, we shall consider these explicitly only in so far as they affect the two main classifications.

An Analytical Framework for Evaluating the Determinants of the Different Forms of International Economic Involvement

Using the typology of Table 1.1, it is possible both to group international transactions into the categories commonly discussed in the

Table 1.1: A Typology of Two-way International Economic Transactions

Organisation of Transactions

Spot Markets → Contracts → Hierarchies

Composition of Transactions		Spot Markets Perfect → Imperfect Comp.	Contracts Perfect → Imperfect Comp.	Hierarchies Perfect → Imperfect Comp.
Inter-industry	Assets →	**A** Arm's-length transactions No cross-hauling Portfolio Investment	**B** Contract transactions No cross-hauling (e.g. of similar kinds of technology) Licensing, management contracts, etc.	**C** Internalised transactions See general theories of DFI and international production Direct foreign investment JVs → 100%
	Products →	H-O-S Neo-factor trade Neo-technology product-cycle trade	Subcontracting (See explanations of Watanabe et al.)	Intra-firm trade
Inter-intra-industry	Assets →	**D** Some cross-hauling of broadly similar assets/products	**E** As above (see explanations of Lall, Telessio, Contractor, Alchian and Demsetz et al.)	**F** Moving towards plant specialisation within hierarchies Vertical and horizontal direct foreign investment
	Products →	Mixture of H-O-S trade — (Burenstam-Linder, Dreze, Gray, Krugman, Barker explanations)		Intra-firm trade (Helleiner and Lavergne, Lall)
Intra-industry	Assets →	**G** Cross-hauling of identical or closely similar assets/	**H** Cross-hauling of identical or closely similar assets/products Some control/influence exerted in contract Cross-licensing, e.g. in chemical industry	**I** Importance of economies of synergy and transaction-cost minimising (See explanations of Williamson, Caves, Teece, Casson, etc.) Horizontal direct foreign investment MNE oligopolies Intra-firm trade
	Products →	(Dreze et al. and Grubel & Lloyd, Brander, Finger, Hesse et al. explanations) Trading Oligopolies	Cross-subcontracting as in auto industry	

literature and to suggest an analytical framework for identifying their determinants.[7] Table 1.2 sets out these characteristics using the framework of the eclectic paradigm of international involvement (Dunning 1981a). This asserts that the extent, structure and form of a nation's international economic involvement will depend first on the endogenous competitive advantages of its firms relative to those of other nationalities — the so-called ownership (O)-specific advantages; second on the structure of its own resource endowments and other characteristics exogenous to its firms, for example, consumer needs and tastes, market structure, government policy, etc. — the so-called location (L)-specific advantages — and third on the organisation of international transactions, and, in particular, the advantages of administering these transactions within the same firm, that is, internalisation (I) advantages, rather than using external markets. Although the OLI framework of analysis has so far been used mainly to explain one-way foreign production, there is no reason why it should not be used to explain other forms, and the totality, of a nation's international involvement.

At a micro level, for a firm to export to or produce in a foreign country, it must generate output from assets which it is able to acquire and utilise at least as, if not more, successfully than its competitors. The literature identifies two kinds of assets, namely, those which are immobile in their use, for example, land, and those which are spatially transferable, for example, technology and most kinds of human capital. It also distinguishes between assets which are exclusive or proprietary to their owners, and those which are accessible to all economic agents. The former are referred to as ownership (O)-specific assets.[8]

For trade in goods to take place, there must be some reason for assets to be used in a country other than that in which their outputs are consumed. In some cases, trade is solely determined by the geographical disposition of location (L)-specific but non-exclusive assets, in others, by a mixture of L- and O-specific assets. But it is also axiomatic that these assets are employed by the firms which own or acquire them, for example, O advantages are internalised rather than leased to foreign firms.

However, since mobile assets do not need to be exploited in their country of origin, other forms of involvement might be preferred to trade in the products embodying them. In particular, two options may be possible. First, the rights to these assets may be sold on the spot market or by contract to foreign firms. Alternatively, their export may be internalised via DFI. But in some cases, there may be no market for

Table 1.2: Two-way International Economic Transactions: Significance of OLI Determinants (Some illustrations)

	Spot Markets (Perfect → Imperfect Comp.)		Contracts (Perfect → Imperfect Comp.)	Hierarchies (Perfect → Imperfect Comp.)
	Perfect	Imperfect Comp.	Imperfect Comp.	Imperfect Comp.
Inter-industry — Assets →	$OaOt^0$ L^+ I^0	Oa^* Ot^0 L^{***} I^0	$Oa{\rightarrow}^{***}$ $Ot^0{\rightarrow}$ $L^*{\rightarrow}^{***}$ $I^0{\rightarrow}^*$	$O^{**}{\rightarrow}^{****}$ Ot^0 L^{***} $L^*{\rightarrow}^{***}$
Inter-intra-industry — Assets →		Oa^* $Ot^0{\rightarrow}^*$ $L^*{\rightarrow}$ I^0	$Oa{\rightarrow}^{***}$ $Ot^0{\rightarrow}$ $L^*{\rightarrow}$ $I^0{\rightarrow}^*$	Oa^{**} $Ot{\rightarrow}^{***}$ L^* I^{***}
Intra-industry — Assets →		Oa^* Ot^* $L^*{\rightarrow}^{***}$ I^0	$Oa^*{\rightarrow}^{***}$ $Ot{\rightarrow}^{***}$ L^* I^*	$Oa{\rightarrow}^{***}$ $Ot^{**}{\rightarrow}^*$ L^* $I^{**}{\rightarrow}^{***}$

Notes:

0	=	zero influence
$+$	=	exclusive influence
$*s$	=	degree of influence between 0 and +
Oa	=	asset advantage of ownership
Ot	=	transactions advantage of ownership (including scale economies)
L	=	location advantage
I	=	internalisation advantage

O-specific advantages. This is likely to be so wherever these advantages rest not in the possession of a particular asset, that is, what have been called asset or production cost advantages (Dunning, 1983; Teece, 1983), but on the ability of a firm to organise multiple assets and intermediate products in a more efficient or less risky way than if they were organised under separate ownership. This capability has been referred to as governance-efficiency of interdependent activities or transaction-cost minimising advantages (Teece, 1983).

Given the presence and geographical distribution of O- and L-specific assets, and the nature of the international market for them, the extent and form of international economic involvement will depend on a variety of contextual variables, notably country-, industry- and firm-specific characteristics. But normalising for these variables, one may imagine two extreme situations. One is typified by a Heckscher-Ohlin-Samuelson (H-O-S) world (see Cell A in Tables 1.1 and 1.2) in which all transactions are conducted in perfect spot markets; there is no government intervention; goods are homogenous and consumer tastes are similar between countries. In this situation, all inter-country transactions will be inter-industry and based upon the distribution of L-specific but non-exclusive assets. At the other extreme, all transactions may be conducted within multinational hierarchies (see Cell I). Here, although immobile and non-specific assets may influence the location of economic activity, it is the distribution of mobile and specific O assets that are likely to be fashioned by the desire to exploit advantages from the common ownership of separate activities. Since, too, the largest MNEs are usually oligopolists, their behaviour, for example, with respect to the inter-penetration of national markets, will also be influenced in this direction.

In between these two extremes, we illustrate seven situations which depict a variety of OLI configurations. But as one moves from the left to right in the matrix in Tables 1.1. and 1.2, risk minimising and other internalising advantages become more important. This simply reflects a growing inability of markets to transact goods efficiently, and the importance of transaction-cost minimising O advantages, relative to L advantages, as a determinant of a nation's competitiveness. Similarly, as one moves downwards from top to bottom of any three columns in Table 1.1, the more important transferable O-specific advantages relative to immobile and non-specific L advantages become in influencing the international disposition of economic activity.

In this chapter, we are especially interested in one particular kind of economic involvement, namely, intra-industry production. How does one explain cross-hauling of similar goods via the foreign production of MNEs of different nationalities? In terms of the matrix in Table 1.1, we wish to explain the determinants of that part of Cells F and I dealing with production (via internalised asset-transfer) rather than intra-firm trade of goods (Cells D and G). However, as we shall argue, there are common characteristics between this and other forms of international involvement and these also require consideration. Indeed, we shall hypothesise that intra-industry production is determined by both those forces making for international economic involvement in general and those specific to (a) hierarchical rather than market transactions and (b) trade in similar rather than different products.

Explaining International Production and Other Forms of International Involvement: The Matrix Analysed

Inter-industry Transactions (Cells A, B and C)

Through Spot Markets (Cell A). Various theories of trade and asset (or rights) transference may be used to explain these arm's-length transactions. The former range from H-O-S type theories, which assume a situation of pure competition in the goods markets, through neo-factor to neo-technology theories which embrace some degree of market imperfection.

One common feature of these approaches is that they are all variants of the factor-endowment explanation of trade, and allow no exogenous intervention, for example, by government. They also implicitly assume zero risk in international transactions. Trade is presumed to arise as each nation seeks to exploit the resources in which it is relatively well-endowed, and which are assumed to produce goods different from those produced by resources in which they are relatively disadvantaged.

Similarly, transactions in assets or asset-rights may be conducted in the spot market. Although historically this has mainly taken the form of portfolio investment, some kinds of technology and managerial skills might have transferred in this way; the import and export of these is also assumed to reflect the disposition of factor endowments.

In such a situation, the allocation of L-specific assets primarily determines cross-border flows. In the H-O-S and neo-factor theories it exclusively determines such exchanges. In the neo-technology model, some O-specific advantages are acknowledged, in so far as it is accepted that technology may be proprietary to particular enterprises. However, it is also implicitly assumed that either the technology is embodied in end-products which are sold in nearly perfect markets, or that technological rights are sold in such markets. There is no acknowledgement of internal markets. In the H-O-S world, one may reasonably presume that firms engage in single activities and that no O advantages from externalities in production- or transaction-cost economies. It is also worth noting that inter-industry trade and portfolio investment can be either substitutable or mutually reinforcing.

Through Contracts or Quasi-markets (Cell B). Contracts may replace spot markets whenever some kind of market failure exists. Let us illustrate by taking risk as symptom of such failure. Two kinds of risk might be considered. First, there is that associated with supply of inputs. Firms are concerned with regularity, quality and price of their purchases, and may wish to engage in long-run contracts with suppliers which protect themselves against the vagaries of a spot market. Second, firms may wish to engage in forward-risk minimisation to protect themselves against external consumers of intermediate products or asset-rights doing anything to lessen the goodwill of the supplier or the continuity of demand for his output. They suggest some degree of exclusivity in a trading relationship, and, from the contractor's viewpoint, some O advantages (for example, product quality) which he wishes to protect.

Contract-trade in goods is likely to be confined to one of a kind or idiosyncratic transactions for which there are no or highly imperfect spot markets, yet where it is comparatively easy to arrive at mutually acceptable terms of exchange. Contract-asset or asset-rights transactions will occur where O advantages are fairly explicit, for example, take a codified form like patents, formulae, blueprints, design specifications, trademarks, etc. yet where the contractor believes he can fully appropriate the economic rent on his assets, and protect himself against the vagaries of the market.[9] Contract-asset transactions will not occur when the main O advantages of the firms lie in the economies of synergy of interdependent activities.

In determining the international allocation of contract-related activities, the distribution of mobile and intangible O assets is likely to pay a more important role than in spot market transactions. But, since the origin of at least some of these assets is itself likely to be country-specific, neo-classical trade and investment theory may still be relevant. Again, in the absence of government intervention, contract trade and factor flows may be either substitutable or mutually reinforcing. It is also worth noting that quasi-market transactions have been rapidly increasing in the last decade; indeed, some commentators

(Billerbeck and Yasugi, 1979) have argued that activities supported by such non-equity resource transfers ought to be treated as a form of international production.

Within Hierarchies (Cell C). All cross-border transactions within hierarchies suggest that there are ownership linkages between the individual production units. This, in turn, implies an investment equity stake by the parent company sufficient to allow it some overall control of influence over decision-making. At one extreme, asset and intermediate-product markets may be completely replaced by internalised transactions. For MNE hierarchies to exist, they must possess O advantages sufficient to overcome the entry barriers of competing with local producers. For single-product-activity MNEs, these arise from the possession of property rights which cannot be fully appropriated via the spot or contract market, and which the firms prefer to combine with at least some L assets in a foreign location. For multi-activity MNEs producing in several countries, there are other benefits — external to any one activity but internal to the firm — associated with transaction-cost economising. Such assets have no external market.

DFI as a form of international economic involvement may sometimes substitute for trade in goods. This will occur where it becomes economical to relocate the use of O-specific but mobile assets as foreign markets expand; or it may be induced by non-market forces, for example, import controls. In other cases, foreign production might increase both imports and exports (which could be either intra- or inter-firm) or replace inter-firm by intra-firm trade. Indeed, intra-firm production is a prerequisite for intra-firm trade; but intra-firm inter-industry trade is likely to be limited to inter (and one-way) industry production.

Inter-industry hierarchical transfers of assets are broadly of two kinds. The first leads to vertical production. This will occur where the gains from contract transactions are insufficient to overcome the costs of market failure earlier identified. The second leads to horizontal production when firms that produce abroad replicate what they are producing domestically; here, the market failure is usually associated with the transfer of asset-usage, for example, trademarks and licenses. The gains include the protection of proprietary rights, and the monitoring of quality control (Casson, 1982), the risks and costs of which will reduce the appropriation of economic rent.

We have suggested that inter-industry production may be trade-creating or trade-replacing. By pursuing import substitution, governments may replace imports by home production. They do this by tilting L-specific advantages in their favour. But, in consequence, they often cause firms to replace an external flow of one kind of transaction by an internal flow of another, that is, they affect the organisation of non-resident economic involvement. These measures are more likely to impinge on the totality and balance of transactions rather than on their composition. However, discriminatory intervention may affect the composition of transactions in two ways. First, it might encourage self-sufficiency and support convergence in economic activity between countries. Second, it might steer inward DFI to those sectors in which the investing firms have O advantages and the recipient country has an L advantage, while promoting outward DFI in those sectors in which indigenous firms have O advantages while the investing country has an L advantage. It is sometimes claimed that Japanese DFI meets these criteria while its US counterpart, promoted for defensive oligopolistic reasons, is of the trade-replacing kind (Kojima, 1978). While this is a simplistic view, it may be reasonably predicated that the nature and degree of market imperfections in the final-goods market will influence the character of international production and its relationship with other forms of transactions.

Inter-intra-industry Transactions (Cells D, E and F)

Through Spot Markets (Cell D). Except where goods are perfect substitutes for each other, the division between inter- and intra-industry transactions is bound to be arbitrary in two respects. First, there is no definitive criterion by which products or activities may be grouped. Sometimes it is by their technical or supply characteristics, sometimes by their substitutability in consumption. Second, the degree of fineness of the classification obviously affects the extent of intra-industry trade; the broader the concept of an industry, the higher the intra-industry trade ratio is likely to be.

The rationale for spot market inter-intra-industry transactions may derive from the disposition of immobile factor endowments, and so be explainable by some variant of the H-O-S model. Alternatively, it may be derived from a similarity in income levels and consumption patterns, or economies of specialisation of economic activity based upon factors other than those associated with the cost and availability of factor endowments.

In the literature, two types of inter-intra-industry trade are usually distinguished. We shall consider each of these in turn. The first type, *vertical* trade, arises whenever intermediate goods at sequential stages of production are classified in the same industry and there is trade between them. Such trade is assumed to be partly based on different factor intensities, that is, is of the H-O-S or neo-technology type, and partly to arise as a result of plant specialisation and scale economies within such sectors (Krugman, 1981). These suggest that national markets are of limited size and such economies can only be gained if output is spatially concentrated.

As with other types of trade, vertical inter-intra-industry trade flourishes in the absence of tariffs and other artificial barriers. Depending on the opportunities for cost reduction, it tends to be particularly sensitive to such barriers. There are certainly market imperfections as firms are faced with downward sloping demand curves; and, there may be others due to the exclusive possession of mobile O assets. Spot market transactions, however, imply that there are no economies of interdependence between asset usage.

The second type of inter-intra-industry trade, *horizontal* trade, is of two kinds. The first is where there is substitutability in production but not in consumption. In this case, the technical characteristics of the final products are similar, but they serve different groups of consumers. Examples include large-engine and small-engine cars. At one end of the scale, these meld with genuine intra-industry trade to gain cost advantages through plant specialisation; at the other, they reflect different L-specific advantages of countries or O advantages of firms which may strongly reflect their country of origin. Like specialisation, based on vertical trade, in the spot market, such inter-intra-industry trade flourishes in unrestricted markets; however, as consumer tastes may not be uniform across national boundaries, the characteristics of individual markets may play a more important role than vertical trade.

The second kind of horizontal inter-intra-industry trade arises where the production of the goods in question requires different technologies and factors of production, but where the goods themselves are fairly close substitutes in consumption, for example, leather and rubber shoes, nylon and cotton shirts, wooden and plastic chairs. As an explanation of this kind of trade, the disposition of factor endowments probably assumes a more important role; indeed, not only may goods be traded across countries, but between different firms in the same countries. Yet, sometimes there may be an element of complementarity in production, such that the groups of products demand similar inputs, an obvious example being marketing. Therefore, O-specific advantages that relate to transaction-cost economising might move in the opposite direction to L-specific advantages.

Through Contracts (Cell E). The motives for engaging in contract trans-actions in goods and asset-usage are similar to those in the case of inter-industry transactions, but the nature of market imperfections may be different. While the desire to minimise the risks of supply instabilities may dominate contract inter-industry trade, quality control aspects are more likely to be important in its inter-intra equivalent. In this case, the O advantages enjoyed by the contractor are likely to be in the area of codifiable knowledge, while the contractee gains access to the markets of the contractor. In cases of shifting L advantages away from the country of the contractor to that of the contractee, and in later stages of the product cycle, process and marketing technology may be a more important ingredient of competitiveness.

It is a comparatively short step from subcontracting in goods to licensing and management contracts, where mobile-asset usage is being traded. Again, O advantages are assumed to relate to a specific item of proprietary knowledge rather than the governance of interrelated activities. However, unlike inter-industry transactions, these may be more *firm-* than country-specific, that is, have to do with size, strategy, degree of multinationalisation, etc. rather than a favoured access to country-specific mobile resources, for example, certain types of techno-logy and management skills' or to markets. Asset contracts may com-plement or substitute for contract or spot market trade. Government intervention both to reduce imports and to avoid hierarchical asset-transfer might lead to an increase in import-substituting asset contracts. Such measures, however, are more likely to be directed to improving the L advantages of host countries rather than to encouraging plant specialisation economies, which thrive under conditions of free inter-national commerce.

Through Hierarchies (Cell F). Inter-intra-industry foreign production may be of three kinds. The first kind, import-substituting production, is host country market-oriented, and involves the substitution of horizontal-trade type imports by local production via DFI. In this case, it is assumed that there is cross-hauling of production, without cross-hauling of final products. Such cross-hauling will be particularly likely in the case of firms competing in international oligopolistic markets and where location strategies dictate the interpenetration of terri-tories. The second kind, vertical production, is complementary with inter-industry trade and embraces the exploitation of immobile endow-ments of countries by non-resident firms, where, because of market failure, subcontracting or licensing does not allow the economic rent of their O-specific assets (or rights) to be fully appropriated. The third kind, rationalised production, occurs whenever firms are multi-activity oligopolists and can benefit from the co-ordination of related but separate activities across national boundaries. Because there is no market for this kind of function, outside the firm providing it, it has to be internalised.

The third kind of inter-intra-industry foreign production is partly an extension of the first kind, where the internalising economies arise from the externalities to which the separate activities gave rise; and, partly it is an extension of the activities associated with multi-product firms, which find it to their advantage to locate the output of different activities in different places. As suggested earlier, the criteria for locating the horizontal distribution of activity may be less obvious than that of the H-O-S kind; yet patterns of consumer tastes, size of markets, income levels, technological capacity and government regulations may all play their part. The reason why US consumers prefer large cars and European consumers small cars is a case in point. But the kind of cross-hauling by companies like Philips Eindhoven typifies the horizontal inter-intra-industry trade; and, this is internalised under common ownership because of the additional plant economies (centralised purchasing, market control, spreading of R and D, etc.) which makes it worth while. The rationalisation of IBM, although in terms of inter-mediate rather than final products, comes even closer to pure intra-industry trade.

Such inter-intra-industry production is directly complementary to intra-firm trade and rests on the practicability of inter-country plant specialisation and the failure of external markets to organise trans-actions involving interdependent activities. It tends to be closely related to the extent of an enterprise's multinationality and to evolve out of the first two kinds of foreign production. Indeed, the growth of the common ownership of assets across national boundaries, by facilitating the rationalisation of the production, marketing and inventory control of similar products or processes in different countries, may well have been one of the most important forces in the expansion of inter-intra-industry trade. In the mid-1970s, intra-firm trade accounted for between 35 per cent and 40 per cent of all trade in industrial plants of OECD countries, outside Japan (Dunning, 1981a); and, the greater part of this was in sectors in which intra-industry trade is above average (Helleiner and Lavergne, 1980).

Intra-industry Transactions (Cells G, H and I)

Through Spot Markets (Cell G). At the opposite extreme to H-O-S type transactions are those in identical or almost identical goods, that is, which are substitutable both in production and in consumption. Theoretically, unless one assumes zero transfer-costs, there can be no such trade under conditions of atomistic competition. Allowing for differences in the production functions of firms, or for economies of scale, it is possible to conceive of one-way trade. But for two-way trade, one has to accept a different kind of country-specific O advantages, for example, those that relate to product quality, brand image, advertising, packaging, etc. and the willingness of firms to penetrate each other's markets, in spite of the additional transfer and other costs involved (Hirsch, 1976). This is most likely to be the case where the international market structure is oligopolistic, and constituent firms prefer to produce in each other's territories rather than adopt an alternative strategy.[10]

Once one permits some degree of product differentiation, the possibilities for intra-industry trade are enlarged. This suggests a desire for variety on the part of the consumer. It also suggests that the trademark-type O advantages of firms between countries give rise to products for which there is at least some demand in foreign markets. It is a typical monopolistic competition situation where a consumer in one country is willing to purchase not only domestic goods, but also product variants produced in other countries. Indeed, in smaller industrialised countries, export markets may dominate the pattern of product innovation.

It is not difficult to spell out the conditions in which spot market intra-industry trade is most likely to occur. These include:

(a) The stronger the opportunities for scale economies in the production and marketing of the goods traded,

(b) the lower the transport costs and other barriers (for example, psychic distance),

(c) the greater the scope for product differentiation and the promotion of brand images, but where the O advantages associated with such competitive weapons are spread across producing countries.

(d) An absence of government intervention in trade flows between countries.

(e) A broad similarity of consumer tastes (for example, for cigarettes rather than particular types of cigarettes).

Such trade is likely to occur between countries of similar economic characteristics, and to become relatively more important as and when the levels of income, structures of resource endowment and market structures converge, tastes become internationalised and barriers to trade are reduced. The activities of MNEs, by their tendency to engage in inter-country plant specialisation, lead to a similar result. Hence the great increase in this form of international involvement in Europe since 1957.

Intra-industry spot trade partly reflects the country-specific ownership characteristics of enterprises and partly those related to their size, product range, etc. It also mirrors some differences in resource endowments and consumer tastes making for different forms of product differentiation. Again, however, it is assumed that markets for the goods traded are reasonably perfect and that O advantages of firms arise from asset efficiency and from that part of transactions efficiency related to scale economies. The asset disposition will be made on similar criteria as the above, but intra-industry trade may not necessarily imply intra-industry asset flows. For example, South Korea both exports and imports automobiles but only imports technology for automobile production.

Contracted Trade or Asset Flows (Cell H). Everything written about contracted trade for inter-intra-industry trade applies in the case of intra-industry trade. There is, however, unlikely to be as much subcontracting of goods *per se*, but a good deal of cross-licensing, at both firm and industry level where knowledge is codifiable. Many inter-country technology transfers in the chemical and motor vehicle industries are of this kind, particularly where there are constraints on DFI (for example, Japan and South Korea in the 1970s). Again, contracted trade or asset-usage is likely to be dominated by large firms. It may be complementary to other forms of international involvement, including intra-industry production. Certainly, there is a good deal of cross-licensing and subcontracting in the European automobile industry, although the assembling firms are mainly owned or controlled by MNEs.[11]

A good example of intra-industry contractual asset flows leading to spot market (invisible) trade flows is the international hotel industry. UK hotel chains conclude management contracts with US hotels, which earn foreign currency for the United States from foreign tourists; while US chains conclude management contracts with UK hotels, which similarly benefit the United Kingdom. But contract intra-industry asset flows might also be a defensive response to trade and investment curbs, that is, of an import-substituting kind. Such flows reflect the geographical spread of O-specific assets, which are best exploited via non-equity foreign involvement because of the location of immobile assets. In this respect, at least, there is a parallel with *inter*-industry contractual transactions.

Intra-industry Production (Cell I). A casual inspection of the extent and structure of international production today suggests that:

(a) It is quite highly concentrated: the top 5 per cent of companies undertaking DFI account for about 80 per cent of such production.

(b) Within manufacturing industry, 75 per cent of such production is undertaken by firms from and located in the advanced industrialised countries; and of this amount, about 80 per cent is within sectors in which inter-intra-industry or intra-industry trade is above average.

(c) Several industries are largely dominated by MNEs which also account for the bulk of both inter- and intra-firm trade. At the same time, there is some evidence that industrial concentration ratios among the leading MNEs is falling (Dunning and Stopford, 1983).

(d) In the 1970s, the composition of inward and outward DFI among industrialised nations has become more similar (Dunning, 1981b). Moreover, intra-industry production has increased relative to inter-industry production. It seems not unreasonable to suppose that these movements will continue in the 1980s as some countries, which already engage in a great deal of intra-industry spot trade and contract transactions, for example, Japan, increase their MNE activity.

(e) At least as far as industrialised or industrialising countries are concerned, there is some suggestion that a modified form of the investment development cycle (Dunning, 1981a) might help explain the evolvement of international commerce from inter-industry trade and one-way DFI to intra-industry trade and finally intra-industry production. This last stage of the cycle is reached when:

(1) MNEs emanate from several countries, and are multi-product and geographically diversified.

(2) Similar goods and services are produced in these countries.

(3) The O advantages of the MNEs are based less on country-specific than on firm-specific characteristics and have more to do with transaction-cost minimising than asset (including innovatory) efficiency.

(4) There is reasonably free trade between countries.

Let us concentrate on this latter set of issues. Essentially there are two kinds of intra-industry production. The first is where such production is a direct substitute for intra-industry trade. Where, for example, there is inter-penetration of markets by oligopolists engaging in trade in similar products, and trade controls are imposed by both the exporting and the importing governments, than import-substituting production may replace trade. However, this is unlikely to occur if the original *raison d'être* for the intra-industry trade is to exploit the internal economies of plant specialisation. In such cases, a dispersion of plants may not be economical, and increased production for the home market by indigenous firms may replace inter-market penetration. However, in oligopolistic conditions, firms may seek to protect *existing* markets, in spite of loss of advantages of specialisation; but more to the point, where the O-specific advantages of MNEs lie not in the production economies of individual plants but in the co-ordination of activities under common ownership, then international production may still be profitable.

There are other reasons for expecting intra-industry production to arise when the goods being transacted are almost perfect substitutes in production and consumption. Such products are unlikely to exist in the early stages of the product cycle. Consequently, O advantages are liable to be firm-specific and related to factors such as product differentiation, brand image and marketing expertise.

In such industries, DFI is likely to arise as an oligopolistic defence against (or in anticipation of) rivals' actions that undermine the profitability (and feasibility) of market servicing by exports (Knickerbocker, 1973). The market conditions that are likely to lead to cross-hauling of assets rather than goods can be identified by using a variant of the model developed by Norman (1983). Essentially, the more geographically diversified are producers of a particular product group, the greater the proportion of transfer costs any one producer will have to absorb in order to be able to export to distant markets. Therefore, the weaker are economies of scale or the lower are additional costs of setting up a foreign operation, and the greater are the transfer costs (including tariff and non-tariff barriers) between home and distant markets, the greater will be the incentive to switch from exporting to foreign production.

It can further be argued that barriers to entry into a particular industry are likely to be lower:

(1) in large markets;

(2) in markets characterised by a sophisticated economic and social environment;
(3) for products produced from a reasonably standardised technology.

Where these conditions are met, it will be more difficult for MNEs from any one country to control the entry of firms from other countries producing substitute products embodying similar technologies. As a result, oligopolistic uncertainty will increase, as will the incentive to serve foreign markets by international production (Casson and Norman, 1983).

The other type of intra-industry production arises through the integration of multi-product but geographically diversified activities. It leads to plant specialisation via DFI *and* to intra-firm trade. It requires all the conditions of intra-industry spot trade *plus* the advantages (as perceived by the firm) of joint ownership of productive activities. For example, ten firms under separate ownership could be producing a similar but not identical refrigerator in ten countries and exporting to the other nine. Alternatively, the ten firms could be under common ownership, in which case if the trading pattern continued to be the same, there would be cross-hauling of international production.

Such rationalisation may occur under two sets of conditions. The first is whenever the internalisation of asset and trade flows (for example, through acquisition) improves the efficiency of plants or leads to extra-plant economies to the firm. These latter include economies of R and D, product differentiation, market rationalisation, purchasing, organisation, financing as well as those of risk diversification. The more the boundaries of firms are pushed out, the more such economies — which are essentially *firm-* rather than *country*-specific — become important. There is also reason to suppose that multinationality produces its own particular internalising economies, including those arising from government-induced market failures.

Such internalising economies may have two effects. First, they may lead to greater efficiency of resource allocation by lowering transaction costs. But secondly, and in common with the first type of intra-industry production, firms may try to control assets overseas for strategic reasons, or to exploit or safeguard a monopolistic position. In this event, although the MNE may gain, the citizens of the country in which they operate may not, and intra-industry production may lessen welfare rather than increase it.[12] In particular, this is argued implicitly by those who are concerned with the substitution of inter-by intra-firm trade.

Which of these two outcomes is the prime consequence of rationalised international production among the world's leading MNEs is a matter for debate. Certainly, some commentators would aver that since the MNEs operate in an oligopolistic market environment, their behaviour is bound to be influenced by strategic factors which, promoted by private goals and influenced by imperfect situations, will not necessarily advance efficiency (Kojima, 1978). Others, notably Caves (1980), Williamson (1981) and Boyer and Jacquemin (1983) assert that such evidence as can be adduced supports the contention that large industrial corporations improve economic welfare rather than reduce it. Much, however, appears to rest on what is assumed to be the 'next best' situation.

This then suggests that for intra-industry production of this second kind to take place — which is concerned more with *who* owns plants in different countries than *where* they are located — requires two sets of conditions. The first applies to intra-industry inter-firm trade. These are that there are gains to be achieved by inter-country plant specialisation; there is free trade between countries; there is similarity of consumer tastes; and there is scope for product or process variety.

The second set of conditions which supplements rather than contradicts the first, explains why much of the inter-firm trade is internalised within the same firm. This asserts that there are advantages of the common ownership of plants producing similar products across national boundaries. These advantages may be of a strategic kind (what Kojima (1978) has referred to as pseudo-economies of the firm) and arise from oligopoly or monopoly power; and those which are genuine economies of transaction-cost minimisation or the exploitation of extra-plant intra-firm economies of multinationalisation and product differentiation.

Conclusion: Towards a Developmental Model

We conclude where we started. Intra-industry DFI or foreign-production is a form of international economic involvement between countries which has many of the characteristics of both inter-industry production and intra-industry trade. Like intra-industry trade, it reflects the advantages of producing similar goods in different countries, and can be partially explained by the distribution of mobile and immobile assets, and of consumer preferences. But, like inter-industry production, it also implies that international transactions are undertaken within the same hierarchy, rather than between independent firms. However, unlike inter-industry production, the nature of which can be explained by an extension of the H-O-S and other factor-endowment approaches to international resource allocation, intra-industry production rests on the advantages of product concentration and plant specialisation, plus the desire of consumers for some degree of product variety to satisfy the same want.

One final observation. We have suggested there is some reason to suppose that intra-industry production is the final stage in the evolvement of international economic transactions which began with inter-industry trade and one-way asset transfer based on country-specific O advantages of single-product MNEs. Inter-industry production or intra-industry trade follows, and then finally — where there are advantages of the common ownership of plants located in different countries — we get intra-industry production, based on firm-specific transaction-cost economising advantages of multi-product MNE oligopolists from different countries.

Over the last century, this progression has been the result of economic and technical events which have weakened the role of immobile non-specific resource endowments, relative to those mobile specific assets in determining the allocation of economic activity; and the reduction in the transaction costs of organising multi-activities in hierarchies relative to those imposed by unassisted markets (Dunning, 1983). As industrial countries have more closely converged in their income levels, resource endowments, market structures and consumer tastes; as the scope and incentive for promoting brand images and widening product ranges have increased; as technological advances have favoured plant specialisation and easier intra-firm communication; as enterprises have become larger and more diversified; as markets have become more international yet more oligopolistic in structure; so conditions have increasingly favoured intra-industry production. Provided that governments allow a relatively free exchange of inputs and outputs, and adopt a liberal stance towards inward and outward DFI, it seems likely that this form of involvement, and its complement, intra-firm trade, will continue to flourish and grow in significance.

Notes

1. International production is defined as production financed by direct foreign investment (DFI), that is, production undertaken by firms outside their national boundaries. Since data on foreign production are not usually published, those on the foreign capital stake or DFI are often used as a proxy for such data.

2. Described in Dunning (1981a).

3. That is from where there is zero to where there is infinite cross elasticity of demand and/or supply.

4. Using goods in the generic sense to embrace assets, asset rights, products and services.

5. These may be individuals, private enterprises or public institutions. For the purpose of our argument, we shall concentrate on the activities of private enterprises.

6. In the literature, technology is sometimes construed as an asset, sometimes as an asset right, and sometimes as an intermediate product. We think it is useful to distinguish the technology of an intermediate product from the capacity to create technology, by referring to the former as an asset right and the latter as an asset.

7. For an alternative classification of types of intra-industry trade, see Willmore (1979).

8. We use this term rather than 'firm-specific' which we confine to other attributes of particular enterprises, for example, size, management style, etc.

9. For an examination of the kind of influence a contractor may have over the operations of a contractee see, for example, Lall (1980).

10. For an elaboration of this thesis, see Brander (1981), Norman (1981) and Tharakan (1982).

11. For example, British Leyland has several licensing agreements with Honda, while Ford and General Motors in the United Kingdom have subcontracting arrangements with continental European component-suppliers.

12. One obvious example is where MNEs engage in transfer-price manipulation which, while increasing the net profits of the MNE as a whole, might reduce those of its subsidiary(ies) and the local value-added to the host country(ies).

* * *

COMMENT

Raymond Vernon

The utility of attempting to develop a taxonomy of the sort found in the chapter by Dunning and Norman cannot seriously be questioned. Their effort has the satisfying quality that it obviously is being attempted by scholars who have thoroughly mastered the main ideas and studies that bear on the process of direct foreign investment (DFI). Besides, their treatment is not inconsistent with a strong and compelling line of reasoning out of the mainstream of economic theory. This is an approach that looks on DFI mainly as a means of minimising transaction-costs, an approach whose origins are generally attributed to

Coase (1937) and whose elaboration owes a great deal to various respected scholars in the United States and Great Britain.

One strong attraction of that line of analysis for well-trained scholars is that it can be pursued without straying very far from the comfortable pastures of static general equilibrium theory. If DFI can be thought of mainly as a manifestation of the firm's desire for cost minimisation, the analysis can go a long way in analysing the firm's behaviour without involving the untidy, underdeveloped and generally unsatisfying concepts that are entailed as a rule in dynamic analyses. Moreover, looking at DFI as a cost-minimising response allows the economist to retain a firm link between microeconomics and macroeconomics, between the behaviour of the individual firm and the behaviour of the economy in which the firm is located; this again is in contrast to generalisations that emphasise the sequential behaviour of the firm interacting with other firms, where the macroeconomic implications of the generalisation can easily be lost. For instance, during the 1950s, so-called product-cycle exports from the United States may well have been so important that an essentially microeconomic phenomenon could be used to explain the overall characteristics of US merchandise trade. But by 1983, even though product-cycle concepts may still have been useful in explaining exports by many US industries, such exports no longer appear to have dominated the US trade patterns.

But the strength of the Dunning and Norman approach also is the source of its weakness. The static approach to intra-industry production represents a procrustean bed, unable readily to accommodate much of the loose and dispersed body of knowledge that has been accumulated on this difficult subject. I emphasise the losses that are incurred by the Dunning and Norman approach not because I think it has negative yield but because the economic community is already so strongly predisposed to follow the line of inquiry that it exemplifies, neglecting rich rewards of dynamic analysis. Several chapters in this volume tend to confirm my concern rather than to allay it. McCulloch and Rugman, while displaying their familiarity with the dynamic literature, for the most part sail in the less turbulent waters of the static cost-minimising approach. Graham, who has been associated in the past with some of the more provocative dynamic theories of DFI, turns to an analysis in which the investor is seen as exercising perfect foresight to maximise a future flow of earnings from a present stock of technology. The pursuit of dynamic processes is encountered primarily in the chapters and comments contributed by authors from the US regulatory agencies. They perhaps are under somewhat less compulsion than academics to cling to the orthodoxies of economic theory.

There is no need to summarise here what the dynamic approach has so far contributed to the understanding of intra-industry DFI. That appreciation can be picked up piecemeal from the various chapters in this volume. Let me nevertheless highlight several emphases stemming out of the dynamic approach that I think are critical for an understanding of intra-industry production.

One point that gains strength from the dynamic analysis is the central role of *uncertainty* in determining the behaviour of oligopolists. When DFI is involved, prospective investors commonly do not know some basic facts. They do not know if the ore in the ground will assay at the value needed for commercial exploration, if the costs of manufacture will be lower at point A than at point B, if the demand for their product will be sufficient to justify a world-scale plant – and, for the most part, they know that they do not know these critical values. Spending more on the acquisition of information in order to reduce these uncertainties is often not available as a practical alternative. Hedges against the uncertainties are not to be had as a rule; and, even if they were, their cost would prove so formidable as to expose the hedger to the devasting competition of an unhedged oligopolistic rival. There is nothing novel in this set of observations; the same points have been made repeatedly in the literature, casting considerable doubt on the utility of models which assume that oligopolists allow their behaviour to be guided primarily by their best estimates of costs and prices. But on a dark street, those that seek the truth tend to look under the street lights. And so it is with scholars who have mastered the enormous power of the general-equilibrium approach.

If hedging is not available, orthodox theory would have the oligopolist reduce his risk through diversification – largely through geographical diversification in the case of DFI. There are indications that some oligopolists in fact do use geographical diversification as a risk-reducing tactic. But an oligopolist cannot use such a tactic with impunity if it risks leaving him with a higher cost structure than a threatening rival. Moreover, the oligopolist can sometimes afford to neglect any cost-reducing possibility as long as he is reasonably sure that no rival will seize it. It is for this reason that interaction between the rivals is thought of as so dominant a part of the behavioural patterns of oligopolists, and why imitative behaviour figures so importantly in the dynamic literature.

Another emphasis that emerges, when the analysis stresses the dynamic elements of intra-industry production, is the fact that the strategy of the multinational enterprise (MNE), rationally enough, is aimed at improving the position of the firm as a whole, not at maximising the profit of each of the individual segments. In some cases, subsidiaries are set up without any expectation that they will generate profits for themselves; the principal object of such subsidiares is to increase the profits of the rest of the system or to reduce its risks. For example, some European firms have established subsidiaries in the United States primarily in order to expose their respective networks to the technological environment and the marketing demands of the US economy. The knowledge acquired by the subsidiary, it is thought, can help the system as a whole not only when competing in the US market but also when competing in other countries. In the same vein, MNEs have been known to set up subsidiaries for the development of raw materials in order to hedge against the possibility that they might be threatened by rivals that were developing such materials in the same areas.

The dynamic approach tends to bring out still another point. MNEs draw their inputs from global markets, not from their home markets alone. This is especially true of inputs in the form of technological information and capital. One justification for the creation of an overseas subsidiary, therefore, may well be the enlargement of a net that is available for use in connection with the next strategic advance of the firm. In a formal sense, the country characteristics, firm characteristics and ownership characterists emphasised in the Dunning and Norman chapter could conceivably capture this point. But the static approach tends to miss the nature of the process that its analysis reflects.

Some of the dynamic sequences worth pursuing in order to understand intra-industry production decisions are processes that go on inside the firm rather than in interactions between firms. Overwhelmingly important in this context is the role of experience or learning-by-doing. I would like to draw attention to Vernon and Davidson (1979), which provides some extensive data on sequences pursued by MNEs in the establishment of product lines and subsidiaries abroad. The firms covered in the study exhibited a preference for geographical areas in which they already had some experience over those that they did not know; they tended to reduce the time intervals between successive introductions of new products in any given foreign market; and they exhibited other signs of preferring to do what they had already done in the past. All this, of course, represents rational behaviour, in as much as perceptions of risk tend to decline and transactions costs tend to shrink as familiarity grows. Once again, however, it will require a dynamic approach in order effectively to pick up important trends of this sort.

The last point I need to make runs counter to the basic emphasis in my remarks. The structure of world industry is changing; in many product lines, the number of firms is increasing and the barriers to entry declining. In industries such as these, some of the conditions that justify traditional static analysis tend to grow more relevant. Meanwhile, however, new oligopolistic industries are likely to appear that are characterised by new barriers to entry. Accordingly, both the static and the dynamic approaches to an analysis of industry behaviour are likely to continue to be relevant; the challenge is to find the right balance.

* * *

COMMENT

Paul R. Krugman

Let me start with my reactions to the way Dunning and Norman map international economic relations. On my first look at their chapter, I found myself having some trouble because the way the map was drawn was not the way I usually think of drawing maps in this area. Then I realised that was just my particular mind-set. There are various ways to do a mapping. The way I had been accustomed to map in this area was to start by thinking about the different motives for international economic relations and to try to map out the implications of that for different types of trade and investment.

I tried initially to read the Dunning and Norman map and chapter in that way. But I realised, after a while, that that was not going to work. Dunning and Norman actually map the other way. They start with the typology of the way things turn out and then attempt to map back to causes. If I have counted the various implications correctly, there are 72 boxes in their tables. They then look at each particular box and ask what types of motives would cause an enterprise to land in that box.

I have some problems with their way of mapping because I am not sure, if you do it that way, how you know what is an appropriate continuum along which to measure things. As usual, I ended up with a problem, with the question of what we mean by intra-industry or, to put it another way, what we mean by industry. The definition given by Dunning and Norman is in terms of products that are close substitutes in production and/or consumption.

I am not certain, however, why we should use that definition in general. Rubber shoes and leather shoes may be close substitutes in consumption. It is not clear to me why discovering that we have international trade or any other kind of international linkage in that form makes a difference. For me the only valid criterion for classification is in terms of some kind of model of the process. In other words, fundamentally, the mapping of Dunning and Norman has to be done the other way. You have to start with notions about what causes what you see, to urge you to decide if what you see is important.

In particular, I had a problem with the whole notion of intra-industry direct foreign investment (IDFI) because I am not sure what is a relevant industry from the point of view of DFI and I am also not sure whether I know which way DFI is going.

First, as regards the relevant industry issue, those of us who tried to produce models of intra-industry trade ended up defining intra-industry in terms of what it was not. It was not related to comparative advantage, that is, did not involve trade based on differences in factor endowments. Therefore, an industry was a group of products within which you could not distinguish according to the criteria which give rise to the more conventional sorts of trade. Since I am not sure what the conventional theory of DFI is, I am not sure how to distinguish a group of products to which it does not apply, which gives me a little bit of pause.

Secondly, I am not certain which way DFI is going even when you see it. Suppose I see that Nixdorf operates in West Germany and in the United States, and I also see that Digital Equipment operates in West Germany and in the United States. Of course, in terms of where they are registered — Nixdorf is a German company and Digital Equipment is a US company — there is no problem. But I am not quite sure about the criterion for declaring which way the DFI is going, since the one thing we know definitely, after two decades of intelligent thinking about DFI, is that whatever it is, it is not an investment. It is an extension of control. Once you have an entity that sprawls across borders, which way do you say the sprawl is going?

What I think we have in mind, certainly in technology-intensive industries, is an exportation of technological know-how that is generated in one place and then applied somewhere else. Then I get still more confused in terms of these things because, certainly, Nixdorf is employing many programmers and systems developers in Massachusetts. The question becomes more obscure, still.

It is clear, however, that we do have two-way exportation of technological know-how, even within what appear to be relatively closely related groups of products in terms of the type of technology that is used in them. That, presumably, is the right definition of an industry here. Semiconductors is probably an industry because there are certain things that you have to know to make semiconductors and the resource — if you like the comparative advantage — is the possession of a pool of people who can do that type of work. Yet we do see two-way trade and two-way DFI in the sense that there are firms producing in more than one country using knowledge developed in more than one country.

Before giving my interpretation of that, let me discuss the ownership (O)-location (L)-internalisation (I) (OLI) framework of Dunning and Norman. The question is: although certainly a good way, is it a *complete* way to look at things? It is quite sensible in a way. Suppose we pose the problem: Who produces what and where? Then it is natural to ask: Who has the special advantages, that is, the know-how or whatever those intangibles that constitute a corporate culture are? What are the costs of producing and distributing when you base in various locations? What are the advantages and disadvantages of having production in different locations under a single organisational umbrella? Those are the O, the L and the I questions, respectively, in the framework of Dunning and Norman. Asking those questions is certainly a very good way to approach the problem.

I am not sure that it is a complete way to approach the problem, even if we ignore the dynamic aspects emphasised by Vernon in this volume. Whenever I look at anything international, I think of economies of scale and search for some examples. I am not certain how they would fit into the OLI framework.

Take two automotive examples. The first example: US firms produce automobiles in Mexico. Certainly, much of that fits under the O and the L. The O, yes, because General Motors and Ford have some firm-specific advantages that the locals do not have. The L, yes, because the existence of a protected market in Mexico induces them to produce there.

There is, however, also two-way trade in automotive products between the United States and Mexico. The primary reason for it is that the Mexicans allow an offset. They allow a firm to strike a deal whereby it produces a narrower range of products in Mexico, exports some of those, and imports more components, or whatever, than it might have otherwise. That turns out to be worth while even though the average cost of production is higher there, simply because it lets the firm get better economies of scale. Perhaps we can fit that into the OLI framework by some sufficiently Talmudic interpretation but it does not strike the mind immediately.

The second example: General Motors, Ford and Chrysler produce automobiles in both the United States and Canada. Again, it is quite true that, taking a sufficiently short time-horizon we could say, well, that is because they have some firm-specific advantages that help them in that. Yet, somehow that it too contingent. Surely, had Alfred Sloan never existed we would still have the same automotive companies on both sides of the border. Definitely, we want a more ultimate explanation that hinges on the economies of scope. There are very good reasons why a North American automotive firm should exist. Again, there may be some way to put that into the OLI framework, but I do not see it.

What does it come down to? If I had to make a first pass at studying IDFI, I would start by asking: Why do two countries both undertake the development of products and processes in a single industry? Presumably, because they both have the kinds of resources needed for that. Why do they not create two identical industries, two sets of firms that do exactly the same thing so that there is no need for economic interchange? The answer must be some form of economies of scale. That is the ultimate reason. You do not expect the Japanese and US high-technology industries to be exact duplicates of each other because there are certain incentives for firms to specialise in producing a limited range of products.

The final question is: Why is some of the interchange of knowledge produced by R and D taking place through DFI rather than trade? That question has to do with the cost of conducting trade versus the cost of internalising transactions within the firm.

My preferred map used to be one that had some measure of the importance of economies of scale along one axis and some measure of the extent of comparative advantage (the difference between countries) on the other axis. I understand that if you try to get into DFI that is not enough. If I had to put in a third axis, it would be some measure of the difficulty of conducting transactions within the market as opposed to within hierarchies. I do not know what to call that variable. I would like to propose the term 'Coaseness' for that variable.

I think that the approach taken in the Dunning and Norman chapter is very stimulating and it is a good way to go about exploration. I believe, however, that eventually one has to run the map inside out. It has to go from the fundamental causes to the effects and not the other way around.

2 THE DETERMINANTS OF INTRA-INDUSTRY DIRECT FOREIGN INVESTMENT*

Alan M. Rugman

Introduction

This chapter focuses upon the analytical determinants of multinational activity, that is, the reasons for international production. A multinational enterprise (MNE) is defined as an organisation that engages in the production of goods or services in two or more nations. An important aspect of international production arising from MNE activity is intra-industry direct foreign investment (IDFI). This is defined as cross-border DFI by MNEs of similar industry groups in each other's home countries. For example, in terms of the automobile industry, IDFI means an investment by the German-owned Volkswagen in the United States and an investment by US-owned Ford in West Germany.

Since IDFI must be done by MNEs — or else it would not be DFI — this chapter applies theories of the MNE to the subset of multinational activity undertaken within the same industry groups. For example, this chapter studies cross-investments by MNEs in manufacturing sectors such as chemicals, computers, electronics, automobiles, petroleum and food. Also studied is IDFI in service sectors such as banking and hotels.

It is shown that the appropriate theory of the MNE is a firm-level theory and that it is necessary to understand the determinants of IDFI at the firm-level rather than at the industry-level. Industries are just statistical abstractions whereas firms are real, live MNEs, where managers, workers and stockholders all have inputs into their efficient operation. The theories of the MNE to be applied here are first, the transaction costs theory of Coase (1937) and Williamson (1975) as applied to MNEs by Teece (1981 and 1982) and Hennart (1982), and, second, internalisation theory, as explained most recently in Rugman (1981).[1]

The Linkage of Multinational Enterprises to Intra-industry Direct Foreign Investment

Why does IDFI take place? It does so only when it is less costly to service foreign markets by IDFI than by exporting or licensing. Normally, a firm has a choice between at least these three methods of inter-national transactions. In a frictionless world of perfect competition, the firm can contract at arm's-length prices, whenever such competitive prices exist. Foreign markets can be serviced by exports or licensing. Unfortunately, for many products, especially intermediate products such as knowledge, there are no arm's-length prices. Then the firm has to overcome the market imperfection implicit in the lack of arm's-length prices. In this case, it makes an internal market, using a hierarchical structure to control the allocation and distribution of resources and goods within the firm. Foreign markets can now be serviced by DFI, in addition to exporting or licensing.

Contractual arrangements with independent foreign partners are favoured when there are high costs associated with internalisation and relatively lower costs with licensing. This occurs, for example, when the risk of dissipation of the firm-specific advantage of the MNE is small and when the costs of incurring contractual agreements are relatively low. Transaction costs exist for the MNE in making a con-tract with another firm. They include the conceptual costs of inventing a contractual agreement plus the operational costs of administering and enforcing it. For the MNE these transaction costs are often high since it lacks information about the foreign nation, while the other party to the contract has some environmental familiarity. For the partner the costs are also high due to lack of knowledge about all the details and elements of the product, process or service being purchased.

Evidently, IDFI originates at the firm-level when a typical MNE has to determine the relative costs of internalisation versus contract-ing (assuming that the arm's-length choice of exporting is even more costly to the firm due to various other market imperfections such as tariffs and other barriers to trade). Furthermore, it is a convenient starting point to assume that international exchanges by MNEs in the same industry group will be motivated by a similar set of factors, that is, all MNEs will seek the most efficient mode of exchange, subject to the information constraints imposed on them. These environmental or country-specific factors can be taken as parameters to start with.

This chapter is an attempt to explain the motivation of IDFI. It starts by assuming the exogeneity of the country-specific advantage (CSA) and other environmental parameters. This approach is different from that of Kojima (1978) and some others who emphasise the locational, trade-specific characteristics of DFI. In this context, the exogeneity of the CSA is supported by Gray (1982a, p. 192) who finds that 'national characteristics play only a minor part in the determination of the patterns of trade and [DFI] among industrial nations'. His major conclusion is that macroeconomic theories of DFI 'conceal as much, if not more, than they reveal', and that a micro-level theory of the MNE, which identifies firm-specific advantages, is required.

Within this framework of an exogenous CSA, the strategic choices open to MNEs in the same industry grouping can be considered only in terms of the limited choice of entry mode between exporting, DFI and licensing. While it is important for MNEs to re-evaluate their firm-specific advantages (FSAs), market niches and other attributes, it is not feasible to model these ongoing DFI choices as other than changes in the original DFI decision, such that a new set of entry modes needs to be considered. However, this still permits some analysis of how industry rivals operate on a world-wide basis and how IDFI occurs. Here the work of Porter (1980) on competitive strategy provides useful clues to IDFI when adapted to a global context.

In particular, Porter's identification of entry and exit barriers is a useful method of classifying changes in IDFI due to dynamic adjustments in the FSAs of MNEs. Due to their internal markets MNEs are better equipped to bypass both entry and exit barriers (such as R and D, advertising and scale-economies) than are domestic or host-country rivals. This ability of MNEs to move into new world markets, switch modes and enter and exit at lower costs than domestic firms is an important reason for the increase in IDFI on a global basis. In this case, IDFI is following the growth of MNEs in general, rather than signalling any significant new international development. IDFI is a passive response to the changing FSAs of MNEs.

In this chapter, the linkages between IDFI and intra-industry trade, as well as the linkages of IDFI to the theory of MNEs are explored. A bridge is built between the concepts. The model developed allows us to explain why MNEs (each with an FSA) in the same industry will operate in different countries, when there is no apparent difference in the CSAs, such that traditional trade explanations of international activity are insufficient in explaining trade and investment patterns. This model is shown to have some policy implications for the treatment, or neglect, of IDFI in the recent literature on international trade and investment, especially that branch of it concerned with MNEs.[2]

Definitions

On a definitional note, only one key distinction is necessary, that between inter-industry and intra-industry trade. I assume that intra-industry trade and intra-firm trade are the same, that both are done by MNEs, and that IDFI is thereby linked to them as shown in Table 2.1. I assume that cross DFI is the same as IDFI, as defined earlier. In practice, some MNEs may engage in intra-firm trade which is inter-industry (in different goods) rather than intra-industry (in the same goods) but I ignore this complication. Intra-industry trade is defined by Grubel and Lloyd (1975) as the value of total trade left, after subtracting out the inter-industry trade (net exports or imports of the industry).

Table 2.1: Relationships of Key Terms

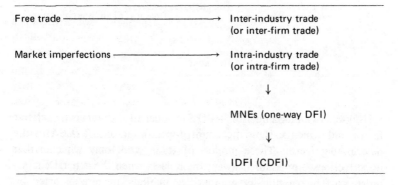

Free trade ──────────────→ Inter-industry trade (or inter-firm trade)

Market imperfections ──────→ Intra-industry trade (or intra-firm trade)

↓

MNEs (one-way DFI)

↓

IDFI (CDFI)

Towards a Model of Intra-industry Direct Foreign Investment

The relationship of intra-industry trade to IDFI is illustrated in Table 2.2. It will be shown that intra-industry trade is a natural companion to IDFI. In the left panels appear the elements affecting trade; in the right panels appear those affecting investments. As demonstrated in Rugman (1981), free trade and MNEs are alternative mechanisms for allocating goods and services to world-wide markets.[3] When barriers to trade (such as tariffs or other government-induced market imperfections) exist, then the MNE replaces trade. When this occurs much of the inter-industry trade is replaced by intra-industry trade and IDFI.

The reasons for trade in homogeneous products are determined by differences in relative goods prices between nations. These rely either on traditional Ricardian explanations of comparative advantage or on

Table 2.2: A Model of Intra-industry Trade and Direct Foreign
Investment

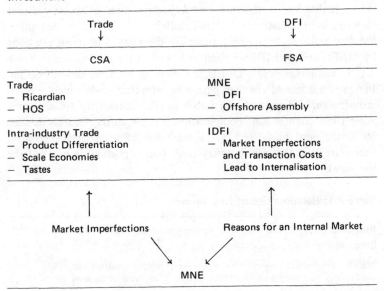

a Heckscher-Ohlin-Samuelson (H-O-S) model of differences in relative
factor endowments. Here the country-specific advantage (CSA) is the
determining factor. These models of trade work only when market
imperfections are assumed away, or at least when the general characteristics of internationally competitive markets are not distorted by
gross deviations from a neo-classical type equilibrium.

The reasons for MNEs are determined by the need to internalise
a firm-specific advantage (FSA), as explained in detail in the next
section. The FSAs arise for the MNEs when there are either natural
or government-imposed transaction costs. Internalisation takes the
form of DFI when there are barriers to trade (which deny exporting)
or a risk of dissipation of the FSA (which denies licensing). As a special
case, some MNEs engage in off-shore assembly to take advantage of
cheap foreign labour, a situation where the foreign CSA is a dominant
consideration to the MNE.

In the international economics literature, intra-industry trade builds
upon a related analysis of market imperfections, specifically, trade in
differentiated products. Intra-industry trade arises because a good (or
'industry' in terms of the H-O-S model) has many characteristics. The

simple H-O-S model looks at a good as a homogeneous product, but statistics of trade, being somewhat more related to the real world than the H-O-S abstraction, pick up the heterogeneous characteristics of a good. Yet intra-industry trade is more than a statistical curiosity, and the literature has advanced theoretical arguments which serve to reconcile it with H-O-S type trade.

These arguments revolve around factors on both the production and the consumption side. First, on the production side, the differentiation of the product, and the related need for it to be produced by large firms that enjoy scale-economies, provide an explanation of intra-industry trade. The reason is that scale is a type of market imperfection in terms of the H-O-S model. Second, on the consumption side, there is increasing congruence of consumers tastes, especially in the high-income advanced nations of the Northern hemisphere, between which most trade takes place.

The theory of IDFI is developed in the next section. As an introduction it can be stated that the theory of IDFI which emerges here is based entirely on an identification of market imperfections. It has been shown previously (Rugman, 1981) that various natural transaction-costs and 'unnatural' government-imposed regulations lead to internalisation by MNEs of their international production. Here it is argued that since *MNEs* undertake IDFI, a theory of IDFI is a theory of MNEs. In turn, it will be shown later that IDFI has the same basis as intra-industry trade and that there is a natural linkage between them.

It is generally accepted that intra-industry trade is compatible with one-way DFI, and that both can be motivated by government interventions. The contribution of this chapter is its focus on the market imperfections which lead to IDFI. We find that the same types of market imperfections occur in all nations and that they motivate the DFI carried on by MNEs. No separate theory of IDFI is required once the spotlight is on the micro reasons for MNE activity.

Both IDFI and most intra-industry trade are being undertaken by MNEs, which are responding to exogenous market imperfections. Indeed, the types of externalities identified by intra-industry trade theorists, such as scale-economies and differentiated products, are good examples of the market imperfections required to build a model of the MNE. It can be concluded that the MNE is the keystone on the erection of a theory of IDFI.

Determinants of Intra-industry Direct Foreign Investment

Caves (1982) states that the MNE is a multiplant firm and that the key decision is where the boundary falls between the allocation of resources in either an internal market or a regular (external) market. MNEs emerge when their internal markets experience lower transaction-costs than those that arise in arm's-length markets. MNEs are of three types:

(1) horizontally integrated multiplant firms,
(2) vertically integrated multiplant firms,
(3) diversified multiplant firms and conglomerates (which reduce risks).

Horizontally Integrated Multinational Enterprises

Horizontally integrated MNEs have a transactional advantage in using a hierarchical administrative structure to control their international production. Firms use their internal markets when these either have lower costs or generate higher revenues, that is, they have lower net costs than any alternative market or contractual system. This principle applies internationally and explains the need for MNEs.

Usually each MNE has a special FSA in the form of an intangible advantage or asset. The FSA can be in the form of technological knowledge, management skills or marketing know-how. Often the FSA is patented. Each MNE attempts to differentiate its product or service, so the first question to ask when examining an MNE is about the nature of its unique FSA.

The natural market imperfections identified by Caves (1971 and 1982) as facing horizontally integrated MNEs are of two general types. The first type is the public-good nature of knowledge, which leads to the appropriability problem, identified initially for the MNE by Johnson (1970) and Magee (1977). The second type is information impactedness, opportunism and buyer uncertainty aspects of market failure raised by Williamson (1975) in a domestic context and applied in an international context by Calvet and Naim (1981) and Teece (1982). These market imperfections are classic reasons for the internalisation of markets by MNEs.

As an example of the application of the concept of internalisation to IDFI, it is of interest to study the pricing of pharmaceuticals by horizontally integrated MNEs. There is an externality in the production and pricing of pharmaceuticals. Multinational drug firms engage in expensive R and D to develop, produce and market a new product.

Some estimates have found that it costs up to $70 million to put a new drug on the market. Most of this expense is incurred for the animal and human testing required to guarantee the safety of the product in order to pass strict government health-regulations.

These huge expenses need to be recovered by the MNE; so, it places a patent on the product. This gives the firm exclusive property rights over the manufacture and distribution of the product in the domain of the patent. In nations where patents are not respected, or when the MNE fears that licensing or a joint venture can lead to dissipation of its FSA, the MNE has an incentive to keep the proprietary knowledge within the firm. It does this by making an internal market, that is, keeps control of the knowledge by using wholly-owned subsidiaries to supply host-nation markets with a brand name product. Multi-national drug firms thereby appropriate a fair return on their invest-ments and bring their new health-related products to consumers around the world.

We would expect to observe a high degree of IDFI in the drug in-dustry due to the need for internalisation as a protection against dissipation of the FSA of the MNE. Each nation's drug MNEs have the same incentives for internalisation. Therefore, IDFI takes place as a response to both natural and unnatural market-imperfections.

There is some potential for rent-seeking behaviour of the MNEs. They have a monopoly over the use of their knowledge, and the more effective their method of internalisation of the FSA on a world-wide basis, the greater the opportunity for them to earn rents. However, data on the profitability of drug MNEs reveal that they do not earn excess profits over time. Nor is there any evidence of systematic exploitation of host nations. This is partly explained by the problem facing the drug MNEs, that of ongoing R and D expenses in the search for the few successful new product lines.

There is a probability distribution of successful drug innovations (just as there is for oil wells or mines). Many drugs are impossible to market as they are not sufficiently different from competitive products. Others provide little revenue to the firm due to their inability to pass health standards, regulatory codes or other restrictions. Only a few drugs are successful and these have to finance future investments. The dynamic FSA of a drug MNE relies on costly ongoing R and D in new product lines.

Recent policy actions in Canada have severely affected the drug industry in that country as discussed in detail by Gordon and Fowler (1981). In the early 1970s, both the federal and provincial governments

enacted legislation for compulsory licensing by MNEs to generic producers. The MNEs were given only three years to sell their products in
the Canadian market before being required to license host-country
generic producers, who in return paid the MNEs a small royalty of 4
per cent on sales.

The effect of this compulsory licensing requirement was to virtually
destroy the drug industry in Canada. It became prohibitively expensive
for MNEs to maintain any R and D capacity in Canada, since patents
on new drugs would not be respected for a long enough period for them
to recover R and D costs. Therefore, such R and D as there was in the
Canadian subsidiaries fled back to the parent MNEs, for whom there
was no risk of appropriation at such a low price by the host nation of
their FSA in knowledge. It can be observed in the context of this paper
that such environmental changes in the Canadian CSAs disrupted the
normal pattern of IDFI. We can anticipate this violation of the exogeneity of the CSAs to be repeated elsewhere.

Paradoxically, it is impossible for a viable Canadian-owned drug
industry to develop since the Canadian market (of 20 million people)
is too small to support the huge R and D costs of new drugs. Canada
lacks scale-economies in R and D, production and marketing.[4] As other
nations, especially developing nations (such as India), Italy and the
Eastern European countries, do not respect international patents, it is
not feasible for a Canadian-based MNE to rely on foreign sales or
production to recover its costs of drug development. Thus the lack of
scale-economies in Canada, coupled with the mercantilistic policies of
other nations, shut Canadian firms out of the world market for drugs.

In the future, IDFI in pharmaceuticals may well be reduced by the
breakdown of internationally accepted patent laws. As other forms of
international servicing, such as licensing or exporting are not desirable
due to the risk of dissipation of the knowledge advantage of the MNE,
world welfare and health losses will be experienced. Only by respect-
ing the property rights of MNEs, either US, Canadian or foreign-owned,
will it be feasible for brand-name drug producers to recover their
position in host countries such as Canada. Without internalisation it is
not possible for MNEs to provide social benefits in the form of R and
D, employment, taxes, and health services.

Vertically Integrated Multinational Enterprises

The second area in which the modern theory of the MNE is relevant
for an understanding of the determinants of IDFI is for vertically
integrated MNEs, such as oil or mineral-resource firms. In the case of

vertically integrated multiplant firms, the internal market can be used to establish control and minimise transaction costs. This gives another sort of FSA to the MNE. Let us look at oil firms as a case study of vertically integrated MNEs.

In the case of petroleum companies, the type of FSA that may be controlled within the MNE is always one determined by external market imperfections. Aliber (1970, pp. 19-20) puts it this way:

> Efficiencies may be realized by co-ordinating activities that occur in several different countries within the firm. Thus an international oil company co-ordinates the production, transport, refining, and the distribution of petroleum at lower costs than individual firms at each stage might be able to by using the market. The economies of vertical integration involve reduction in transactions costs, the cost of search, and the costs of holding inventories.

Petroleum firms engage in vertical integration in response to both natural and government-induced market imperfections. Their control over sources of supply and over markets is justified when a FSA needs to be generated in order to bypass a host of transactions costs involving supply uncertainties, logistics and search costs. The optimal rate of development of an oil field requires co-ordination of the production (refining) and marketing function in a dynamic sense. This is best achieved within a firm, where accurate information about all these functions can be assembled. Such knowledge is not freely available, and the internalisation of extraction, refining and marketing by the MNE gives it a special type of FSA. This assignment of property rights permits the firm to protect its information and gives it a knowledge advantage.

Table 2.3 illustrates this process. There are four stages of vertical integration: extraction, transportation, refining and distribution. Control of the supplies and markets is needed to allow the crucial capital-intensive refining stage to operate at full capacity. An oil MNE can put together this package at lower costs than the market. The MNEs have managed to continue this process even after OPEC disrupted the extraction stage in 1973 and 1979. The oil MNEs retained control over distribution; so, they were able to pass on to consumers the higher costs of crude oil. In return, the oil MNEs only required supplies of oil; price did not matter. Of course, over the last ten years the bargaining over crude oil prices has moved away from firms and towards governments. Yet the oil MNEs still retain the general ability to

Table 2.3: Vertical Integration of Oil MNEs

Extraction
↓
Transportation
↓
Refining
↓
Distribution

overcome the set of transactions costs identified in Table 2.3; so, their role as internalisers will continue in the future.

One of the key benefits of a MNE is that a subsidiary has access to the large set of crude oil supplies owned by its multinational parent. If there is a disruption to part of the supply, action can be taken by the parent to minimise the effect on any one affiliate. Also, an affiliate can always renew its contracts for supplies of crude oil. During times of crisis, a firm with no ongoing relationship with a supplier of crude oil may have difficulty in obtaining adequate supplies of crude oil at any price.

Another benefit for the subsidiary is access to new research and technology produced within the MNE, activities which are controlled and centralised in the parent firm but used optimally by all affiliates. While there are no theoretical problems with the concept of making internal markets, practical issues may arise when it is applied internationally. The key problem is that of sovereignty. The host nation often has a viewpoint different from that of the parent firm. The host nation may look at the same picture as the MNEs and their subsidiaries but interpret it differently. It is for this type of reason that IDFI puzzles governments but is accepted as a natural phenomenon by MNEs.

The amount of IDFI undertaken for reasons of vertical integration will be limited in any case, since oil MNEs operate on parallel tracks between nations rather than across nations. It is only when oil MNEs, such as Exxon, decide upon a strategy of product diversification that their acquisition activities lead into IDFI and then they may not be all that successful since their FSA does not lie in financial management or control.

Diversified Multinational Enterprises

The third type of multiplant MNEs identified by Caves are diversified

MNEs. These, explained by the principles of international diversification, are discussed in detail by Rugman (1979). This type of MNEs also has useful implications for IDFI. The focus on financial diversification means that the conglomerate activity can also be included in this category of MNEs. Conglomerates from different countries can engage in IDFI.

MNEs, by the very nature of their international operations, are engaged in risk-pooling. They are exposed to less variation in sales than are uninational firms confined to a single (domestic) market. Although international diversification is an explanation based on financial factors instead of real-asset factors, it is still relevant for IDFI, since risk-pooling is an excellent reason for cross-industry investments.

The version of international diversification of relevance here is that in which imperfections (in the form of information costs and government regulations) in the international capital market constrain simple portfolio diversification (which individuals could do themselves by buying into the stock indexes of various nations). MNEs, and not individual investors, must do the diversification because it is prohibitively expensive for an individual to assemble an efficient global portfolio by buying into the stock market indexes of various nations. The individual investor has very high information and search costs. There is also political risk, exchange risk and other environmental uncertainties to be considered.

The MNE is a potential surrogate vehicle for financial asset diversification by individuals since it is already operating internationally and the business cycles of nations do not move in perfect tandem. The advantages of real-asset diversification of MNEs arise since MNEs avoid market imperfections by internalisation. This has an implication for IDFI, since there is a type of FSA involved in the financial diversification achieved by the specific MNE. Each MNE is a portfolio of assets, with an FSA something like a brand-name, since the FSA is unique to each individual MNE. There is a close link between the role of the MNE as an international diversifier and the growth of IDFI in recent years.

The capital market model of Aliber (1970) appears at first sight to be applicable to IDFI also. Aliber argues that a country-specific factor, foreign-exchange risk, determines the international pattern of net flows of DFI. The investor's valuation of foreign-exchange risk affects the capitalisation rate attached to earnings in that currency. For example, if the dollar is expected to appreciate, US MNEs can borrow more cheaply than other MNEs and use their lower cost of capital to finance overseas production, although precisely what motivates the MNEs to expand abroad is not made clear. In Aliber's model, IDFI will occur whenever the investor's valuation of exchange-risk changes. The model, therefore, broadly explains the switchover from US to European and Japanese DFI in the 1970s.

In an updated version of the model, Aliber (1983) states that the national Q ratio (representing the market value of a firm over its book value) captures this CSA in exchange risk and determines the country-mix of ownership. Aliber finds that the Q ratio for US firms has been falling during the 1970s, while that of European firms has been increasing. He attributes this to changes in relative exchange rates, with the dollar weakening during the 1970s. The market value of US firms increased less rapidly than the market value of European firms, drawing down the US Q ratio, and reducing the relative amount of US DFI.

If this is true − it would be surprising if such a macro view of DFI is all that matters − then we might anticipate even more IDFI if exchange-risk increases. However, a more micro level explanation of DFI is required. The investment decision of the MNE is determined primarily by an FSA, such as the need to internalise property rights in knowledge, rather than by the type of CSA identified by Aliber. If the CSAs are modelled as environmental parameters, they cannot influence the IDFI decision. If the CSAs are to be endogenised, it must be done on stronger grounds than in the Aliber model. In conclusion, the FSA inherent in the international diversification motive for IDFI is a stronger explanation for IDFI than is the CSA explanation of Aliber's exchange-risk model.

Intra-industry Direct Foreign Investment and Country-specific Advantages

While all the theories discussed here are relevant for an analysis of IDFI, it is less likely to occur for reasons of vertical integration than for those of horizontal integration and diversification. The main motivation for IDFI will be cross-industry DFI in horizontally integrated MNEs with an FSA in proprietary knowledge.[5]

The exogeneity of the CSAs, assumed so far in this chapter, may need to be relaxed to encompass some of the swings in IDFI. For example, the relative advantages of US-based MNEs in technology and managerial know-how have been superseded by those of Japanese and European MNEs. Yet even here I would argue that the changing CSAs are themselves influenced by FSAs and that it is the process of DFI which, at the firm-level, acts to motivate changes in the macro environmental parameters.

The Linkage of Intra-industry Trade to Intra-industry Direct Foreign Investment

Dunning (1981b) has argued that IDFI is broadly determined by the same factors as intra-industry trade and that IDFI patterns follow those of intra-industry trade, with some, as yet unspecified, time lag. The literature on intra-industry trade, for example, Grubel and Lloyd (1975), identifies product-differentiation, scale-economies and converging consumer-tastes as key variables determining intra-industry trade. Tastes are functionally related to *per capita* real income, so the level of development is one of the alternative determinants of intra-industry trade.

Table 2.4, using data for 1967, indicates that intra-industry trade[6] occurs between high-income European and North American nations. At that time intra-industry trade was less important for Japan, although this influence has undoubtedly increased recently. Similarly, Table 2.5 reveals that most intra-industry trade is in technologically advanced, specialised industries such as chemicals and other manufactured goods, rather than in resource-based products.

When applied to IDFI, such broad theoretical and empirical generalisations about intra-industry trade imply that most IDFI will occur between high-income European, Japanese and North American nations. IDFI should also occur in income-elastic and technology-intensive manufacturing sectors such as computers, other high-technology electronics, pharmaceuticals, automobiles, and in service sectors such as banking and hotels. MNEs are very active in these sectors. In most of them horizontal investment predominates, although IDFI may also occur where vertical integration is important, as in the oil, mineral resources and pulp and paper industries.

Data in Dunning (1981b) broadly support this linkage between the composition of intra-industry trade and IDFI. Unfortunately, the table on IDFI reported by Dunning cannot be readily reconciled with the tables on intra-industry trade reported here, as Dunning's work is confined to an analysis of IDFI in each of five nations (USA, Japan, UK, Sweden and West Germany). It is not really meaningful to aggregate these data across all five nations without running into questions of weighting and interpretation. Also nine industry groups are studied instead of ten. However, for what it is worth, I have reworked Dunning's tables, to rank his nine industries in decreasing order of IDFI, in Table 2.6. These rankings can be compared to those for intra-industry trade, both based on Dunning's own data, and

Table 2.4: Intra-industry Trade by Country

Name of Country	Intra-industry Trade as a Percentage of All Trade for 1967, at the 3-digit Level, Across All Industries
Europe	
United Kingdom	69
France	65
Belgium–Luxembourg	63
Netherlands	56
Germany	46
Italy	42
United States	49
Canada	48
Japan	21
Australia	17

Source: Grubel and Lloyd (1975, Table 3.3, p. 39).

Table 2.5: Ranking of Industries by Percentage of Intra-industry Trade

Rank	SITC Class	Description	Percentage
1	5	Chemicals	66
2	7	Machinery and Transport Equipment	59
3	9	Commodities and Transactions, n.e.s.	55
4	8	Miscellaneous Manufactured Articles	52
5	6	Manufactured Goods Classified by Material	49
6	1	Beverages and Tobacco	40
7	4	Animal and Vegetable Oils and Fats	37
8	0	Food and Live Animals	
9	2	Crude Materials, Inedible, Except Fuels	30
10	3	Mineral Fuels, Lubricants and Related Materials	30

Note: This is the unweighted average of the percentage of intra-industry trade at the 3-digit level in ten 1-digit level industries across ten countries for 1967.
Source: Grubel and Lloyd (1975, Table 3.2, p. 37).

analysed in comparison to Table 2.5.

As Dunning has noticed, his data produce rankings which are approximately the same between IDFI and intra-industry trade. In Table 2.6, for five of the nine industries there is only a deviation of 1 in the ranking, while for two of the industries there is a deviation of 2. The industries where there is a major difference in rankings are paper and allied products, which has much higher IDFI than intra-industry trade, and transportation equipment where the reverse holds.

Table 2.6: Ranking of Industries by Percentage of Intra-industry Direct Foreign Investment (IDFI)

IDFI Rank	Description	IDFI Percentage	Intra-industry Percentage	Trade Rank
1	Other Manufacturing	77	74	3
2	Primary and Fabricated Metals	74	85	1
3	Chemical and Allied Products	67	74	2
4	Paper, Printing and Publishing	67	39	8
5	Electrical Engineering	63	72	4
6	Mechanical and Instrument Engineering	54	71	5
7	Food, Drink and Tobacco	48	39	9
8	Textiles, Leather, Clothing and Footwear	44	53	7
9	Transportation Equipment	33	62	6

Note: The data were recalculated from Tables 1 and 2 in Dunning (1981b) for 1965, as this is the year closest to the Grubel and Lloyd (1975) data year. The unweighted average of Dunning's five nations was found.
Source: Dunning (1981b, Tables 1 and 2).

Grubel (1979) also finds a very high correlation between IDFI and intra-industry trade of Germany for 1976. IDFI, or what Grubel calls 'the index of intra-industry trade in long-term assets' is 99 per cent, while the index of intra-industry trade itself is 95 per cent. Grubel suggests that the German figures are representative of other nations, and while data on IDFI may not always be as high in other nations as for Germany his 'casual inspection of the data reveals the existence of two-way trade in assets to be a wide-spread phenomenon' (Grubel, 1979, p. 72). I tend to agree. My general conclusion is that the empirical evidence available (inadequate as it is) indicates a close relationship between IDFI and intra-industry trade. It is a moot point whether further empirical work on IDFI will really provide much useful new information.

One difference worth noting between intra-industry trade and IDFI is that the latter will still take place under government-imposed imperfections, such as tariffs and other controls on trade and investment. Internalisation theory explains MNEs and MNEs undertake the IDFI. Therefore, Dunning (1981b) is open to question when he states that intra-industry trade flourishes in the absence of tariff barriers and import restrictions and then goes on to accept that the same conditions permit IDFI. The region in which this statement may be correct is the European Economic Community (EEC), and perhaps other major customs unions. The progress of economic integration will indeed increase both intra-industry trade and, by reducing its costs, IDFI. However, the EEC is a good example of an organisation where, while nominal tariffs have been lowered, other market imperfections still exist, especially regulations affecting factor markets such as that for labour. Therefore, IDFI occurs in the EEC since some natural and unnatural (government) imperfections remain. As long as there are transaction costs to trade, this leads to internalisation or contracting by MNEs and statistics will report this activity as IDFI.

IDFI occurs in service sectors as well as in manufacturing sectors. The theory of the MNE has been shown by Casson (1982) and Dunning and McQueen (1982) to explain activities in the international hotel industry. Dunning and McQueen demonstrate that MNEs in the hotel industry have ownership-specific advantages (or FSAs) in the form of high quality, reliable and efficient 'experience goods' (services) which reduce the transaction costs (buyer uncertainty) of customers. These internalised advantages are slightly different but are common to all major hotel MNEs, for example, Holiday Inn, Inter-Continental, Hilton, Sheraton and Trusthouse Forte.

Cross-investment in the hotel sector is taking place despite the prevalence of US-owned MNEs. Dunning and McQueen (1982) report that the United States has 50 per cent of foreign-associated hotels, France and Britain each 15 per cent but West Germany only 2 per cent. Country-specific factors help to determine this degree of foreign ownership; a multiplant domestic base is required for overseas hotel chains. Yet the underlying FSAs are clearly necessary, if not sufficient, conditions (in Dunning's eclectic model) for successful IDFI. An example of recent IDFI in the United States is Canadian ownership of the Four Seasons hotel chain and the purchase of the Howard Johnson hotels by Imperial Tobacco of Britain. The latter is more of a conglomerate DFI than a DFI based on FSAs related to recovering transaction costs such as reducing buyer uncertainty.

For similar reasons of horizontal integration, IDFI will exist, indeed prevail, in international banking. Each multinational bank has an intangible knowledge advantage which lowers such transaction costs as opportunism and buyer uncertainty. IDFI in banking will increase as the FSAs become more apparent. We notice that European, Canadian, and Japanese multinational banks are increasing their presence in world markets, although US banks still dominate. Grubel (1977) and Rugman (1979) have discussed this in more detail, while Tschoegl (1982) provides empirical support.

Intra-industry trade and IDFI are particularly important for small open economies, such as Canada, Belgium and Switzerland. These nations lack domestic markets of sufficient size to provide indigenous firms with scale economies and the full benefits of specialisation. Instead, many small-scale plants with short production runs exist. These inefficient plants only survive due to protection by tariff or non-tariff barriers. Yet, as the world moves towards greater trade liberalisation, with the General Agreement on Tariffs and Trade (GATT) rounds reducing nominal tariffs, firms are having to engage in contracting out and other types of rationalisation in order to achieve greater economies of specialisation. This increases IDFI.

McCharles (1983) has documented this strategy for the Canadian case. He finds that although subsidiaries of US MNEs have been attracted to Canada in the past by tariffs, now they too need to contract out and seek more efficient suppliers. Again, this leads to an increase in both intra-industry trade and IDFI.

Policy Implications

The paradigm of internalisation has been shown to offer powerful insights into the linkages between MNEs, intra-industry trade and IDFI. All three are spokes on the wheel of internalisation. What policy implications arise from this analysis of the determinants of IDFI? In order to provide a framework, let us relate these to some of the relevant questions on IDFI raised by Erdilek (1983).

IDFI is a significant economic phenomenon but it does not require a new theory for its explanation. The theory of internalisation explains it very well. Identify the relevant FSA of the MNE and the reason for cross-investment will have been found. Alternative theories of the MNE seem to have more trouble with IDFI; for example, the eclectic approach of Dunning (1981b) involves some convoluted reasoning before the link can be made between intra-industry trade and IDFI. His main conclusion is that IDFI is following the trend of intra-industry trade. The second link of IDFI to the theory of the MNE (and especially the internalisation component) is surprisingly not made by Dunning, although his work lends itself to such a linkage.

The product cycle model of Vernon (1966) does not relate all that well to IDFI either, since it has to consider both the sequencing of net exports over time between groups of nations and the reasons for changes in the rate of standardisation of the product. This involves juggling changing combinations of CSAs and FSAs all in an oligopolistic framework where (dynamic) strategic rivalries are in play. While defensive DFI is a potentially good reason for cross-investment, it is not clear exactly where the trade-off comes between relevant CSAs and FSAs when explaining IDFI.

Both of these general theories of the MNE are too broad; a convenient simplification is required to apply them to IDFI, such as the assumption of exogeneity in the CSAs. However, as both the eclectic and product-cycle approaches use the key element of internalisation theory, namely the importance of modelling market imperfections (which leads to identification of the FSAs), it can be inferred that both are useful variations in explaining IDFI. Also relevant will be sibling theories of the MNE which have focused on one or another type of market imperfection, a point made in the context of the general nature of internalisation theory in Rugman (1981, Chapter 2). As market imperfections persist, indeed increase, we can expect more FSAs to develop, leading to even more IDFI.

From this comes a simple but penetrating insight into the policy issues raised by IDFI. As a limiting case, IDFI will disappear with the removal of the market imperfections that generate it. In a world of perfect markets and no externalities, that is, where knowledge can be priced on a regular market and no government-imposed imperfections exist, there is not a logical reason for IDFI. Indeed, free trade is all that occurs in such a first-best world. Since transaction costs and government regulations do exist in practice, all policy discussion is about second-best measures. What policy means in this context is unclear. All we can do is look to the first-best solution as a guideline. For example, if the GATT can liberalise trade by removing tariff and non-tariff barriers, then the motives for IDFI are simultaneously reduced. No separate policy on IDFI, or indeed on MNEs, is required. If the market imperfections can be removed at *source*, the MNEs and IDFI will fade away.

To the extent that MNEs are replacements for the first-best world of free trade, they increase allocative efficiency. Internal markets are a method of getting towards the elusive benefits of perfect markets. In a world of transaction costs and government imperfections, arm's-length market prices simply do not exist for many goods and services. Internalisation is an efficient response (from the perspective of the firm) to such market imperfections. To the extent that IDFI is done in the internal market of MNEs, IDFI is efficient in comparison to the second-best world from which it springs.

Data on the performance of the world's largest MNEs reveal that

Table 2.7: A Comparison of the Performance of the World's Largest
Multinational Enterprises, 1970-9

Part A	Rate of Return on Equity	
	Mean	Standard Deviation
50 Largest US	13.46	3.28
50 Largest European	8.23	4.52
20 Largest Japanese	10.19	4.13
10 Largest Canadian	11.48	5.64
Part B		
10 Largest US	14.22	3.31
10 Largest European	9.13	5.35
10 Largest Japanese	10.69	3.95
10 Largest Canadian	11.48	5.64

Source: Rugman and Lecraw (1985, Table 5.5) (forthcoming).

they are 'efficient' in the sense that they earn a normal rate of return.
Summary data on the performance of the 50 largest US, 50 largest
European, 20 largest Japanese and 10 largest Canadian MNEs are
reported in Table 2.7 for a ten-year period. Profits are shown by the
return on equity (ROE) defined as net income-after-taxes divided
by the value of stockholder's equity.

These groups of MNEs earn mean profits which are insignificantly
different from those earned by uninational firms of similar size. The
European MNEs' average ROE is lower than that of other nations
because the 14 state-owned enterprises (SOEs) are included in the
group. Rugman (1979) showed that US MNEs had more stable profits
than non-MNEs of similar size over the 1960-9 period, and the proxy
for risk reported in Table 2.7 (the standard deviation of earnings over
the ten-year period) lends some support to this finding for the 1970s.

In conclusion, IDFI is a replacement for trade, and IDFI is linked to
intra-industry trade. The explanation for increasing IDFI is not to be
discovered by looking at statistics on the volume, pattern and balance
of trade. Rather it is to be identified by considering the plethora of
natural and government-induced 'unnatural' market imperfections
which lead to the development of internal markets and MNEs in the
first place.

The trade 'policies' of nations are often no more than sanctified
statements of official wishful thinking. They are not tablets of stone.
MNEs and changes in IDFI react to governmental policies, rather than
initiate them. When governments create distortions in the market-

place (for distributional or other non-efficiency reasons), they are effectively advertising for replacement internal markets, which the MNEs provide and IDFI signifies.

IDFI is the result of world-wide innovation as MNEs use internal markets to retain their FSAs. MNEs provide goods and services to consumers which embody this intangible asset, thereby transferring technology and increasing global economic welfare. Diffusion of technological know-how is confined to MNEs until the products become relatively standardised, at which time the risk of dissipation of the FSAs becomes negligible and indigenous producers in host nations take over the provision of the product or service.

The United States, like other nations, benefits from IDFI, since this is a replacement for international trade, with the MNE as a vehicle for efficient world-wide allocation and distribution. Clearly, in the long-run, efficient industrial development is dependent upon the acceptance of IDFI. Even in the protectionist atmosphere of the United States, it does not pay to restrict inward DFI, for the same reasons of economic efficiency that US outward DFI has always been supported. IDFI is superior to short-term interventionist policies which preserve the interest of owners and workers at the expense of national economic welfare.

The symmetry of MNEs to free trade is a guiding light in the jungle of government intervention, regulation and restriction of international economic activity. If protection and restrictions on trade increase, MNEs or contractual arrangements will increase. If more restrictions are imposed on intra-industry trade and IDFI together, then either alternative methods of international exchange will develop or world welfare will contract.

Notes

* Major substantive comments were received from Asim Erdilek and Donald Lecraw, while Mark Casson, John H. Dunning, Peter Gray, Herbert Grubel, Rachel McCulloch, Gordon Roberts and Clas Wihlborg provided helpful advice. I am alone responsible for any errors.

1. For antecedents of internalisation theory see Buckley and Casson (1976) and Dunning (1977). For a modern application of internalisation theory to services, see Casson (1982). Internalisation theory is similar to the eclectic approach of Dunning (1979); see Rugman (1982, especially Chapter 1).

2. In order to better relate my work to that of Dunning and Norman in this volume, I should note that my model has their location-specific factor (L) as an exogenous CSA. The other two elements of their model, the ownership (O) and

internalisation (I) advantages are both included in my FSA. For my purposes, it is approriate to assume that the internalisation advantages of the MNE are operationalised through its ownership of them. The theory of the MNE and of IDFI is a firm-driven, micro theory; so, there is no need to segment ownership and internalisation, as Dunning and Norman do in their OLI framework. I am attempting to derive predictive statements, rather than erect a typology of all possible cases, although the latter is a perfectly respectable way to proceed. Again, in the terms of the OLI framework, my analysis is focused mainly on the key diagonal cells in the Dunning and Norman matrix; the off-diagonal cells clearly follow as minor sub-cases once the principal elements are known and understood.

3. The work of Krugman (1983) has come to a similar conclusion, albeit in terms of very restricted and simplified trade-type models of imperfect competition. In a product differentiation model of monopolistic competition where R and D (or know-how) is assumed to be a fixed cost, there is trade in information by MNEs. Krugman (1983, p. 64) finds that for horizontally integrated MNEs 'trade and multinational enterprise are substitutes, just as trade and factor mobility are substitutes in the Heckscher-Ohlin model'. However, Krugman's second static trade model, for vertically integrated MNEs, leads (in a world of no uncertainty) to the contrary finding that 'trade and multinational enterprise will be complements rather than substitutes' (ibid., p. 64). This peculiar result is due to his neglect of the fact that vertically integrated MNEs benefit from greater security of supplies and markets, as argued above. Of more consequence is Krugman's failure to recognise that the crucial aspect of the MNE is that it overcomes transaction-costs and operates an efficient internal market. This process of internalisation gives the MNE a special, unique FSA that is robust enough to predict why MNE activity replaces trade or licensing under most conditions of imperfect markets.

4. For more details of these points and evidence across other industries besides drugs, see Rugman (1980b and 1983).

5. Peter Gray (1982b) has gone as far as to argue that *only* horizontal DFI is a determinant of IDFI. He states (pp. 73–4):

When tariffs are high, it is quite possible for a single industry to have foreign production in two countries simultaneously. This is the [DFI] equivalent of intra-industry trade. If individual firms in different countries have product-specific proprietary know-how (for which there is no substitute) which is not available to firms in the other country, then both countries will have firms producing in the other country. The prime examples of such behavior are the chemical and pharmaceutical industries in which different firms have quite distinct commercial patents which enable them to manufacture abroad.

6. Grubel and Lloyd (1975) define intra-industry trade in industry (i) as the total of its exports (X) plus imports (M) less the amount of net exports. The index of intra-industry trade, R_i, is:

$$R_i = [(X_i + M_i) - /X_i - M_i/] \times \frac{100}{(X_i + M_i)}$$

The second term $/X_i - M_i/$ is net exports, or conventional inter-industry trade.

* * *

COMMENT

Irving B. Kravis

There are two broad approaches to the theory of intra-industry direct
foreign investment (IDFI). The one adopted by Rugman in his insight-
ful chapter is what may be termed the 'fallout' approach. In this
approach, the theory of direct foreign investment (DFI) is set out and
applied to firms in different parent countries. The theory thus explains
why firms in a given industry but in different countries will invest
abroad. Among the locations chosen for such investment may be the
parent countries of other firms also engaged in DFI. Hence there will
be some cross-investments in the same industry, that is, IDFI. The
inflows into each parent country need not be attributable to the fact
that the country already has local production and outward DFI.

The other approach tries to explain the cross-flow directly; here, the
existence of local production and outward DFI help to explain the
inflow. The approach draws heavily on the presence of oligopolistic
rivals in different parent countries and their establishment of productive facilities in each other's home market as part of a counter-threat
strategy. Hymer and Rowthorn (1970), for example, interpret the cross
penetration of markets by US and European firms as responses to the
challenges each feel presented by the other.

A more general theory of IDFI than is afforded by either of these
approaches requires three components. The first is a theory of the
location of parents. The second is an explanation of the establishment
or acquisition of affiliates by the parents, that is, why some firms
become multinational enterprises (MNEs). The third is a theory of the
location of affiliates. Dunning's writings on DFI and IDFI, for example,
Dunning (1981c), have included all three of these components although
in a different framework.

Location theories turn largely on country characteristics. Rugman,
concentrating on explaining the behaviour of existing firms, tries to
exclude country characteristics, but they keep forcing their way back
into his analysis (for example, his reference to the shift in relative
managerial know-how as between Japan and the United States). The
explanation of the location of parents can be approached by accounting for the location of industries in general terms. If an industry is
found in a country but none of its firms invest abroad, that should be
explained by the second component of the theory.

The location of industries can be explained in terms of country-specific factors falling to two broad categories. The first set of factors is the level of development which is correlated with the kinds of production that are likely to be carried on. It may be expected, for example, that textile production and construction are more dispersed among countries than many other activities, while computer production tends to be concentrated in high-income countries. Also, a high-income country is likely to have a greater diversity of industries, population and other things being held constant. Since the presence of home production is a prerequisite for overlapping IDFI in the important set of cases in which DFI in both directions is based on horizontal integration, high-income countries are on this account more prone to high ratios of IDFI than low-income countries.

The second set of factors consists of those familiar with the theory of comparative advantage, namely, differences among countries in factor endowments and differences among industries in factor intensities. Although Rugman downplays the role of these factors in explaining both trade and DFI, it seems fair to say that the view that emerges from the recent literature is not so negative in evaluating the role of country-specific factors in explaining trade flows. For example, Stern (1980) estimated that over 40 per cent of US exports and three-fourths of US imports could be explained in terms of Ricardo (natural-resource content) or Heckscher-Ohlin factors. (He classified the rest of US trade mainly as high-technology, product-cycle goods.) Also, it may be easier to explain the pattern of production in terms of factor proportions than the pattern of trade (Krueger, 1977).

Country-specific factors not only explain what industries are likely to develop and give rise to firms that will become MNEs, but may also determine the nature of the firm-specific advantage (FSA) that enables the MNE to produce competitively in a foreign country. It is possible, for example, that the firm-specific advantages of US and Japanese MNEs are different. The former may arise more from the prevalence in the United States of technological advances based on R and D, and the latter may be attributable to a greater degree to superior management methods rooted in part in distinctive sociological factors.

The relevance of these country-specific factors in explaining the industry composition of DFI and, therefore, the possibility of IDFI is more clearly seen by examining sources of foreign investments other than those of large countries with diversified industrial production. The bulk of Swedish DFI, for example, is in two raw-material-based industries — forestry and mechanical engineering — the latter an outgrowth of the availability of phosphorous-free iron ores (Carlson, 1977).

Two caveats about this advocacy of a role for a theory of parent location are in order. First, its usefulness is in proportion to the importance of horizontal integration in DFI. The case for including country-specific characteristics is much weaker in explaining DFI representing vertical integration and very weak indeed for DFI based on conglomerates. (However, it is not unusual to hear the political and economic stability of the United States mentioned as a motivation for the inflow of DFI. The diversification motive sometimes given for conglomerates becomes somewhat more plausible here.) Secondly, the underlying presumption is that the industrial distribution of a country's outward DFI is related to the industrial distribution of its production, or, alternatively, that a country's shares in world DFI in various industries is related to its shares in world production. These caveats can be regarded as hypotheses that lend themselves to empirical verification or rejection.

The second component of a theory of IDFI, the explanation of why firms establish or acquire affiliates, is, as already noted, the main concern of Rugman's chapter, and has been extensively treated in the literature both on industrial organisation and on MNEs. No further comment will be made here. The factors that lead a parent to choose one location over others in establishing affiliates have also been investigated quite extensively.

Reasons often given for choosing foreign over domestic production include saturation of the home market (with oligopolistic rivals ready to defend their market shares or vigilant antitrust officials ready to oppose a rise in the firm's share), the need to circumvent trade-barriers, and, for parents in countries with exchange controls, the possibility of getting access to foreign exchange. In the choices of MNEs among different foreign locations, political and cultural factors appear to have played large roles. Historically, US outward DFI was concentrated in Canada and Latin America, and currently it still favours the UK among European countries, despite larger markets in France and Germany. Important destinations for the outflow of DFI from the UK were the areas of the Empire-Commonwealth, especially Canada but also parts of Asia and Africa.

Among the economic factors attracting US MNEs to particular host countries, the size of the market seems to have been more clearly of significance than the cost of factor inputs (Kravis and Lipsey, 1982). This is explicable in terms of the opportunities for scale economies that large markets afford. Also, in the past all but a small share of affiliate production was typically sold in the host country's domestic market, although this has been changing (Lipsey and Kravis, 1982). Costs of entry may be an important determinant; the difficulty of establishing a foothold depends on the size and marketing sophistication of potential investing firms in the potential host-country. This may help explain the choice of less developed country (LDC) locations by MNEs with headquarters in other LDCs and the relatively late entry of some European MNEs into the US market.

As this suggests, interactions between the characteristics of the parent country and those of the host country may also be important. For example, firms investing abroad from a home base in a developing country have often adapted the large-scale technology of advanced countries to the needs of the small home-market, using more labour-intensive methods and simpler machinery. They then invest abroad in other developing countries where markets are also small (Wells, 1977). Country characteristics are thus seen to determine the nature of the specific advantage of parent firms while foreign-country characteristics determine where that advantage can be exploited.

This way of formulating the determinants of IDFI suggests some hypotheses that lend themselves to empirical investigation:

(a) The ratio of IDFI ought to be higher for pairs of countries with diversified production.

(b) When a country is rather specialised (for example, Sweden), its ratio of IDFI should be low when paired with another specialised country having different industrial specialties.

(c) For countries with overlapping production, the ratio of IDFI should be higher the greater the proportion of the overlap in concentrated industries. (This draws on the link between DFI and concentration ratios, often cited in the literature, though not mentioned previously in this comment.)

(d) The IDFI ratio should be higher between countries with similar markets in terms of *per capita* income, size (total demand) and sophistication of marketing techniques.

With respect to public-policy implications, there does not appear to be anything about intra-industry investment that calls for different treatment than inter-industry investment flowing in and out. One possible consequence of larger inter- and intra-industry flows into the United States may be a change in the bargaining positions of different countries regarding the treatment of DFI. The United States may become more tolerant of other countries' restrictions on DFI or may use its inward DFI as leverage to obtain better treatment of its outward DFI. Other policy implications, such as those related to antitrust considerations and to the diffusion of technological knowledge, seem more likely to turn on the inflows and outflows each with its own effects without regard to the extent to which they represent cross-flows.

* * *

COMMENT*

Donald J. Rousslang

Direct foreign investment (DFI) takes place when a firm has a production advantage that it can exploit more efficiently in foreign markets by locating production abroad than by exporting or by licensing to foreign firms. Rugman uses the theory of internalisation to explain why a firm may find foreign production more profitable than exporting or licensing. According to this theory, a firm will absorb intermediate markets between production and ultimate consumers in domestic and foreign markets if transaction costs in these markets can be reduced by making the markets internal to the firm. These transaction costs may occur naturally, such as transportation costs and the costs of bringing buyers and sellers together, or they may occur as a result of government interference, such as restrictions on imports.

The theory of internalisation is a necessary part of any explanation of intra-industry direct foreign investment (IDFI), and Rugman provides an excellent statement of the theory both here and in earlier work (Rugman, 1981). Of course, a complete theory of IDFI also requires an explanation of why the firm has an advantage that it can exploit in the foreign market. Rugman distinguishes between two types of advantages: country-specific advantages (CSAs), such as a relative abundance of capital in the home country, and firm-specific advantages (FSAs), such as technological advantage held by a particular firm. He argues that CSAs are not likely to play a significant role in determining IDFI, or even in determining DFI in general. He cites Gray (1982a, p. 192) that 'national characteristics play only a minor part in the determination of the patterns of trade and [DFI] among industrial nations'.

However, one can offer the alternative view that changes in CSAs are probably a major factor in the growth of IDFI. In the years immediately following the Second World War, the United States was relatively abundant in both capital and technology. US firms made substantial DFIs abroad, whereas DFI in the United States by foreign firms was insignificant. Later, as other countries accumulated capital and technology, the CSA of the United States in these factors became less important, and there was more opportunity for the two-way flow of investment. International differences in technology between individual industries became more important than overall CSAs in determining investment flows among developed countries. Finally, differences in FSAs within the same industry became important enough to cause IDFI.

According to this view, the growth of capital and technology abroad relative to their growth in the United States, and the consequent reduction in the CSAs of the United States, is the major cause of the growth in IDFI. This view is not inconsistent with Rugman's analysis. However, it places a different emphasis on the factors that determine IDFI, and it has slightly different policy implications. For example, someone who adopts this view is less likely to attribute the growth of such investment to an increase in market power of individual multinational enterprises (MNEs) or to increased efficiencies from internalisation.

Another important factor that influences the amount of IDFI is the classification scheme used to define industries. The definition of industries is somewhat arbitrary, and one would expect the amount of IDFI to depend heavily on the classification scheme used. A greater degree of homogeneity of goods within an industry is likely to reduce the amount of IDFI, just as it reduces the amount of intra-industry foreign trade. In particular, more aggregate industry classifications are apt to contain more of this investment.[1] Rugman notes this point, but I would give it greater emphasis than he does. The amount of IDFI, the reasons for it and its policy implications all depend heavily on the degree of aggregation used to define 'industry'.

The above statements do not disagree with Rugman's analysis, but they place greater emphasis on factors besides internalisation that determine IDFI. Rugman states that IDFI 'is a significant economic phenomenon but it does not require a new theory for its explanation. The theory of internalisation explains it very well. Identify the relevant FSA of the MNE and the reason for cross investment will have been found.' My point is that explaining the origins of these FSAs is an equally important part of a complete explanation of IDFI. I believe this part deserves a greater emphasis than it is given by Rugman.

In his conclusions, Rugman mentions the benefits of IDFI. He argues that such investment 'helps remove the effects of government-created market imperfections'. He also states that this investment 'is superior to short-term interventionist policies which preserve sunset industries and the interests of owners and workers at the expense of national economic welfare'. This does not appear to me to be one of the more important benefits of this investment. 'Sunset' industries are usually the result of a loss in national comparative advantage, and these industries are unlikely to attract significant DFI. For example, I would not expect inward DFI in the US shoe, apparel and steel industries to significantly alleviate the problems of those industries, or to reduce the adverse welfare effects of import restrictions in those industries.

Rugman fails to point out that the ability of DFI-flows to respond to trade restrictions may in some instances reduce overall economic efficiency and welfare. This is true because governments may deliberately impose trade restrictions in order to attract DFI. Examples of this endogeneity of government policies abound. Witness the popularity of performance requirements, such as those Brazil and Mexico impose on their local automotive industries. Canada has apparently sometimes imposed import restrictions as a means of attracting DFI in specific industries. Local-content requirements have recently been proposed for the US automotive industry, at least in part to encourage inward DFI. Foreign governments often require that US DFI accompany their purchases of military equipment. Small countries often use tax incentives and subsidies to attract DFI as one of the few means available to them to effectively provide fiscal stimulus, with consequent adverse effects on the efficient world-wide allocation of resources.

An important benefit of IDFI that occurs to me – and one that Rugman does not mention – is that this investment is likely to increase economic welfare by increasing competition in industries where scale economies or other natural barriers to entry tend to result in too few domestic producers. The increased competition will reduce the market power of domestic firms in these industries, and should improve the allocation of resources by reducing the gaps between rates of transformation in production and rates of substitution in consumption in the domestic economy.

Notes

* The views expressed here are those of the author, and do not necessarily reflect the views of the US International Trade Commission.
1. A good description of the effects of aggregation on homogeneity in an industry is given by Finger (1975).

3 INTRA-INDUSTRY DIRECT FOREIGN INVESTMENT, MARKET STRUCTURE, FIRM RIVALRY AND TECHNOLOGICAL PERFORMANCE

Edward M. Graham

Introduction

This chapter discusses the effects of intra-industry direct foreign investment (IDFI) on market structure of industries and conduct and performance of firms within them. The aim of the discussion is to clarify certain public-policy issues regarding IDFI. These issues include:

(1) Is it in the interest of the United States to regulate further the direct investment entry of foreign firms into the US market?

(2) Does IDFI reduce rivalry among firms globally, and if so, does this call for an international antitrust approach to regulation of competition?

(3) Should (and can) the United States encourage further inward DFI?

It is not the goal of this chapter to provide definitive resolutions of these issues — such a goal would be far too ambitious — but rather to examine these issues in light of what is known (or hypothesised) about the effects of IDFI on competition and performance of firms in affected industries. In this spirit, a discussion of the three issues *per se* is postponed until the end of this chapter, where the discussion is presented in the context of the analysis developed earlier. The analysis and discussion are limited to effects of IDFI on rates of technological progress in manufacturing industries. Firm and industry performance are viewed primarily under the criterion of the rate of creation of new technology, rather than the more usual criteria of price and static efficiency. This focus seems appropriate because IDFI mostly occurs in manufacturing industries for which, in the long-run at least, technological progress is by far the most important determinant of welfare gains. It further seems appropriate because much recent writing on the multinational enterprise (MNE) has concentrated on this type of firm's market power in terms of ability to control the rate of creation and diffusion of new technology and consequent effects on national capabilities to generate technological progress.[1]

Some Preliminary Considerations

It is impossible to understand the effects of IDFI without some knowledge of its causes. And while it is not the purpose of this chapter to review the large and growing literature on the determinants of DFI, a few preliminary observations are none the less in order.

There seem to be two distinct 'families' of theories of DFI which are to some extent competing.[2] One family is typified by Dunning's 'eclectic theory' of the MNE (Dunning, 1979, 1980). The 'eclectic theory' is actually a synthesis of a number of paradigms, all loosely derived from neo-classical theories of trade and locus of production (location theory). Dunning posits that a firm invests in operations outside of its (geographical) home market when the firm holds proprietary assets (usually technology or differentiated products) which can be efficiently exploited internally within the firm but not within the home market. Thus, DFI is the matching of (internalisable) firm-specific advantages (FSAs) with location-specific advantages (LSAs).

Under the 'eclectic theory', DFI would generally enhance static welfare in the sense that the allocation of resources would be improved as a result, assuming FSAs do not accord to their owner monopoly power in world markets. Dunning has argued that IDFI has tended to be on the increase among developed countries whose economic structures are similar, leading to greater rationalisation of activities by MNEs within these nations, that is, these firms increasingly site activities according to different LSAs. If so, the effects doubtlessly are to increase intra-firm trade and to enhance static welfare. In effect, the MNE moves each nation closer to realising its (factor-proportion determined) comparative advantage. Kojima (1977, 1982), however, has argued that at least some IDFI has resulted from efforts by firms to circumvent government-imposed trade restrictions. In such cases, the results could be trade- and welfare-reducing.

Whether or not the MNE optimises dynamic welfare, however, is open to considerable debate (Dunning, 1982). Much of the debate is about the effects of MNE operations on host countries' technological capabilities. It has been argued that in order to maintain its FSAs (specifically, its technological advantages), the firm must exercise market power to eliminate or at least to reduce the threat of rivals imitating these advantages (Magee, 1977, 1981). Thus, it is held that MNEs will attempt to squelch local entrepreneurs in host nations who might, in the absence of the MNE, engage in innovative activities to the greater benefit of the local economies. This sort of complaint against MNEs is most often voiced by developing nations (Stewart, 1981). However, similar arguments have been voiced in Europe, where it has been claimed that US-based firms have acted to put technologically dynamic local rivals out of business, sometimes by acquiring them. If indeed the MNE does succeed in doing this, it can distort long-run dynamic comparative advantages, that is, nations or regions could fail to develop specific technologies which might be the basis for future changes in patterns of international trade. And, to an undesirable degree, technological innovation would become concentrated in the home countries of MNEs.[3]

Of relevance to these considerations is the source of the alleged market power of the MNE. This, according to most authors, comes from two sources:

1. The ability of the firm to economise on transaction costs (including, importantly, costs of information) via internalising the buying and selling of certain factors of production, raw material inputs, or intermediate goods. The possibility of savings via 'internalisation', rather than participation in open (external) markets is argued to imply a market failure (Buckley and Casson, 1976; Teece, 1982).

2. The ability of the firm to use rents garnered in one market to cross-subsidise activities in some other market.

It has been widely noted, however, that DFI takes place largely not in industries which are monopolies or dominated by a single firm, but in ones which are oligopolistically structured and within which interdependence among several sellers is significant (Behrman, 1969). This observation has led to a second family of theories of the determinants of DFI, those that see this investment resulting, in part at least, from oligopolistic reaction. There exists no synthesis of oligopolistic reaction paradigms, but the essence of them all is that DFI is undertaken by an oligopolist in order to counter, check, or forestall a move by some rival oligopolist. The first family derives loosely from location theory, the second from game theory.

As noted, the two families are to some extent competing ones. If a firm's motivation for DFI is to respond to or anticipate the action of a rival, that firm will not necessarily act to match a FSA to some LSA. Investments motivated by oligopolistic reaction hence do not necessarily improve allocative efficiency. The best example might be where an MNE enters a local market in order to foreclose a rival's participation in it, and, in doing so, obtains trade protection for an inefficient local subsidiary. This, of course, requires host-government acquiescence (Parry, 1979). But neither do such investments invariably work against allocative efficiency. More importantly, as will be demonstrated as one of the central themes of this chapter, oligopolistic reaction might act to offset some efforts of MNEs to exercise market power to defend FSAs. If so, the effect of the offset will be to enhance the rate of technological progress.

A central and largely unresolved issue of economics is the extent to which the conditions for allocative efficiency correspond to those for dynamic efficiency, that is, for optimisation of the rate of technological advance. (Elements of this dilemma are reflected in the discussion of the eclectic theory.) In most general terms, this rate is determined by two sets of causal factors (Nelson, 1981). First are the opportunities for creation of new technologies, which are a function of the state of knowledge applicable to technical problems faced by a particular industry. At any given time, different industries face different opportunities. *Ceteris paribus*, progress will occur most rapidly in those industries where the opportunities are such that expected costs of innovation are low relative to expected revenues (quasi-rents).

However, the second set of causal factors violates this *ceteris paribus* assumption. These are the structural characteristics of the industry. Exactly what characteristics have which effects is a matter of controversy. On the one hand, it is argued that considerations of appropriability require that innovating firms be able to hold a monopoly over exploitation of a new technology. This would suggest that innovating firms must hold some element of market power and hence that a degree of distortion of allocative efficiency must be tolerated if technical progress is to occur (Magee, 1981). But it is also argued that if a firm (a well co-ordinated oligopoly) possesses too much market power, that is, barriers to entry are too high, that firm might withhold new technologies from the market in order to amortise fully investments based on existing technologies. Thus, some element of inter-firm rivalry is also essential for high rates of technical progress. This leads to the dilemma posed by Schumpeter (1950): A firm's propensity to innovate is affected by a 'carrot', that is, the potential to earn supra-normal profits by means of a monopoly (albeit most probably a temporary one) on a new technology, and a 'stick', that is, the potential for loss of profits if rivals pre-empt development of the technology. Given any set of technological opportunities, the 'carrot' will be stronger, the greater the market power possessed by the firm *ex ante*. But the greater the market power possessed by a firm the less will be the power of the 'stick' to induce the firm to undertake investment in the new technology.

The interaction of these causal factors is captured in a simple conceptual model developed by Scherer (1967).[4] In Figure 3.1, curve C represents the expected discounted present value of costs associated with new product development opportunities as a function of development-time. The exact shape of the curve is a function of the technical opportunities facing the firm, as described above. In general, the curve is downward sloping because there are extra costs associated with accelerating the development of a technology, not incurred if development-time is extended. Curve V_1 represents the discounted present-value of expected quasi-rents from the technology as a function of the time of its commercial introduction. Delay in introducing the technology reduces this value mainly because the earlier the introduction, the longer the innovator can tap the technology's profit potential before imitators enter the market.[5] T_1 indicates the optimal development-time from the viewpoint of the firm, that is, that which maximises the difference between expected quasi-rents and expected development-costs.

Increasing rivalry will in general reduce both the time during which an innovator can monopolise the market by introducing a new technology ahead of rivals and the share of market which the innovator can expect to gain if the introduction is delayed. Moreover, the firm might increase its estimate of the probability that during any given interval of time a rival will pre-emptorially launch the innovation. The net effect is both to lower curve V_1 and to increase its slope. The result is shown as curve V_2 in Figure 3.1. The expected maximum profit of the innovator is less than before because of the reduced ability to appropriate quasi-rents from the commercialisation of the technology, but the optimal development-time is contracted.

If the amount of rivalry becomes excessive, expected present value of quasi-rents will always be less than costs, and a profit-maximising firm will not choose to undertake the development of the technology. Curve V_3 depicts this case in Figure 3.1. Such a situation arises as the structure of the industry approaches perfect competition, the structure which is held to maximise allocative (static) efficiency.

The Scherer model can be used to analyse the effect of aggressive

Figure 3.1: Present Values of Expected Quasi-rents and Expected Costs in Product Innovation Without Oligopolistic Collusion

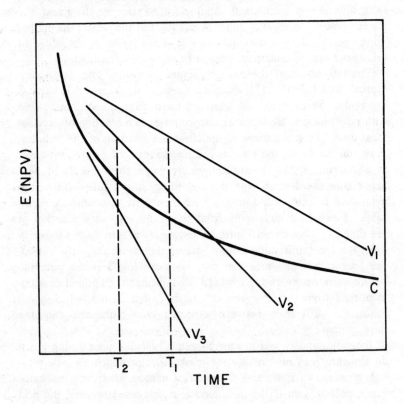

Note: E(NPV) is Expected Net Present Value.
Source: Scherer (1980, p. 367).

new entry by a firm into a market dominated by a single firm. From the dominant firm's point of view, *ex ante*, that is, before the new entry, the situation might appear as depicted by curves C and V_1. But *ex post*, the situation might appear more as depicted by curves C and V_2. Scherer (1980, p. 428) himself concludes that

> a monopolist or a company that already dominates the market . . . has little to gain from speeding up the introduction of new product improvements as long as other firms refrain from doing so . . . But if their market position is threatened by the intrusion (of a new rival)

Figure 3.2: Present Values of Expected Quasi-rents and Expected Costs in Product Innovation With Oligpolistic Collusion in Domestic Markets

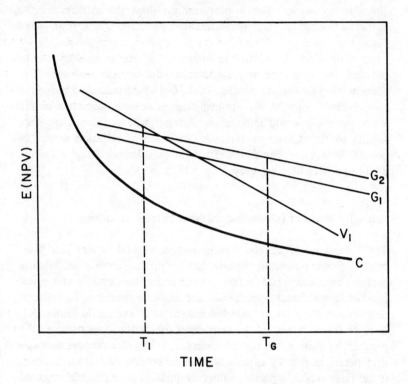

. . . they have a great deal to lose from running a poor second . . . (the model predicts) that dominant firms will be potent innovators when their market-shares are endangered.

Scherer's model and others similar to it embody Cournot-like assumptions that firms can neither collude among themselves successfully nor know with certainty what their rivals' responses to their moves will be. It is of some utility to ask what, in terms of the model, would be the effects of successful collusion. Suppose that in the absence of collusion, the situation faced by the firm was a depicted by curves C and V_1 in Figure 3.2. Successful collusion assures that the new product innovation, when launched, will be launched by all firms simultaneously. This reduces the expected quasi-rents associated with early introduction, because there is no longer any opportunity for any firm to monopolise, even briefly, the innovation. But the expected quasi-rents associated with later introduction are increased, because there is no chance that a rival will pre-empt the market with an earlier introduction. The net effects are captured by curves G_1 and G_2 in Figure 3.2.

In conclusion, the rate of introduction of new technology will be reduced, but it is indeterminate whether the collusion will reduce or increase firm's expected profits. Curve G_1 would indicate a reduction of expected profits at the optimal time of new product introduction while curve G_2 would indicate an increase. Whether or not expected profits would increase or decrease as a result of collusion would, of course, have some significant effect on the likelihood that collusion could be successfully achieved.

A Rivalry Model of Intra-industry Direct Foreign Investment

The Scherer model can be used to analyse why DFI might take place in an oligopoly possessing opportunities for product innovation. Suppose that the expected present-values of costs and quasi-rents of a major new product development opportunity for any one firm as a function of development-time are as depicted by curves C and T_1 in Figure 3.3. Because the costs exceed the quasi-rents for all development-times, the product innovation will not be undertaken. But also suppose that one firm perceives that by exploiting the new product in foreign markets, it can raise expected present values of quasi-rents to the level depicted by T_2. The slope of T_2 is greater than that of T_1 because the overseas market itself will be characterised by some rivalry. Hence the curve (not shown) depicting expected present-values of overseas quasi-rents will be downward sloping. The summation of the domestic and overseas markets will result in a curve of greater slope than the curve of either taken alone.

One conclusion which can be drawn from the model is that DFI activity may be stimulated by technological opportunities which would go untouched *ceteris paribus* but in the absence of the opportunity to trade or invest abroad. Another conclusion is that the rate of technological progress will increase as a result of the greater slope of the curve for the combined domestic and overseas markets.

Thus, the opportunity to garner additional quasi-rents from foreign markets might be an important motivation for firms to expand their activities overseas. There is evidence that the magnitude of these

Figure 3.3: Present Values of Expected Quasi-rents and Expected Costs in Product Innovation With Oligopolistic Rivalry in International Markets

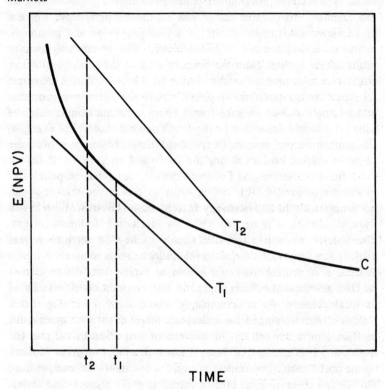

quasi-rents for US firms is substantial (Mansfield, Romeo and Wagner, 1979). Of course, firms have a number of options for exploiting technologies in overseas markets, including exportation, licensing and DFI. The lattermost can be accomplished via either take-over of existing firms or green-field investment. The option chosen by a firm is a function of several static and dynamic considerations, including those posited in the eclectic theory, that is, opportunities for achieving 'internal' economies (Dunning and Norman in this volume). The choice may also be affected by the degree to which the firm has accumulated overseas experience (Aharoni, 1966). To the extent that gaining such additional experience leads the firm to increase DFI relative to other overseas activities, this might be viewed as a learning phenomenon, that is, the firm's learning of exactly what internal economies can be realised.

A firm's decision on how to exploit overseas opportunities is not taken in a vacuum; government policies can have a major bearing on this decision. An obvious case is one mentioned previously, where a host-country government grants to a firm protection and monopoly rights as an inducement to invest locally. The investment decision might not be optimal from the point of view of the firm, but the firm might face exclusion from the market in the event that it does not acquiesce to the government policy. Conversely, certain government policies might induce (or even force) a firm to refrain from investment where this would otherwise be the firm's optimal choice. For example, US semiconductor manufacturers might have chosen to service the Japanese market via DFI during the 1960s and early 1970s, as indeed these firms did service the European market. But Japanese policy was to discourage inward DFI, and in order to service the market at all, US firms largely had to license their technologies (Borrus, Millstein and Zysman, 1982). Government policies, including indirect (macro-economic) ones, can affect the choice of how to service overseas markets in a variety of other ways (McCulloch in this volume).

Even if a firm chooses and is able to exploit the foreign market via DFI, government policies might still affect exactly how it establishes its local preserve. As an example, it would seem reasonable that a foreign entrant holding technological advantages might wish to establish itself in a local market via the buy-out of a significant local rival (or rivals), and hence to reduce rivalry.[6] But such a move might be blocked by the host-country government in order to maintain local competition. The foreign entrant might thus be forced to make a green-field investment. In some cases, however, the host government might actually encourage acquisition of a local firm by the foreign entrant in order, for example, to upgrade the local firm's technological capabilities.

Expansion of firms into foreign markets adds a new element to the dynamics of rivalry among product innovators in home markets. Selling in overseas markets can augment the expected revenues from introducing a new product. This is especially so if the firm can act as a monopolist in some segment of the overseas markets. If the firm brings to these markets new products not produced by local competitors, it might establish itself as a dominant firm by virtue of being first with these products. Alternatively, its dominance might be achieved by means of acquiring the strongest local firm already producing substitutes. It could then derive quasi-rents from overseas which would not be immediately available to rivals at home. The potential of these quasi-rents would stimulate the firm to accelerate its new-product development efforts at home, and this would be perceived as threatening by rivals. If entry barriers to the foreign markets could be overcome, these rivals might themselves become multinational in order to equalise the advantage held by the multinational firm, creating a clustering of DFI in the industry.[7]

Of course, the model thus far describes one-way DFI and not IDFI. A useful starting point in dealing with IDFI is to examine the host country effects of one-way DFI by advanced countries in other advanced countries, for example, the effects of entry by US firms into Europe. What is of particular concern here is what happens within specific industries of the host country after entry by strong foreign rivals. Let us focus on penetration of European markets by US-based manufacturing MNEs during the decades following the Second World War. One interpretation might be that these firms behaved exactly as discussed earlier, that is, attempted with some success to eliminate technologically threatening local rivals. While there was concern during the 1960s that this might indeed have been happening (Servan-Schreiber, 1967), in retrospect, it appears that European technology has staged a remarkable comeback.

In many industries, US MNEs in Europe were not powerful enough to eliminate local rivals, however desirable that might have been in principle from the viewpoint of US MNEs.[8] In some cases, of course, US MNEs were prevented from acquiring dominant local producers of substitutable goods, since such acquisitions might have given the US entrant a locally dominant market position. However, US MNEs often did have enough market power to be able to disrupt existing patterns of conduct among local firms. Thus, they may have acted not unlike the new entrant into a market characterised by a dominant firm or by a small number of firms behaving similarly to a dominant firm. In fact, some observers, for example, Behrman (1972), Dunning (1958, 1970) and Caves (1971, 1974a) have suggested that entry by US firms served to stimulate local technological innovation rather than suppress it. Thus, while indigenous European firms in most industries thus proved to be too strong and resilient to be broken by the power of US multinationals, this power was great enough to provoke the indigenous firms to accelerate their efforts to generate new technologies. Also, in their efforts to become more dynamic technologically, in some cases European firms received considerable assistance from their national governments.

No matter how dynamic a technological response indigenous

European firms might have shown, the US-based MNEs entering into their markets retained some advantages which posed a threat to uni-national rivals. One principal source of the threat lay in the US MNEs' ability to cross-subsidise activities internally within their organisations. For example, they could use rents generated in external, that is, US markets, to cut prices locally to increase their market shares. They could continue to transfer technologies developed abroad, at low marginal cost, to local subsidiaries in order to gain renewed advantages over domestic rivals. Operating multinationally, they could view the costs and benefits of new product development differently in compari-son with local uninational rivals. In terms of Figure 3.3, the US MNE might calculate the expected present-value of quasi-rents from develop-ment of some new product as lying along T_2, while a local firm, having more limited marketing horizons, might calculate the quasi-rents it could appropriate as lying along T_1. As a result, the US MNE might proceed with development of technologies, which, if successful, would give it advantage over local rivals.

Some of this threat could be countered if a European firm were to become multinational itself, in particular to enter the home market of its US-based MNE rival. It would thus expose itself to the same set of economic conditions which give to the US MNE its source of advantages. Empirical evidence presented by Flowers (1976) and Graham (1978) indicates that entry of European firms into the United States has followed entry of US rivals into Europe in several industries, suggesting that the European DFI indeed might have been stimulated by the earlier US penetration of European markets.

European firms would have options in servicing the US market. Many of the considerations in deciding which option to take would be the same as those in the initial expansion of US firms into Europe. One additional consideration, however, would favour the DFI option. Operating in the home market of its principal multinational rivals, the European firm derives two benefits which would be absent were it to have limited its operations to its own European home markets. First, the European firm is better able to replicate the cost and benefit trade-offs faced by its US rivals in the development of new product technologies, that might be used to advantage by the latter in European markets. Second, once its gains a foothold in the US market, the European firm is able to pose a threat to its US rivals on their own 'home turf'. The European firm can then, for example, counter its US rivals' cross-subsidisation, to increase market shares in Europe, by initiating similar behaviour in the United States. More generally, the fact that the European-based firm and its US-based rivals would be able to counter aggressive rivalry in one market area with retaliation in another may lead to alteration of conduct in all major markets. This collective ability to pose a counter-threat is enhanced if all firms actually operate in one another's markets via DFI. Otherwise, a firm's activities might be blocked by government intervention. If, for example, one firm services a foreign market via exports and attempts to cross-subsidise expansion of the local market share, it might wind up facing local import-restrictions triggered by antidumping or counter-vailing measures actions (Graham, 1978).

The internationalisation of firms via cross-penetration of markets thus significantly increases seller interdependence. The prospects of such an increase has led some authors to conclude that the inter-nationalisation of European firms will significantly reduce long-run competition and rivalry among firms world-wide in numerous indus-tries. Hymer and Rowthorn foresaw a future when, after a decade wherein

> both US corporations and non-US corporations try to establish market positions and protect themselves from the challenges of each other . . . the cross penetration . . . has as its logical end a stock equilibrium where all of the dominant oligopolists have a similar world-wide distribution of sales. (Hymer and Rowthorn, 1970, pp. 81–2)

They saw a gradual but turbulent reduction in the authority of the nation-state as the power of international oligopolies grows.[9]

The transitional state envisaged by Hymer and Rowthorn wherein corporations try to 'protect themselves from the challenges of each other' is clearly one in which aggressive rivalry among MNEs could occur. In developing strategies for entering into the United States, for example, European firms often introduced new-product technologies which were at least as disruptive to established conduct of local firms as were earlier introductions of new-product technologies into Europe by US MNEs. Here the model of the new entrant into an industry dominated by single firm or like-minded oligopolists seems apt (Faith, 1971; McClain, 1974; Franko, 1976). Also, European firms have often located their US operations in regions of the United States far from where their domestic rivals are located in order to take advantage of non-unionised labour and other locational advantages (Daniels, 1971). This practice too has shaken up patterns of conduct in domestic US industries.

As one example where entry by a major European firm significantly accelerated new-product introduction by domestic US rivals, let us examine the tyre industry. Prior to the entry into the North American market in 1971 of the French firm Michelin (first into Canada and then into the United States), domestic US firms lagged behind their own European subsidiaries in introducing radial tyres to the market. The domestic industry was characterised by a small number of producers (four firms dominated the market) and quite high barriers to entry. All of the four largest US producers had major subsidiaries in Europe where there were also several large local firms, of which Michelin was one. In Europe, radial tyres were introduced in the late 1950s. By 1970, 65 per cent of all tyres sold there were radials, many of which were produced by subsidiaries of US MNEs. By contrast, in the United States only 7 per cent of tyres sold in 1970 were radials, mostly imports and considered to be speciality tyres. Following the DFI entry of Michelin and its local production of radials, however, US tyremakers began quickly to switch to production of radials themselves. As a result, by 1980 the majority of tyres sold in the United States were radials.

This example might in fact tell two stories. First, in Europe, where entry by US firms intensified rivalry in the tyre industry, the rate of introduction and diffusion of new product technology was more rapid than in the United States itself. Arguably, this situation has existed in other industries as well – the automotive industry comes to mind. One explanation might be that US firms tacitly colluded to withhold radials from the US market in order to maximise rents in the United States. They might have wished to amortise fully existing physical capital that was specialised in the production of biased tyres before introducing the newer radial technology. Their rents, in turn, could have been used to build European market shares by price cutting. But Michelin's entry into the United States ended this possibility, if it existed. Indeed – and this is the second story – the Michelin entry apparently accelerated greatly the introduction and diffusion of new product technology in the United States.

But such rivalry, leading to increased rates of new-product introduction, might be viewed by those who accept the analysis of Hymer and Rowthorn as a transitory phenomenon. So the question remains: In the long-run, after transitional phenomena have died down, will cross-penetration of each other's home markets by US and European MNEs through IDFI lead to a stable oligopoly-equilibrium world-wide, as predicted by Hymer and Rowthorn, or will some other outcome ensue?

The outcome is exceedingly difficult to predict; no one can make the prediction with confidence. As will be demonstrated — again with the aid of the Scherer model — the outcome is likely to be industry-specific.

Fundamentally, the effect of IDFI as depicted here is to increase rivalry and seller interdependence in industries where it occurs. In terms of the Scherer model, the effect as observed by any one firm is both to displace downward and to increase the slope of the expected present-value of quasi-rents curve, that is, the shift depicted in Figure 3.1 from T_1 to T_2 (or even from T_2 to T_3). (This, as previously noted, assumes no collusion exists and that the entry is not accomplished via acquisition of potential rivals.) The initial effect of transnational expansion, however, is to displace this curve upward. Therefore, even after the downward displacement caused by IDFI, the curve may be higher than it would have been in the absence of any internationalisation. In line with the Scherer formulation, what may be termed the 'pure rivalry effect' (the increase in slope of the T curve) acts by itself to induce firms to accelerate new-product development. But what might be termed the 'appropriability effect' (the downward shift of the T curve) reduces appropriable quasi-rents. If this is excessive, firms may not develop the new product at all.

The lattermost possibility — an increase in competition so great that technological progress stops entirely — strikes me as a most unlikely possibility. Thus, from the Scherer model we are left with the expectation that IDFI will generally act to accelerate new-product development and introduction. This seems to be the most likely consequence for most industries. There might be exceptions, however, where collusion among large rivals will act to reduce technical progress. Then public agencies would have a legitimate role to act against them.

It should be noted that IDFI can increase effective rivalry even in cases where it has no effect on industry concentration. For example, consider the case with two nations where (before IDFI) an industry was monopolised in each nation by a local firm. Globally, the Herfindahl index of concentration in this industry would be 0.5. But so long as neither of the two firms attempted to compete in the market, there would be absolutely no rivalry in the industry. After IDFI, however, whereby each of the two firms penetrated the other's home market and, by assumption, held equal market share in its 'foreign' market, rivalry would clearly increase. There would be duopoly in both national markets in place of monopoly, but the index of concentration would remain at 0.5. Of course, the duopolists might collude to behave jointly as monopolists. That is less likely, however, than a true monopolist behaving monopolistically.

Although the Scherer model assumes no collusion, we cannot rule it out altogether among MNEs from different home countries. But even so, interpenetration of national markets by MNEs based in different countries — assuming that no merger of major rivals results — acts to reduce the likelihood that collusion can be successfully undertaken globally. That is if collusion can occur in an industry after IDFI, it is likely that the conditions for collusion were even riper before IDFI. The more rivals in any given market, the more likely that at least one firm will cheat on any collusive effort.

A qualification is in order. If a global industry is marked by one-way DFI, for example, US firms operate in Europe but European firms do not operate in the United States, behaviour of firms might be characterised by rivalry in the DFI-penetrated market but by collusion in the market not penetrated by DFI. It has already been conjectured that this situation might have existed in the tyre industry before the arrival of Michelin in North America. In such a case, IDFI could conceivably result in not greater rivalry but collusion. (In the tyre industry case, for instance, an implicit bargain might be struck between US and European producers that the latter will ease off on new-product development in exchange for no further increase in European market share by the former. Such a bargain could be more readily enforceable after IDFI because of the European firms' ability to launch new products in the United States.) If this were to be the case, little change would occur in the home market of the original MNEs. On the other hand, the technological dynamism of the original host market would suffer. Arguably, however, if a slowdown in the rate of technological advance occurs in any geographical market of the industry, it will ultimately induce slowdowns in other markets. None the less, while this qualification does not negate the earlier point that IDFI generally reduces the likelihood of successful globally collusive behaviour.

But can global collusion in fact succeed in any industry characterised by IDFI? In principle, it is most likely to succeed if existing firms in the industry can erect and maintain high barriers to entry and if collusion increases maximum attainable profit for all parties to the collusion. (This is the case depicted by curve G_2 in Figure 3.2.) Conversely, if potential new entrants can surmount barriers to entry, efforts at collusion are likely to break down. One characteristic of the past decade indeed has been considerable such new entry into most industries. This role, often played by firms from Japan, has reduced considerably opportunities for and incidents of successful collusion. Furthermore, new entry into an industry enlarges the number of rivals. The more rivals in an industry, the more likely that some firm will find it worth while to break away from any collusive arrangement.

One additional consideration. It has been widely observed that tendencies towards collusion and cartelisation are strongest during periods of recession or depression. The Great Depression of the 1930s was marked by numerous effective international cartels.[10] Furthermore, especially during periods of depression, firms can somehow agree to refrain from rivalry based on new-product introduction while competing effectively along other dimensions.[11]

The likelihood of successful collusion is clearly reduced if firms perceive that they can potentially increase profits by pre-empting rivals in product innovation (the case depicted by curve G_1 in Figure 3.2). Whether such potential opportunities exist depends both on the market structure faced by the firms and on the technological opportunities relevant to the industry. These variables vary considerably among industries. Thus, the likelihood of successful global collusion would differ substantially from industry to industry. Attempting to identify in which specific industries, if any, the potential for such collusion is significant is beyond the scope of this study. Such identification might be one direction for future research. On the whole, however, I believe that such potential is not great for most industries characterised by IDFI under the present circumstances.

The more important research issue is whether the central hypothesis of this chapter — that IDFI is motivated to a significant extent by inter-firm rivalry — is a difficult one to test. If rivalry does act as a motive, it can act in tandem with others. Even if rivalry is the major motive for penetration of foreign markets, the exact form that the penetration takes is likely to be strongly affected by government policies, internal firm economies and factor proportions. Exactly how significant are rivalistic considerations as a motive for DFI is an issue that will not lend itself to easy empirical and definite resolution (Caves, 1982, Chapter 4).

Public Policy Issues

In light of the preceding analysis, an effort is now made to address the three public policy issues posed in the opening paragraph of this chapter.

*Is It in the Interest of the United States to Regulate Further the Direct
Investment Entry of Foreign Firms into the US Market?*

If 'to regulate further' is taken to mean 'to restrict or inhibit' such
entry via mechanisms not already in place, the analysis of this chapter
strongly suggests that no such regulation would be desirable. IDFI tends
to increase rivalry among firms which often serves to accelerate the rate
of technical progress. The major possible exception would be the case,
discussed earlier, where IDFI acts to reduce rivalry in the host nation
market into which DFI had entered prior to the counterflow of DFI
into home nation market. But the regulation of reverse DFI into the
home nation market in such a case would be a clumsy way of ensuring
continued rivalry in that market. Moreover, it is not certain that situations such as the one described do actually exist.

This is not to say, however, that US inward DFI should be entirely
unregulated. There are certain types of IDFI which definitely warrant
scrutiny. In general, those cases warranting the most scrutiny are those
which could facilitate collusive behaviour among industrial rivals. The
recent decision of General Motors and Toyota to produce jointly an
automobile in the United States may be an example. It is not clear to
me why, if Toyota is to produce directly in the United States, it must
do so in a joint venture with the dominant domestic firm. It does not
require much imagination to hypothesise that an undertaking of this
sort might reduce rivalry between two large competing firms rather
than increase it. Here, of course, the objection is largely to the particular form of the DFI and not to the fact *per se* that Toyota is undertaking DFI in the United States.

Overall, the objective of scrutiny and regulation of US inward
DFI should be that it does not reduce rivalry among major competing
firms. But the fact that US inward DFI should be subject to some
scrutiny and regulation where appropriate does not mean that new
mechanisms for control are needed. Existing government apparatus for
regulation of competition, that is, the Antitrust Division of the US
Justice Department and, to a lesser extent, the US Federal Trade Commission, has historically been able to provide this scrutiny. In some
cases, the US Government has actually blocked inward DFIs deemed to
have potentially anticompetitive effects, as discussed by Faith (1971)
and McClain (1974). In most such cases, foreign firms have sought to
enter the US market via acquisition of ongoing domestic firms. Much
criticism in the past has been of the sort that such regulation has been
overzealous, that is, has often served to block acquisitions by foreign
firms of marginal domestic firms which might have actually increased

effective competition in the United States. Very little evidence or even opinion exists that inward DFI historically has been underscrutinised.

Should There be an International Antitrust Approach to Regulation of Competition Among Multinational Enterprises Based in Different Countries?[12]

A full response to this issue would require a discourse on the merits and demerits of antitrust as a means of regulating competition. Such a discourse will not be attempted here. There is some opinion that the antitrust approach is increasingly ineffective (Thurow, 1980, Chapter 6). However, accepting that there is some merit to antitrust regulation, the case is strong that such regulation should be pursued at an international level. The reasons are clear: large firms possessing market power, those to which antitrust regulation is largely directed, increasingly operate on a global level. Also, to an increasing degree, firms from a multitude of nations have gone multinational. Consequently, the antitrust lawyer's concept of the 'relevant market' spills over national boundaries. In numerous important industries, the 'relevant market' is virtually the whole world, at least a substantial portion of it.

How to pursue antitrust regulation at an international (multilateral) level is a matter not easily addressed. Such regulation, to be at all effective, would require a ceding of a significant element of sovereignty by all major nation-states, a most unlikely occurrence. However, there is an example of supranational antitrust regulation: Directorate General IV of the Commission of the European Communities. Although its experience has been mixed, it has not been abandoned. Whether (and how) such regulation might be promulgated, say, at the level of the Organisation for Economic Cooperation and Development is an issue worthy of further exploration.

Should (and Can) the United States Encourage Further Inward Direct Foreign Investment?

As already suggested, the United States should not discourage further inward DFI. Should it provide additional incentives to lure such investment? I believe that incentives are not necessary. Inward DFI has grown rapidly in recent years, possibly for reasons touched upon in this chapter and possibly for other reasons as well. In the medium-term, there is little reason to expect an abatement of this investment (Erdilek, 1983). Furthermore, research has repeatedly shown that host-country incentives do not significantly affect DFI decisions. Most often they serve to subsidise an investment which would have taken place anyway.

The major case where such incentives do have an effect on the DFI decision is where an investor, having decided already to invest, is nearly indifferent between two locations in different jurisdictions. In such a case, the availability of a subsidy may tilt the decision to the jurisdiction offering the subsidy. Should the other jurisdiction get wind of this, however, it might counter with a subsidy of its own. Instances have been recorded where this leads to a bidding war to the benefit of the investor and at the expense of the taxpayer in the jurisdiction that eventually wins the war. In such instances, both jurisdictions might be better-off simply to agree to offer no incentives at all.

A related question is whether the United States should pursue efforts to encourage additional DFI in trade-impacted industries, that is, those industries in which imports have recently gained significant increases in market share and in which domestic employment has declined. After all, some argue, trade and DFI are alternative ways for foreign firms to service US markets; DFI can serve to bring to the United States market many (but not all) of the benefits from trade while preserving domestic employment.

This is a complex issue, and it can only be touched upon here. Let us see which benefits from trade are preserved by the DFI alternative and which are lost. Preserved are most of the dynamic benefits: the stimulus to technological innovation created by enlargement of markets and increase in effective rivalry among firms. I have argued in this chapter that these are possibly the most important gains from the internationalisation of business activities. I should also note, however, that when DFI is forced by government action, in mosts cases by trade restrictions, the result falls short of the happy marriage of firm-specific and location-specific advantages linked by internal firm economies, as depicted in the eclectic theory of DFI. Instead, there is likely to be some important element of mismatch of these three elements, leading to misallocation of resources. Such a misallocation comes at some cost, which is not trivial. One element of the cost, for example, is the retention of resources in activities from which, over the long-run, the host nation might do better to disinvest.

It would be simplistic and dogmatic to argue that such costs are never worth paying. In some cases, the short-run costs of too fast a rate of disinvestment in an activity might far exceed the present value of the costs of any distortions due to import restrictions accompanied by inward DFI. And even if such a calculus is not favourable from a purely economic perspective, DFI, by preserving most of the dynamic benefits of trade, could be an acceptable second-best solution to otherwise intractable political pressures, which otherwise might lead to the exclusion of foreign firms from the US market.

Be this as it may, it would seem highly unwise to encourage DFI as an alternative to trade as a 'policy in a vacuum'. Rather, such a policy, if pursued, should be carried out against a backdrop of specific goals with respect to which industries should contract at what rates relative to the economy as a whole and which should expand. What is implied, of course, is some effort to determine how the nation's spectrum of comparative advantages is likely to change over time and what adjustments will be required by these changes. To some observers, such an effort is tantamount to industrial policy. Industrial policy is viewed by some individuals as an anathema but by others as the future solution of the US economic problems. But no matter what view one takes, one must recognise that a policy of encouraging foreign firms to substitute DFI for trade as a mode of doing business in the United States represents government intervention in the marketplace. No such intervention should be attempted without some knowledge of what the effects will be and whether these effects really are in the nation's best interest.

Notes

1. The recent thinking – that is the thinking of the past ten years or so – is summarised in Dunning (1982).

2. There exists a third 'family' which views the MNE as simply an institution for international financial intermediation. Under this reasoning, DFI occurs simply to enable investors to diversify asset holdings across international barriers. Such reasoning is of limited plausibility, and hence this third family is not further discussed here.

3. The reasons why an MNE might wish to concentrate its R and D efforts in its home country are explored by Vernon (1974). Possible distortions resulting therefrom are discussed in Vernon (1981).

4. A similar but more rigorous (or mathematical) model is presented by Kamien and Schwartz (1978).

5. Even if the nominal value of the stream of quasi-rents were unaffected by the timing of the introduction of the innovation, a delay in this introduction will reduce the present value of the stream. Thus, the curve will be downward sloping even in the absence of any rivals.

6. If a foreign entrant into a local market possesses firm-specific advantages not held by potential local rivals – so that the market value of the local rivals would be increased were they to gain access to these advantages – the entrant may be willing to pay a premium over *ex ante* market value of one or more of these local firms in order to integrate them into its global operations. Of course, the local equities market might recognise the value of the potential acquisition to the foreign firm, and might demand some premium, but so long as the total asking price were to be lower than the internal value of the acquisition to the

acquiring firm, the acquisition would be realisable. In such a case, the acquisition would be of benefit to the shareholders of both the foreign and local firms but might be contrary to social welfare interests.

7. Such a clustering indeed has been observed by Knickerbocker (1973) in the DFI activities of US firms.

8. Indeed, one well-considered interpretation (the product cycle theory) of US firms' DFI would hold that this DFI was motivated in large part by fear on the part of US firms of losing European markets to local firms. In the absence of such a defensive motivation for DFI, US firms would have serviced the European market by exports from the United States (Vernon, 1966).

9. This theme and variations on it have been raised by other authors, such as Behrman (1971) and Vernon (1971, Chapter 8).

10. For an account of these see Hexner (1945). The origins of many of these cartels, however, predated the Great Depression (Domeratzky, 1928).

11. This certainly occurred during the Great Depression, which, as noted, was a period marked by numerous international cartels (Edwards, 1944).

12. The antitrust and IDFI issue is explored in greater depth by Nelson and Silvia in this volume. See also Caves (1982, Chapter 10).

* * *

COMMENT

Jean-François Hennart

Introduction

Graham's study is a contribution to the long-standing debate on the causes and effects of direct foreign investment (DFI) on world competition. Graham focuses on intra-industry direct foreign investment (IDFI) and argues that it can be explained in terms of game theory. It arises when oligopolists based in different countries 'counter, check or forestall each other's moves' by investing in each other's home markets. Thus, recent European DFI in the United States can be explained as a response to earlier investments by US firms in Europe. IDFI is likely to increase the degree of international rivalry, particularly by accelerating the development and introduction of innovations.

The Oligopolistic Theory of Intra-industry Direct Foreign Investment

Hymer and Rowthorn (1970) were the first to view DFI as caused by oligopolistic reaction. They predicted that DFI by US firms in Europe would trigger counter-DFI by European firms in the United States. Increased multinationalisation by European firms would lead to cross-penetration of markets, greater concentration and increased collusion.

Graham (1974 and 1978) and Flowers (1976) tested the Hymer–Rowthorn hypothesis and confirmed its general validity. Graham argued that European retaliatory DFI in the United States would temporarily disrupt oligopolistic stability, but that cross-penetration of markets through IDFI would likely result in international collusion between large US and European multinational enterprises (MNEs), and even perhaps in world-wide monopolies. Only continuous entry by new firms might prevent such collusion from occurring.

His present study marks therefore a change in Graham's views. IDFI is still undertaken with the intent of reducing competition, but this result is unlikely to be attained. Graham now believes that 'inter-penetration of national markets by MNEs of differing nationalities always acts to reduce the likelihood that collusion can be successfully undertaken globally.'

I share Graham's view that the recent wave of IDFI by European and Japanese firms will lead to increased competition. But my optimism stems from my belief that many IDFIs cannot be explained by oligopolistic reaction, and that those that can be are inherently pro-competitive.

Types of Intra-industry Direct Foreign Investment

'Exchange of threats' probably accounts for a small share of what statistics show as IDFIs. Some of them are statistical illusions caused by the level of data aggregation. When French firms produce dairy products in the United States, and US firms manufacture cookies and crackers in France, these appear as IDFIs when seen at the two-digit Standard Industrial Classification (SIC) level. Yet they are not really IDFIs, since yogurt and crackers are not close substitutes, and there-fore, in a strict sense, do not belong to the same industry.

The second type of IDFI — which probably makes up the bulk of such investments — arises when firms in the same industry manufacture differentiated goods in each other's home markets. Because tastes and factor-cost proportions vary between countries, and because of histori-cal accidents, firms based in different countries often possess specific types of proprietary know-how. In many cases, these assets are most efficiently exploited through DFI (Hennart, 1982). MNEs may thus manufacture overseas products which, although they belong to the same industry group, have medium or low cross-elasticity. Examples are ethical drugs with different therapeutic uses, different types of machinery and different types of chemicals.

A special case of the above occurs when domestic suppliers follow their customers overseas. Banking provides an interesting example. US banks have followed their customers to Europe; European firms are now establishing branches in the United States. Branches of foreign banks are able to compete with domestic banks because their parents' nationality gives them specific advantages, such as a deposit base in a specific vehicle-currency, ready access to a particular stock of information and commercial intelligence and privileged ties with longstanding domestic customers (Caves, 1982; Yannopoulos, 1983). In such cases, the degree of product differentiation may vary from medium to high. Firms which are in the same industry are now somewhat insulated from the moves of their rivals. Oligopolistic reaction and 'exchange of threats' is then less of a factor.

We have IDFIs *stricto sensu* when the products sold by oligopolists within an industry are only slightly differentiated, and their cross-elasticity is therefore high. Such investments are made by mature oligopolies producing fairly homogeneous goods. These constitute a subset of all horizontal direct foreign investors, which are in large part firms producing new and differentiated products. In mature oligopolies, the degree of seller interdependence is high, and oligopolistic rivals will take into account the effects of their actions on one another. Oligopolistic reaction may then be a motive for such IDFIs.

Oligopolistic Collusion and Intra-industry Direct Foreign Investment

'Exchange of threats' hypothesis thus explains one of the three possible types of IDFIs, that undertaken by oligopolies producing basically undifferentiated products. Is IDFI an effective tool to reduce oligopolistic interdependence and to reach a *modus vivendi* in such industries? Or does it signal an inability or unwillingness to collude, and is it likely to result in increased competition? Both theory and history show that cross-penetration of national markets is a second-best strategy to reduce competition. Oligopolistic collusion is much easier to obtain in the absence of IDFI.

To industry participants, higher prices are a public good. Cartels experience therefore the same problems as those encountered by providers of such goods. Positive and negative incentives must be found to prevent cheating (Olson, 1965). Governments are often enlisted to police the cartel, either directly (as in France between the two World Wars) or indirectly, by protecting domestic oligopoly members from foreign competition through either tariffs[1] or non-tariff barriers, such as discriminatory taxation[2] (Olson, 1982, p. 130). Cartel members may also rely on persuasion and social ostracism. Here the crucial variable is the degree of social homogeneity of industry participants, and the similarity of their costs and opportunities.

Inter-penetration of markets greatly complicates the enforcement of cartels. Tariffs are no longer potent against foreign competitors, whose subsidiaries must now be made a party to the agreement. Governmental support for the cartel requires the unanimous assent of the main competitors' home governments. Extension of the cartel to foreign producers also increases the size and the social heterogeneity of the cartel's membership, and thus makes collusion harder to achieve (Scherer, 1980, pp. 211-12; Hennart, 1983).

For all those reasons, domestic cartel agreements are easier to set up and to enforce than international ones. One would therefore expect domestic oligopolies, secure behind trade or investment barriers, to attempt to prevent IDFIs by dividing the world into broad geographical zones reserved for each member of the cartel. Such divisions provide convenient focal points, making the conclusion of an agreement easier to attain than the determination of production quotas for each member firm (Schelling, 1960).

The history of MNE shows that domestic monopolists and oligopolists often successfully blocked the entry of foreign subsidiaries in their home market in exchange for division-of-markets agreements with the potential invaders. We can find numerous examples of such a pattern before the First World War in aluminium (Wilkins, 1970, p. 88), in matches (Wilkins, 1970, p. 100), in steel (Wilkins, 1970, p. 100) and in condensed milk (Wilkins, 1977). In dynamite, US producers successfully aborted two attempts by the Nobel Dynamite Trust to establish subsidiaries in the United States (Wilkins, 1983). In the inter-war period, domestic oligopolies in a large number of industries entered into agreements dividing the world into zones of influence.[3] These cartel agreements drastically reduced the level of DFI (Hexner, 1945; Wilkins, 1974).[4]

In all of the preceding cases, the intruder was ousted without the need for the defender(s) to actually counter-invest in the aggressor's home market. By contrast, we know of much fewer cases of IDFIs caused by 'exchange of threats', and they do not seem to have had unqualified success in reducing competition.

In his doctoral thesis, Graham (1974) describes three examples of how 'exchanges of threats' have resulted in DFI: the American Tobacco-Imperial Tobacco, Standard Oil–Shell, and Procter and Gamble-Unilever cases. Graham also presents two more recent examples: Michelin's entry into the United States and General Electric's investment in OSRAM in response to Philips's investment in the United States. Other known cases include Caterpillar's joint venture in Japan to check Komatsu's threat to its world-wide markets (Hout, Porter and Rudden, 1982) and IBM's development of its Japanese subsidiary to counter Hitachi's and Fujitsu's attacks on its US market (Watson, 1982).[5]

Of all these examples, the American Tobacco-Imperial Tobacco was the only clearly successful one, that is, the only one in which IDFIs resulted in immediate collusion. That was achieved by prompt bilateral divestment and the formation of a joint venture to serve third markets (Wilkins, 1970, pp. 91-2; Graham, 1974, pp. 75-6). In the Standard Oil-Shell case, the parties eventually reached an agreement in 1928, 15 years after Shell had responded to Standard Oil's attack on its European and Far Eastern kerosene markets by establishing production and marketing subsidiaries in the United States (Graham, 1974, pp. 32-8).

'Exchanges of threats' does not seem to have reduced rivalry in two of the other cases mentioned by Graham. Procter and Gamble and Unilever have continued to compete on world markets, with Procter and Gamble gaining the advantage. Michelin's entry into the United States has done little to stabilise the tyre oligopoly; quite the contrary has happened. Ten years after Michelin's entry into the United States, the rivalry between Michelin, Goodyear and Bridgestone has turned to an all-out war.[6] Similarly, there is no clear sign that IBM's and Caterpillar's 'exchange of threats' strategies have worked to dampen competition between them and their Japanese counterparts.

Conclusion

No generalisation can be made from a handful of cases; further empirical research is necessary before more solid conclusions can be drawn on the consequence of 'exchanges of threats' for oligopolistic stability. Nevertheless, the preceding examples do not contradict the view that successful international collusion has historically been accompanied by a decrease, not increase, in IDFIs. These investments reveal the inability of national oligopolies to protect their home market from foreign competitors. By transforming a series of national monopolies into world-wide oligopolies, they have made collusion more difficult to achieve.

Many factors can account for this development. Antitrust enforcement is much stronger today than it was before the Second World War. As noted by Caves (1982, p. 100), multinational production is slowly moving away from homogeneous primary products towards differentiated heterogeneous goods. Collusion has been shown to be much more easily established for the former than for the latter (Hay and Kelly, 1974). Increased diversification by MNEs also works in the same direction.

But the emergence of IDFI is also due to dramatic improvements in managerial techniques which have lowered the costs of operating manufacturing facilities in foreign markets (Graham, 1974; Hennart, 1982). These gains in internal efficiency (especially significant in the case of European and Japanese firms) have made MNEs based in the same (or closely related) industry in another country favoured entrants into national markets previously protected by high barriers to entry (Caves, 1982, p. 100).[7]

There is substantial evidence that the number of actual or potential entrants in many industries has increased since the Second World War (Knickerbocker, 1976). For both theoretical and empirical reasons, I am therefore inclined to believe that cross-penetration of national markets through IDFI does not herald the return of international collusion, but is instead the sign of increased world-wide rivalry in most industries.

Notes

1. For example, US tariffs on copper after the Second World War.

2. European governments have often assessed taxes on automobiles on the basis of horsepower, discriminating against US imports and the products of subsidiaries of US-based MNEs.

3. I thank Mira Wilkins for sharing with me her superb knowledge of these complicated events.

4. In some cases, these division-of-market agreements were cemented by the cross-licensing of patents or by token cross-shareholding. In the 1930s, General Electric purchased minority holdings in its major European competitors (Wilkins, 1974, p. 68). Similarly, the US subsidiary of the German I.G. Farbenindustrie held minority stakes in Du Pont, Union Carbide and other major US chemical firms (Graham, 1974, p. 93).

5. I am thankful to Alan Rugman for calling this reference to my attention.

6. In 1980, Michelin entered the Brazilian market, a Goodyear stronghold. Recently, the main protagonists have substantially cut prices to gain market share.

7. There is some evidence that this phenomenon is taking place in US industry. Jarrett (1979, Chapter 3) thus found a positive correlation between the level of capital-cost entry barriers and inward DFI in US industry.

* * *

COMMENT

William F. Finan

Graham's chapter seeks to explore the notion that inter-firm rivalry, in a specified industry context, can be one possible explanation for the observed phenomenon of intra-industry direct foreign investment (IDFI). It contains several suggestive and interesting threads of argumentation. The central argument, however, is weak. Nevertheless, I would urge that this line of investigation be explored further. Graham's general approach has merit.

Central to Graham's analysis of IDFI is a model of rivalry developed by Scherer. In this model, the focus is on the outcome of rivalrous reactions of an incumbent innovator to attempted market entry by a rival. In terms of IDFI, Graham identifies two benefits for firms whose home markets were invaded by the DFI of the foreign rivals: replication of the rival's cost and benefit trade-offs and threatening the rival on its own 'home turf'.

The threat that the reverse-DFI is seeking to address is the ability of the rival to cross-subsidise activities internally within its organisation. But it is unclear how a multinational enterprise (MNE) of host nation A, whose market has been entered via DFI by an MNE of host nation B, can replicate the cost and benefit trade-offs faced by its rival of country B. Suppose that the MNE of country B is cross-subsidising its operations in the television market by the home-country rents earned in non-television markets. Then any entry by the MNE of country A into B's television market has no effect whatsoever on the ability of the rival to cross-subsidise. Only in the unlikely case that the two firms paired up across all markets could one rival effectively counter the other's ability to cross-subsidise.

Returning to the idea that rivals gain from IDFI by replicating their foreign rival's costs and benefits, another issue which is not addressed well is the problem of scale economies. Implicit in the analysis is the assumption that the industry being modelled is characterised by economies of scale. If a firm sought to respond to a rival's entry by engaging in DFI in the home market of the rival, it could simply raise its overall average costs. This could result from a failure to develop plants of sufficient scale to achieve maximum economies. Excessive fragmentation of its production into small inefficient plants could cause the reacting firm further losses in its relative competitive position.

But beyond these problems, one question never addressed in the chapter is why the reacting firm does not simply export to the home market of its rival. In Graham's conceptualisation, entry via DFI and entry via simply exporting are not distinguished. This is an important oversight. Let me suggest two reasons why a firm would prefer DFI to simply exporting. First, there may be a scarce production factor in both markets, for example, computer software designers. Entry via DFI into the home country of a rival threatens to bid up the cost of its scarce resources. Therefore, a reaction is needed to threaten the rival in its home market lest it succeed in bidding up the costs in its host market.

A second reason could be related to benefits available only to resident foreign operations. For example, US co-operative research associations are restricted in their membership to firms who engage in significant manufacturing operations in the United States. There are several of these co-operative arrangements in the electronics industry. A European or Japanese firm can join these co-operative ventures, but only if they have 'significant' manufacturing facilities in the United States. A similar constraint applies to membership in co-operative programs in Japan. Other government programs, for example, tax incentives, also operate on a similar basis. Thus, a foreign rival may seek to neutralise the competitive advantages of a rival in its home market by establishing qualifying facilities.

Graham concludes that IDFI increases rivalry and seller interdependence. This conclusion is overdrawn. The theory and the evidence he presents do not adequately support this strong conclusion. Likewise, Graham's argument that for most industries IDFI will generally act to accelerate new-product development and introduction is also overstated. First, rivalry can continue in the absence of IDFI. Second, rivalry in the duopoly case, even in the absence of collusion, can result in a deceleration of innovation. R and D expenditures need not be more than a credible instrument to bully a rival into accepting either the existing or a minority market position. What seems to be the more likely outcome is not that most industries will become more innovative, rather that, as Graham suggests earlier in his chapter, the outcome is industry-specific.

Let me now turn to the public-policy issues addressed in the final section of the chapter. First, there is a conclusion that it is almost 'unequivocally' against the interest of the United States to regulate DFI entry because it 'virtually always acts to increase rivalry'. As Graham notes, there can be exceptions such as in the proposed General Motors and Toyota link-up. But this should suggest that we need to look more carefully at the effect of IDFI on competition rather than sliding by the example, dismissing it as a minor exception. DFI can significantly reduce rivalry if the new entrant has the resources to appropriate a scarce factor, whether land or human capital, bidding it away from the market incumbent.

Another situation which needs to be reviewed is the case where a foreign government imposes stiff performance-requirements on new US entrants into its market. If DFI is an essential requirement for achieving market position, US firms would, despite the presence of performance requirements, feel compelled to undertake DFI. But if the foreign rivals freely enter the United States via DFI, relative advantages could accrue to them. In such a setting, it may be necessary to consider restrictions on the entry of the foreign firms, pending negotiations toward eliminating the foreign government's performance requirements on US DFI in their home market.

The second policy issue addressed is antitrust. An international approach to international antitrust regulation is suggested. I find the arguments presented only weakly tied to the bulk of the chapter. The same is true with Graham's policy analysis of the encouragement of inward investment.

In conclusion, a significant amount of Graham's discussion of the effects of rivalry on innovation seems not to depend on whether DFI is part of the story or not. Perhaps this is suggesting that IDFI is an artificial construct with little unique features, at least in terms of its implications for inter-firm rivalry. But the area of investigation regarding IDFI's role in rivalrous conduct seems relevant. On the matter of DFI in the United States, I would not necessarily suggest that in all cases one should maintain strict neutrality. In selected instances foreign governments' restrictions on their inward DFI may necessitate some actions on the part of the United States.

4 ANTITRUST POLICY AND INTRA-INDUSTRY DIRECT FOREIGN INVESTMENT: CAUSE AND EFFECT*

Philip Nelson and Louis Silvia

Introduction

The question of how antitrust law and intra-industry direct foreign investment (IDFI) interact arose naturally from early economic research on the characteristics of direct foreign investment (DFI). For example, Kindleberger (1969) argued that DFI would not exist in a world of perfect competition and thus belonged to the theory of monopolistic competition. Caves (1971) expanded on this view, arguing that oligopolistic market structures normally prevailed where DFI was found. Others, such as Hymer (1970), Vernon (1970) and Newfarmer (1979), went further, taking the position that DFI was a device for restraining competition. Reflecting these and their own findings, Bergsten, Horst and Moran (1978) argued for increased antitrust scrutiny of DFI by US firms.

The interaction between IDFI and antitrust law is not only reflected in the effect IDFI has on antitrust enforcement efforts, but is also reflected in the effect antitrust law has on IDFI activity. What effects has US antitrust law had on IDFI? To answer this question, we look at both the inward and the outward DFI of the United States. When it comes to specific examples of how the law has affected IDFI and foreign commerce more generally, the literature is surprisingly sparse. While specific examples of how antitrust may discourage foreign commerce by US businesses are difficult to obtain, there is one recurring theme that deserves particular attention. Businessmen express uncertainty about what is prohibited by the antitrust laws and argue that they veto projects that may be perfectly legal and undertake the projects in second-best ways that are clearly legal in order to avoid antitrust risks (Brewster, 1958). To the extent that this argument is valid, clearly, antitrust laws not only affect the level of IDFI activity, but also help to shape the form this activity takes.

Statistical tests of the impact of antitrust law on DFI have obtained no clear results. For example, Maule (1968) found that the closing of

97

the asset acquisition loophole in US merger law in 1950 appeared to divert US firms' acquisition activity to Canada, where it triggered a merger wave. Subsequent tests by Reuber (1969), however, revealed a series of statistical problems with the initial Maule (1968) study, suggesting that other factors might explain the initial observations.[1]

While the strength of the interaction remains to be shown, there may be significant links between antitrust law and IDFI. However, many of the important ties between IDFI and antitrust are not the most obvious direct ties. Many of the effects of antitrust laws on IDFI (and vice versa) are indirect. By shaping market structure, antitrust can effect many of the determinants of IDFI. As a result, the interface between antitrust and DFI can only be charted once the analyst has come to grips with the complicated task of understanding the general structural effects of antitrust on the economy. Unfortunately, the outline of these relationships is far from complete and is subject to substantial debate.

Other indirect effects are also apparent, and perhaps open to more precise analysis. DFI is only one method by which a firm can increase its foreign sales. Exports and licensing are other possibilities. To the extent that US antitrust laws alter the desirability of importing into the United States, exporting from the United States and licensing arrangements for foreign production, they can affect the relative return from DFI, and thus the extent to which it occurs.

Direct and indirect effects of IDFI on antitrust enforcement activities are also evident. Clearly, actual and potential DFI alters the structure of US markets, which is key to the focus of antitrust efforts. Furthermore, the threat of DFI may be a structural fact that US-based enterprises take into account when making their competitive decisions. As a result, antitrust analysis must take DFI into account. This chapter attempts to advance the analysis of the relationships between antitrust law and IDFI (and its constituent DFI), by providing some insights into the types of cause and effect relationships which might exist between these two market forces.

Overview of US Antitrust Law[2]

Brief Description of the Basic Antitrust Laws

Antitrust laws focus on activities that involve the exploitation or enhancement of a firm's market power.[3] The principal antitrust statutes are the Sherman Act, Clayton Act, Robinson Patman Act and Federal Trade Commission (FTC) Act. In addition, there are state antitrust statutes and various special laws that provide exemptions from antitrust prohibitions. For our purposes, the most important of the exemption statutes is the Webb-Pomerene Act, which exempts certain export activities.

The antitrust statutes appear to be fairly simple on the surface. For example, the Sherman Act uses few words in condemning contracts, combinations and conspiracies in restraint of trade in its first section and monopolisation or attempts to monopolise in its second section. However, while the antitrust laws have this simple statutory foundation, their effects flow from a long history of judicial interpretation. Given the very general guidance provided to the judiciary by the underlying statutes, it is not surprising that, as the antitrust law has grown through the accretion of precedents, it has become increasingly more sophisticated and complex. As with other laws that rely on growth through precedent, there is some justifiable uncertainty about what the law really is in some areas. While the FTC and the Department of Justice have tried to clarify the law and reduce the uncertainty facing firms by providing guidelines and offering opinions in advance of actions against firms, the possibility of private antitrust suits, particularly in the areas of vertical restraints, has had the opposite effect.

While it is difficult to summarise the proscriptions of antitrust law in a few sentences, there are some basic points that must be kept in mind:

Horizontal Restraints. Price fixing is illegal. However, practices that may support or suggest the presence of price fixing are studied on a 'rule of reason' basis. As a result, information exchange, pricing formulas and restraints on competitive activities may or may not be found illegal.

Monopolisation. Monopolisation involves both the showing of market power and demonstrating that the firm with market power took concrete steps directed at obtaining that power or exploited that power in ways that injured competition, such as deterring the growth of rivals. If the market power is a by-product of honest and successful competition, it is not assailable under current law.

Attempted Monopolisation. Attempted monopolisation requires showing that a firm employed anticompetitive *conduct* with the *intent* to monopolise and that it had sufficient market power to have a *dangerous probability* of success. The market power required under an attempt-

case appears to be less than that required under monopolisation, since the anticompetitive activities receive more emphasis.

Mergers. Horizontal, vertical and conglomerate (potential competition) mergers may be attacked under antitrust law. The Department of Justice and FTC 1982 guidelines include as factors to be studied:

(1) The level of market concentration before the merger;
(2) the change in concentration caused by the merger;
(3) barriers to entry;
(4) evidence of market performance;
(5) efficiency effects of the merger; and
(6) the presence of a dominant firm.

Methodologies for defining the product and geographical markets, which are key to the derivation of the market share statistics, are suggested.

Joint Venture Law. Joint ventures can be attacked under various antitrust statutes. Principally, they may be viewed as agreements in restraint of trade (Sherman Act), as an acquisition (Clayton Act) or as an unfair method of competition (FTC Act). However, legally, they often receive more lenient treatment than mergers, since they may not unite the firms' decision-making apparatus in the same way and they may create new productive capabilities. The Department of Justice's 1977 *Antitrust Guide for International Operations*[4] suggests that among the factors studied by enforcement authorities are: the nature of ancillary agreements, the extent of competition among the partners, the information exchanges that are likely to arise under the agreement and the structure of the relevant markets.

Vertical Restraints. Resale price maintenance is *per se* illegal. Other vertical restraints (exclusive dealing, tying and territorial restraints) are analysed under a 'rule of reason' approach.

Price Discrimination. Firms are prevented from setting discriminatory prices, providing services on a discriminatory basis, or offering advertising allowances on a discriminatory basis where the effect of this discrimination is to lessen competition or to injure competition with other sellers or competitors of the customer. There are defences to a price discrimination charge, including cost justification, meeting competition and changed circumstances.

The International Reach of US Antitrust Laws

The prohibitions against anticompetitive conduct contained in US antitrust laws apply not only to trade within the United States, but to foreign trade as well. Clearly, US laws apply to foreign firms with respect to the business they do in the United States. For example, even the merger of two foreign firms may be challenged if those firms have horizontal overlaps in products produced or sold in the United States.[5] However, antitrust law does not stop at the US border. For example, US antitrust law has been found to apply to the transportation of cement and fertiliser cargoes financed by the Agency for International Development between foreign ports.[6] In the *Alcoa* case, Judge Learned Hand held that restrictive agreements outside the United States and involving no US firm may be within the reach of US law if the agreements affect US imports.[7]

While US antitrust laws historically have attempted to affect foreign firms in the ways noted above, recent legal discussion and cases suggest that the reach of US antitrust is becoming more limited. Perhaps most importantly, it has been held that a firm's action must have a 'direct and substantial effect' on US commerce before it is subject to US antitrust law.[8] In interpreting this, and the *Alcoa* 'effects test', courts have also accepted that it is important to recognise the interests of the other countries that are involved. This is done, in part, by putting the activity in an international context by considering whether there is foreign-sovereign compulsion, whether the activity is related to an act of state and whether comity issues are involved.[9]

Under foreign-sovereign compulsion doctrine, a firm may defend itself against antitrust action by establishing that it was forced by threats of sanctions by foreign governments to act as it did.[10] The act-of-state doctrine proscribes the examination or judgement of the legality and motivation of sovereign acts of a foreign state within its territory. While this principle does not establish a defence to a showing of liability like the foreign-compulsion doctrine, it can make a showing of anticompetitive activity impossible. To employ the defence, the parties must show that the activities were of a sovereign nature, rather than simply commercial, and in the foreign government's territory.[11]

Comity has become an increasing concern of courts dealing with international antitrust issues. The major recent decisions advocate a balancing of factors.[12] Among the factors to be balanced are:

(1) The degree of conflict with foreign law or policy;

(2) the nationality of the parties;

(3) the relative importance of the alleged violation of conduct in the United States compared to that abroad;

(4) the availability of a remedy abroad and the state of related litigation there;

(5) the existence of intent to harm or affect US commerce and its foreseeability;

(6) the possible effect on foreign relations if the court exercises jurisdiction or grants relief;

(7) if relief is granted, whether a party will be placed in the position of being forced to perform an act illegal in either country or be under conflicting requirements by both countries;

(8) whether the court can make its order effective;

(9) whether an order for relief would be acceptable in this country if made by a foreign nation under similar circumstances; and

(10) whether a treaty with the affected nation has addressed the issue.[13]

While there has been this shift towards a balancing of factors which may limit the application of US laws, there is recent evidence that the foreign reach of US antitrust law is still fairly extensive. In a case against several uranium producers, alleging cartel behaviour, the Seventh Circuit Court affirmed jurisdiction over foreign (and domestic) producers.[14] In its argument, the court was closer to the reasoning in *Alcoa* than other recent decisions might have led one to predict.

Empirical Significance of Antitrust Enforcement Activities

While deterrent effects of antitrust enforcement are often crucial, actual enforcement efforts, being the most visible, are the basis for perceptions of antitrust law that shape the actions of firms. We now turn to a brief empirical review of the enforcement of merger and joint-venture law to provide an indication of the level of federal antitrust activity in the areas that are most important to IDFI.[15] The extent to which antitrust enforcers take investigative action with respect to acquisitions or joint ventures can be estimated using data from the FTC's pre-merger notification programme. Under the Hart-Scott-Rodino (HSR) Antitrust Improvements Act of 1976, firms must notify the government before they consummate certain acquisitions

Table 4.1: Numbers of Hart-Scott-Rodino Pre-merger Filings, 1978–82

Year	Number of Filings
1978[a]	355
1979[b]	868
1980	824
1981	1083
1982	1144

Notes: a. The pre-merger notification rules went into effect on 5 September 1979.
   b. Minimum value of transaction was raised from $10 million to $15 million on 21 November 1979.
Sources: Federal Trade Commission, Second, Third, Fourth and Fifth Annual Reports to US Congress pursuant to Section 201 of the Hart-Scott-Rodino Antitrust Improvements Act of 1976. The figure for 1982 was provided by Pre-merger Notification Office, Federal Trade Commission.

and joint ventures. Advance notice is required for transactions in which:

(1) the acquiring firm has total assets or annual sales of at least $100 million; and
(2) the acquired firm has assets or annual sales of $10 million or more.

Since late 1979, reportable transactions must involve more than $15 million dollars in voting securities or assets.[16] The transactions must affect US commerce to be reportable. A transaction involving a foreign firm is considered to affect commerce within the United States if the firm has sales in or into the United States of $10 million or more. In addition to exemptions for relatively small transactions, there are exclusions for regulated industries and transactions, such as some partnerships, where assets are not exchanged.

Table 4.1 presents data on the number of Hart-Scott-Rodino filings between 1978 and 1982.[17] It should be recognised that not every filing leads to a consummated deal, even without government intervention. In 1982, there were filings for 1,144 proposed transactions. This represented an increase of 320 from the 1980 level.

Table 4.2 presents the frequencies of clearance and second requests by the Justice Department and the FTC for 762 proposed transactions in 1981.[18] Clearance is a process employed by the FTC and the Justice Department to minimise duplicative investigational efforts. If either one or both of the agencies decide that a transaction should be investigated seriously, a 'clearance' process is undertaken to assure that only

Table 4.2: Incidence of Clearance and Second Requests for 762 Hart-Scott-Rodino Filings in 1981

Clearance Granted to Federal Trade Commission (FTC) or Department of Justice (DOJ)				
Number		Per cent of 762		
FTC	DOJ	FTC	DOJ	Total
104	62	13.6	8.1	21.7
Second Requests Issued				
Number		Per cent of 762		
FTC	DOJ	FTC	DOJ	Total
51	27	6.7	3.5	10.2

Source: Pre-merger Notification Office, Federal Trade Commission.

one of the agencies proceeds with an investigation. If the agency which undertakes the investigation decides after further research that there is sufficient possibility that there is a need for an injunctive action, it will issue a second request to the firms involved in the transaction. In short, clearance and second requests may be considered as measures of enforcement interest by the antitrust agencies.

As Table 4.2 shows, nearly four out of five HSR transactions fail to generate sufficient antitrust concerns to set off a clearance procedure between the FTC and the Justice Department, and about nine out of ten transactions do not reach the second request stage. Therefore, the overwhelming majority of HSR reportable transactions pass antitrust review with little trouble. Among the 762 HSR transactions for 1981, 115 involved foreign acquisition of US firms (112) or joint ventures with US firms (3). Of these 115 transactions, 18 generated clearance procedures while 11 elicited second requests. Since the percentages for clearance and second requests are lower than those for total samples of transactions, the data suggest that US inward DFI transactions create somewhat fewer antitrust concerns than transactions between domestic firms.

Only a very small number of transactions in the 1981 sample involved either acquisitions by US firms of foreign-controlled entities (15 transactions or 2 per cent of the total), or foreign acquisitions of other foreign-controlled entities (7 transactions or about 1 per cent of the total).[19] Of the relatively small number of US acquisitions of foreign entities six (40 per cent) generated clearance procedures, and three (20 per cent) elicited second requests. Of the seven transactions

Table 4.3: Number of FTC Orders and Complaints Involving
Acquisitions and Joint Ventures, Financial Years 1980-2

Year	Number of Orders[a]	Number of Orders Foreign Firms	Number of Complaints[b]	Number of Complaints Involving Foreign Firms
1980	11	4	5	1
1981	13	2	6	0
1982	6	2	2	0
Total	30	8	13	1

Notes: a. Orders include consent agreements (including both those reached before
and after the issuance of a complaint), initial decisions of FTC administrative
law judges and final decisions by the FTC.
  b. Complaints represent formal, legal challenges by the FTC. Numbers do not
include complaints issued along with final consent agreements.
Source: FTC Annual Reports, 1980, 1981 and 1982.

involving foreign acquisition of foreign-controlled entities, one clearance procedure was undertaken and no second requests were issued.
While these statistics may suggest different average levels of antitrust
concern for US acquisition of foreign entities (higher) and for foreign
acquisition of other foreign entities (lower), as compared to wholly
domestic transactions, the very low number of these two types of
transactions in the sample precludes any strong conclusion regarding
relative levels of antitrust concern. As data from the 1981 HSR filings
suggest, only about 10 per cent of the proposed acquisitions and joint
ventures are sufficiently troubling to antitrust enforcers to warrant
further investigation through the issuance of a second request. However, still far fewer transactions arouse sufficient concern for the
government to attempt to block their consummation.

The FTC opposition to mergers and joint ventures during the last
three fiscal years is summarised in Table 4.3. During the fiscal years
1980 to 1982, the Commission issued 30 orders in this area, which con-
sisted of 20 consent decrees, four initial decisions by FTC administrative law judges and six final decisions by the FTC itself. 13 transactions
were formally challenged during fiscal years 1980 to 1982 with the
issuing of administrative complaints. With the exception of one joint-
venture case, all of these FTC actions concerned acquisitions.[20] Eight
of the 30 FTC orders and one of the 13 complaints involved foreign
acquisition of US firms.[21]

Parallel enforcement activity by the Department of Justice (DOJ)
is summarised in Table 4.4. As the table shows, the DOJ filed suit to
challenge 23 acquisitions between 1980 and 1982. (It challenged none

Table 4.4: Number of Department of Justice Cases Instituted Involving
Acquisitions and Joint Ventures, Calendar Years 1980-2

Year	Number of Cases	Number of Cases Involving Foreign Firms
1980	10	4
1981	4	0
1982	9	1
Total	23	5

Source: Commerce Clearing House, *Antitrust Reporter*.

of the joint ventures formed during this period.) Five of the 23 cases
involved foreign firms. Two of the five challenged the acquisition of
a foreign firm by a US firm, while the other three challenged acquisitions by foreign firms within the United States.

The Effect of Antitrust Laws on Intra-industry Direct Foreign Investment

Antitrust Laws and Intra-industry Direct Foreign Investment: Direct Effects

No antitrust question is likely to arise when a foreign firm enters the
US market through *de novo* entry. However, it is standard practice for
US authorities to scrutinise foreign entries that involve acquisitions
or the establishment of a joint venture with the following questions in
mind: Before the entry, was the foreign entrant a perceived or actual
potential entrant? If it is determined that the foreign firm is either
likely to have employed *de novo* entry or was perceived by established
firms as a likely *de novo* entrant, there may be cause for antitrust
action. The economic theory for such an action would be that the
presence of the entrant on the fringe of the market restrains the pricing
of today's market participants and that *de novo* entry would add to
the competition in the market. However, there are fairly narrow legal
and economic requirements that must be met for this theory of anticompetitive effects to be valid.[22] Among the market characteristics
that courts and economists consider to be relevant in evaluating potential competition cases are:

1. Is the target-market concentrated?
2. Is an alternative method of entry available and feasible?
3. Does the alternative form of entry offer a reasonable chance for

long-term structural improvement or other procompetitive benefits?
4. Are there only a few other potential entrants that are similarly
positioned for entry?[23]

Potential-competition doctrine has been employed successfuly
against foreign firms. For example, the FTC intervened in Yamaha's
efforts to form a US joint venture with Brunswick.[24] Under the joint
venture agreement, outboard motors manufactured by the venture
would be purchased by both Brunswick's subsidiary and Yamaha,
but would be sold in the United States only by Brunswick's subsidiary.
The FTC ruled that the joint venture substantially lessened potential
competition between the parents in the concentrated US market. At
the time of the joint-venture agreement, Brunswick ranked second in
the industry. The FTC also found that independent entry by Yamaha
into the US market was likely.

DFI by US firms is also subject to antitrust scrutiny by US authorities. For example, in *United States* v. *Jos. Schlitz Brewing Co.*, the DOJ
intervened to stop US-based Schlitz's acquisition of Canadian-based
Labatt, since Labatt was a potential entrant into the United States
and Labatt controlled US-based General. The result of these direct
effects may have been to discourage DFI, if the only economically
viable form of entry is subject to antitrust attack. On the other hand,
and perhaps more likely, the presence of antitrust law may have altered
the form of DFI, shifting it to wholly-owned subsidiaries set up through
de novo entry.

Antitrust Laws and Intra-industry Direct Foreign Investment: Indirect Effects

Exports. The reach of US antitrust laws is restricted in the case of US
exports by the Webb-Pomerene Export Trade Act of 1918. Section 2
of this Act states that nothing in the Sherman Act will make it illegal to
form an assocation for the sole purpose of export-trade or for such an
association to form an agreement affecting US exports, provided that
this association and its agreements do not restrain trade within the
United States. More recently, the Department of Commerce (DOC) has
been granted the authority to give immunity from antitrust suits to
export trading companies that are properly set up under the Export
Trading Act of 1982. However, firms are still subject to antitrust laws
if there is 'direct, substantial and reasonably foreseeable effect' on US
commerce, and antitrust analysis will be done by the DOJ and the DOC
as part of the certification process.

To the extent that these regulations achieve their goals of enabling smaller US firms to spread the fixed costs of setting up selling agencies needed to compete abroad through exports, they may encourage exportation relative to DFI, at least in the short-run. However, to the extent that exports are the first step in a dynamic process that leads to DFI – as we suspect is frequently the case – antitrust exemptions which encourage exports may have the effect of changing the dynamic path so that DFI levels are higher. Empirically, the Webb-Pomerene Act does not appear to have had a major impact on US exports (US FTC, 1967; and Larson, 1970).

Licensing. Under US antitrust laws, a holder of a patent has a legal monopoly. Other innovators who have unpatentable or unpatented know-how may also have legal monopolies; however, their protection from competition is less formal, and, as a result, their ability to exploit their advantage is more limited. While a patent holder is given fairly broad rights to exploit his patent, patents have come to be viewed by courts as a privilege 'conditioned by a public purpose'.[25] Basically, this means that a patent holder cannot go beyond attempting to protect his invention against appropriation. For example, while a patent holder can set the price at which the direct output from the use of his patent is sold, increasing restrictions have been placed on the patent holder. Some of the restrictions imposed by courts under their interpretations of the Sherman Act include:

1. A price agreement can only be made when the patent is for the product that is being sold at the set price.
2. When an improvement-patent taken out by a licensee of the original inventor leads to cross-licensing, the members of the patent pool may not be allowed to set prices for the product that results from their combined patents.
3. The licensing agreement usually cannot extend to products that are not related to the patent. Particularly, where the members of a patent-pool dominate an industry, cross-licensing will be scrutinised to determine if the linkage of the patents unduly expands the ability of the firms to restrain competition.

The rights of patent holders are also restricted by the Clayton Act, especially its Section 3 which governs tying-agreements. While patent holders may wish to insert conditions in their licences that require a licensee to use particular machines or products when producing under the licence, tying-clauses may be found illegal, if in the court's opinion the tie may 'substantially lessen competition'.[26]

To the extent that antitrust law makes it difficult for patent holders to license their technology without opening themselves to legal actions and costly remedies, antitrust law decreases the attractiveness of licensing relative to alternative ways of exploiting a technological advantage such as DFI. Particularly, where it is difficult to monitor the use of a patent without a supplemental contract that ties unpatented inputs to the patent-licence, antitrust law can encourage DFI. However, for other firms the choice may be between licensing and no foreign involvement. To the extent that one type of foreign involvement leads to another, this effect may decrease DFI.

Imports. Foreign producers with a technological or organisational advantage over US producers have reason to consider expanding sales to the United States. However, imports into the United States that are priced below prevailing US prices may not only encounter pleadings for relief by US firms before the US International Trade Commission (ITC), but may also face retaliatory antitrust challenges. Specifically, US firms can try to use attempted monopolisation and price-discrimination law to bring the foreign producers into US courts. As in 'dumping' cases before the ITC, US firms can argue that foreign producers are selling below cost to gain market power in the United States.[27]

If it is difficult to measure foreign production costs which are needed to justify delivered US-prices, foreign producers may be encouraged to produce in the United States (assuming that their advantage does not require foreign production), rather than export to the United States, by the desire to avoid antitrust suits. While the desire to avoid antitrust cases may be a factor in some cases, it is likely that ITC filings and political pressures are a more important force in encouraging US production relative to imports. While antitrust action has several advantages over ITC import relief actions,[28] it suffers relative to ITC filings because the injury standards for relief are more difficult to meet (focusing more on injury to competition than on competitors). Furthermore, antitrust actions are subject to counter-claims, broad discovery-rights against the complaining firm, jurisdictional problems and possible delays in fully adjudicated actions.

Because filing before the ITC may be a preferable way to block imports, the question of how antitrust laws affect this competitive tactic is relevant. While the magnitude of the impact is difficult to assess, it appears that antitrust laws discourage some filings before the ITC, and thus may encourage imports. The Noerr-Pennington Doctrine allows competitors to combine in their efforts to lobby government officials. However, the 'sham' exception to this doctrine limits the arguments that can be made before a government body, by requiring that information provided to government officials must be in good faith. Furthermore, antitrust authorities can consider whether the information exchanges that occur during filings are necessary to the filing. Also, the frequency of filings may be studied to determine if they are a cover for collusion. There has been scrutiny of 'informal settlements' between US firms and foreign rivals to determine if market-sharing agreements appear to have been reached illegally.

Market Structure. Critical appraisals of the general impact of antitrust laws cover a wide range. Bork (1978, p. 4) states that modern antitrust laws '. . . significantly impair both competition and the ability of the economy to produce goods and services efficiently.' According to Mueller (1973, p. 323), however, 'antitrust judgments are relatively simple to execute, and they remove the harmful effects of market control by going to the source of the problem'. Depending on which general view of antitrust law one holds, a very different perspective will be taken on its basic impact on market structure, and thus DFI. This debate must be capsulised here by positing both efficiency-stimulating and efficiency-undermining effects of antitrust law.

More specific structural impacts can also be identified. Perhaps most importantly, the antitrust laws themselves are part of the structure which defines the rules of the game, governing the strategies firms can employ. For example, predatory pricing is illegal under antitrust laws. To the extent that the potential for a predatory response by established firms is a concern for the foreign entrant, the presence of this law may encourage entry generally, and thus increase DFI in the United States. Furthermore, predation laws may affect the location of investments. To the extent that US predation law is stricter than foreign law, DFI in the United States will be preferred by firms that feel open to predatory attack. Firms that would be 'first movers' or otherwise benefit from more lenient predatory-pricing rules may prefer foreign markets, since weaker predatory-pricing laws favour them.

Once it is recognised that antitrust laws can shape market structure (both because they define the rules of the game and because they can lead to market actions that alter tomorrow's structure), it becomes apparent that antitrust law can have a wide variety of very intricate

Table 4.5: Indirect Structural Effects of US Antitrust Laws on Intra-industry Direct Foreign Investment: Effects on Inward DFI of the United States

Structural Effect	Effect on DFI
1. Increase the efficiency of US firms or lower the price umbrella.	1. Discourage DFI by foreign firms in the United States by lowering their expected rate of return.
2. Decrease efficiency or raise the price umbrella.	2. Encourage DFI by foreign firms in the United States by raising their expected rate of return.
3. Raise factor input costs.	3. Discourage DFI in the United States due to cost disadvantage of producing there, unless differences in input intensity of production function are in advantage of foreign firms.
4. Lower factor input costs.	4. Encourage DFI in the United States due to cost advantage of producing there, unless differences in input intensity of production function are in disadvantage of foreign firms.
5. Lower entry costs by discouraging predatory pricing.	5. Facilitate entry into the United States and thus encourage DFI in the United States, unless foreign firms are advantaged by ability to cut prices.
6. Discourage acquisition by domestic firms.	6. Increase the chances that the 'high bidder' for a firm is foreign, encouraging DFI in the United States.
7. Discourage joint venturing among US-based competitors.	7. Encourage US firms to form joint ventures with foreign companies, increasing DFI in the United States.
8. Lower barriers by preventing vertical foreclosure.	8. Facilitate entry and thus encourage DFI unless foreign firms would be at an advantage if US-sourced inputs were foreclosed.
9. Raise entry barriers by discouraging product support by retail sellers.	9. Discourage entry, and thus undermine DFI.
10. Change the market structure through increased lobbying strength and profit opportunities of US firms that trade barriers offer.	10. Encourage DFI to the extent that trade barriers are raised by effective lobbying and the presence of trade barriers stimulates DFI.

effects on DFI, and thus IDFI. Indeed the network of effects is probably too complicated to catalogue, once one gets past the most obvious effects. Even the effects that occur to us make a long list. Table 4.5 presents a sample of some of the arguments that have been or could be made for the impact of US antitrust law on DFI in the United States through its effect on market structure. Table 4.6 focuses on how

Table 4.6: Indirect Structural Effects of US Antitrust Laws on Intra-industry Direct Foreign Investment: Effects on Outward DFI of the United States

Structural Effect	Effect on DFI
1. Increase the efficiency of US firms or lower the price umbrella.	1. Encourage outward DFI by leading to comparative advantages that can be exploited abroad or by raising relative profits to be earned by DFI.
2. Decrease efficiency or raise the price umbrella.	2. Discourage outward DFI by reducing comparative advantages to be exploited abroad or by raising relative profits to be earned from domestic investment. Monopoly profits may, however, lead to greater investment, including DFI.
3. Raise factor input costs.	3. Encourage outward DFI to gain advantages of lower factor costs abroad.
4. Lower factor input costs.	4. Discourage outward DFI by removing opportunities for reducing factor costs through foreign production.
5. Lower domestic entry costs by discouraging predatory pricing.	5. Encourage domestic entry relative to foreign entry, decreasing outward DFI.
6. Prevent aggressive competitive tactics in the United States.	6. Increase outward DFI, with higher rate of return due to ability of US firms to employ aggressive competitive tactics.
7. Promote more competitive markets.	7. Reduce monopoly profits, resulting in lower investible funds or R and D, weaker US advantage, and thus discourage outward DFI. Also, decrease oligopolistic rivalry, which may reduce DFI, if one firm's DFI triggers parallel actions by rivals. Increased competition may, however, engender greater R and D, and thus increase DFI.
8. Discourage acquisition of domestic firms.	8. Increase relative attractiveness of foreign acquisitions, encouraging outward DFI.
9. Discourage joint ventures among US firms.	9. Encourage US firms to form joint ventures abroad with foreign firms, thus increasing outward DFI.
10. Lower barriers to entry by preventing vertical foreclosure.	10. Encourage domestic entry relative to foreign entry, and reduce the need to look abroad for secure sources of vital inputs.
11. Raise barriers to entry by discouraging product support by retail sellers.	11. Discourage domestic entry relative to foreign entry, increasing outward DFI.
12. Prevent participation in foreign cartels by US firms.	12. Encourage DFI, since geographical market division is not a feasible strategy.

the US antitrust laws affect US outward DFI through their structural effects. In studying Tables 4.5 and 4.6, it is important to remember that not only will the relevance of the relationships vary across markets, depending on the characteristics of the particular market, but that some of the theories on which the linkages are based are the subject of ongoing debates in the industrial-organisation literature.

Several of the relationships presented in Tables 4.5 and 4.6 deserve specific attention because they have received emphasis in the literature. Among the better known theories is the reactive theory of DFI offered by Knickerbocker (1973) (see Point 7 in Table 4.6).[29] According to Knickerbocker, oligopolists fear that unmatched actions by rivals will allow those rivals to gain competitive advantages (perhaps in the form of physical, financial or human assets). As a result, firms match or 'checkmate' each other's actions to balance the competitive capabilities within an industry.

Although Knickerbocker's theory is included in our list of factors influencing DFI, its validity remains to be established by further work. Perhaps more importantly, this theory requires some but not too much symmetry across oligopolistic firms. If firms are in different positions, could one firm not fail where the other succeeds?[30] Where premature DFI occurs, it should undermine rather than support the oligopolistic balance that is central to Knickerbocker's theory. Additional work on the factors that can determine why a quick response to a competitor's entry is profitable must be done before this theory can be accepted.[31] One basis for 'follow-the-leader' behaviour may be found in the 'first mover' theories (Schmalensee, 1982). If it is true that barriers to entry, or at least entry costs, are higher for late followers than first movers, the firms that follow might have thought later entry would be more profitable, but had to recalculate the optimal timing of entry once they observe entry activity by a rival.

Knickerbocker's theory is also weakened if the internal structures of oligopolists and the environments they face are too symmetrical. When substantial symmetry exists, simultaneous DFI may simply be due to contemporaneous independent assessments of similar circumstances such as changes in tax laws or tariff barriers. To the extent that oligopolists are better positioned to take advantage of foreign opportunities, clustering such as that observed by Knickerbocker could simply reflect relative efficiencies.

These basic problems with Knickerbocker's theory lead us to question his empirical tests. Knickerbocker's use of two- and three-digit Standard Industrial Classification (SIC) code data seems to be another problem, since industries typically are not economically well defined at such an aggregate level.[32] There might also have been biases inherent in the way Knickerbocker analysed these data that could explain the results.[33]

Even if oligopolistic reaction is not key to the pattern of DFI, could there be an empirical relationship between market concentration and DFI? Other studies in this volume suggest that there may be such a relationship. Although the simple correlation between concentration and DFI will stand up over time, it will be hard to discover exactly what is driving this observation. There are several relationships that could produce this basic result. For example, if increased concentration is correlated with profitability or efficiency, increased levels of DFI could be attributable to the greater availability of investable funds and the ability to convert investment ideas into profitable enterprises, rather than directly to increased market power or concentration. Alternatively, market concentration may be correlated with firm size. To the extent that large firms already have the fixed managerial investments, needed to control DFIs, in place and smaller firms do not, the marginal decision that large firms face when deciding whether to expand abroad is different.[34] For the large firms, the incremental costs of DFI will be lower because of the sizeable fixed costs they already have incurred.

Based on the simple positive relationship between concentration and DFI, one might be tempted to argue that antitrust law alters DFI by changing concentration levels. However, the complicated associations between the various market characteristics suggest that more sophisticated relationships between antitrust law, market structure and DFI exist. Recent research by Ozawa (1979a and 1979b) on Japanese DFI drives this point home. Ozawa has found that Japanese outward DFI is not generally undertaken by large firms in oligopolistic industries. Smaller firms looking for competitive advantages, such as lower input costs, have also played a significant role in Japanese outward DFI.

The Effect of Intra-industry Direct Foreign Investment on the Enforcement of US Antitrust Laws

The level and structure of IDFI affect the need for and focus of antitrust activity.[35] Most notably, DFI in the United States by foreign firms should decrease concentration and the threat of future DFI should discourage, or at least restrict, price-fixing agreements by lowering the limit price at which entry will take place. As markets become more competitive with the influx of foreign-based competitors, the need for active antitrust enforcement should be reduced. Is the story really this simple? Or, can DFI increase the need for active antitrust enforcement? Are there more subtle procompetitive effects of IDFI on antitrust enforcement efforts? These are the questions to which we now turn.

Potential-entrant Theory

As is suggested above, when most economists think of foreign entry into the United States through DFI, they think of the provision of new productive assets which expand industry capacity, increase competition, lower prices and enhance consumer welfare. However, this is not the only scenario that may follow from DFI. If the industry in question requires a scarce resource as an input, the addition of new capacity may not be as procompetitive as it first appears, if the addition of the new capacity is accompanied by an increase in the concentration of ownership of the scarce input. For example, DFI that increases US oil-refining capacity may appear procompetitive, but it may not have this effect if the entry also places substantial amounts of US oil reserves under the control of an OPEC cartel member. In this case, the relevant market would be crude oil, and the change in control over crude oil should be the focus of attention. Especially when there is a world market for the product, entry into the United States may be largely irrelevant and may hide increases in world concentration, which is key to the evaluation of potential price and output effects.

Perhaps more importantly, DFI can reduce competition and raise antitrust concerns when it occurs through the acquisition of established firms, rather than through *de novo* entry. As noted earlier, the acquisition of a US firm by a foreign potential entrant into the United States may reduce competition by shrinking the number of perceived or actual potential entrants. Entry into the United States via a joint venture with a US firm raises many of the same antitrust concerns that entry through acquisition does. However, a joint venture offers the possibility that the foreign entrant may retain substantial independence. Only a careful study of the specific joint-venture arrangement will reveal whether the restrictions that accompany the agreement are necessary or overly restrictive. For example, ancillary agreements that limit competition or facilitate disciplining of the foreign firm, should it set out on its own (through imports or independent production in the United States), would raise antitrust concerns.

Potential-entrant theory also recognises the possibility of a 'pre-emptive strike'. A firm from one country may enter a foreign country through acquisition, not so much because it wishes to supply that country, but because it wishes to obtain control over a potential entrant. For such a strategy to be profitable, the foreign firm must clearly be contemplating entry and the firms must agree that it is more profitable to share the wealth than to do battle. Barriers to entry, few existing or potential competitors, the ability to agree on the size and division of the profits and a willingness to sacrifice independence must all be present. If the market is oligopolistic, there may be a 'public goods' problem, since one firm will bear the social cost of acquiring the potential entrant, while all of oligopolists benefit. As a result, it may be easier to allow the firm to enter and co-ordinate post-entry prices and output.

Foreclosure Theory

While it requires a fairly specific set of circumstances, economists have noted that concentration of input markets may facilitate injurious collusion in downstream markets. Entry by a foreign competitor may loosen these foreclosed markets by directly or indirectly providing a new source of supply of the input that is foreclosed. Alternatively, it may increase concentration in the blocked market, adding to the competitive problem. DFI by US firms may have the same two effects. For example, US outward DFI in mining properties that are sources of particular minerals may lead to increased concentration in this mineral, if the acquiring firms are already the dominant producers. Alternatively, the acquisition may lead to reduce concentration, if DFI allows US firms that have been blocked from US sources of the material to gain access to the scarce input.

Infant-industry Theory

When an industry receives a major innovative shock, concentration may be increased, as the competitors with the more advanced technology grow faster than the less efficient competitors. While the efficiency gains from such a technological shift may more than offset the competitive costs of the change in market structure, the ultimate market structure may depend on how fast the adoption of the new technology is and how many firms there are with similar competing technologies. Thus, when a foreign firm enters a market with a superior technology, the entry may prove to be a mixed blessing. While there may be clear short-run gains in efficiency and lower prices, the shock of the new technology may lead to a more concentrated long-run equilibrium. The market may also become concentrated very quickly if the entry by DFI spawns a series of retaliatory mergers.[36] While a higher level of concentration may not be important, as would be the case if barriers to entry were low, antitrust authorities might be legitimately concerned if the early entrants could use their lead to insulate themselves from future competition. For example, if other characteristics of the market, such as learning-curves and sunk costs, support entry-deterring activities, the trade-off between efficiency and monopolisation may arise in both the short-run and the long-run.

Maverick/Mutual Forbearance Theory

Entry by a foreign rival, perhaps with only a small market share, would appear to increase competition. In particular, the foreign firm can have different incentives than its larger US rivals. It is likely to have a smaller share of the market, and thus may perceive itself to be a fringe competitor that can fail to follow the prices of the leading US firms without undesirable consequences. Furthermore, to the extent that its entry is based on a slightly different organisational or technological structure than the US firms it faces, it will have a different cost structure. Therefore, it will find different pricing tactics to be desirable, making collusion difficult. The incentive structure of foreign firms may also be different, weighting the goals of some firm constituents (such as union members) less than established US firms. In short, foreign firms might be expected to be mavericks that would do more to undermine cartel behaviour than existing US firms.

Entry by foreign firms, even at small share levels, may have larger anticompetitive effects, however, that more than offset any pro-competitive effect that accompanies entry. In particular, if the same international firms face each other in many different markets, there is the possibility that DFI in the United States simply completes a web of relationships so that US firms are discouraged from cutting prices in the United States or abroad by the fear that the foreign firms will retaliate.

Economists have modelled mutual-forbearance using extensions of traditional oligopoly models, finding that profit-maximising firms may have incentives to take into account potential responses in one market to their actions in a second market.[37] Theoretically, asymmetrical share configurations appear to be important to this relationship (one firm has a large share where its competitor has a small share and vice versa). Although empirical tests of these hypotheses are in their infancy, some weak support has been found.[38]

In the DFI literature, economists have used informal arguments that bear a close resemblance to the more general mutual-forbearance theory. Basically, it has been posited that in oligopolistic industries, DFI by one industry member will trigger substantial responsive DFI for 'strategic reasons'. However, the 'strategic reasons' are rarely formalised, although there have been efforts to look for cases where firms appear to have been motivated by mutual forbearance notions. For example, Graham (1974) argued that international cross-investment was motivated by the desire to cross-threaten international rivals in such cases as Shell Oil's 1911 investment in the United States (which was a response to Standard Oil's international competitive tactics) and Procter and Gamble's entry into the United Kingdom (which was a response to Lever Brothers' US entry). However, in applying this theory it should be recognised that DFI may not be required to threaten a rival, since, for some products, imports into the rival's market may serve the same purpose.

Perhaps because the economics of mutual forbearance and related practices is still developing, courts have been reluctant to base findings on these theories. For example, in *United States* v. *Marine Bancorporation Inc. et al.*, the Department of Justice argued that a market-extension merger raised competitive problems because it linked oligopolists. However, the court held: 'The Government's underlying concern for a linkage or network of statewide oligopolistic banking market is, on this record at least, considerably closer to "ephemeral possibilities" than "probabilities".'[39]

Conclusion

Caves (1974a, p. 292) concluded that: 'Much of the copious literature on the multinational firm, whether positive or normative, approaches its subject with neither an analytical model of how the beast operates nor a systematic test of the model's prediction.' Our review of the DFI literature, in search of analyses relating to the relationships between DFI and antitrust activity has led us to much the same conclusion. Although the link between antitrust and DFI is frequently recognised, there is surprisingly little in the way of well-specified-hypothesis testing. Perhaps more surprisingly, there is a lack of detailed case studies of DFI decision-making processes. While firms may be reluctant to disclose antitrust concerns, and public records of their thought processes are probably scarce, it still is remarkable that others have not expanded on Brewster's effort with more thorough case specific studies.

This is not to say that the area is totally uncharted. As the preceding discussion illustrates, by combining the research efforts that have been conducted on domestic antitrust policy and firm behaviour, with the fundamental findings of DFI literature, it is possible to sketch the links between antitrust policy and IDFI. The problem is that the strength of these links has gone untested.

Reviewing the essential outlines of the relationship, we find that IDFI is affected directly by antitrust policy, through prohibitions on merger and joint-venture activity contained in the law. Perhaps more importantly, we observe indirect effects through antitrust law's effects on the desirability of alternatives to DFI (that is, exportation and licensing) and through the law's role in defining the market structure in which DFI decisions are made. There are also definable effects of DFI activity on antitrust enforcement efforts. However, as was noted in the discussions of the theories of potential entrant, infant industry, foreclosure, and maverick/mutual forbearance, even the direction of these effects are hard to identify, since the nature of these effects varies so much across specific cases.

Our simple empirical effort does confirm a fundamental fact that future investigators should keep in mind: antitrust enforcement efforts involving DFI are relatively rare; thus, antitrust law's primary effects probably are preventive rather than remedial. One important implication of this finding is that studies which focus on the cases that are actually brought will be based on a biased sample. Only firms that dared to tread close to the gray margin of antitrust law will be included in the sample, while decisions to adopt alternatives that offer less antitrust risk will be missed.

Unfortunately, future investigators will have to face a problem we have ignored until now: We suspect that the overall relationship is not simply an interaction system of linkages in which antitrust law alters DFI efforts and DFI affects antitrust enforcement activities, but a system that also involves a set of exogenous factors that simultaneously shape both DFI and the focus of antitrust enforcement. When attempting to test theories that imply causal relationships, the possibility that the observed linkages between DFI and antitrust activity, which appear to be causal, may in fact be the result of other market characteristics must be kept in mind. Specifically, we are concerned that the set of feasible technological opportunities may simultaneously be contributing to market structures that trigger antitrust scrutiny and to market opportunities that stimulate DFI.

While the theoretical complications of pursuing the analysis appear significant, this should not serve as an excuse to abandon further research efforts, but simply serve to warn off hasty conclusions. Indeed, we view this chapter as a basis for future research. We hope that the introduction to antitrust and the outlines of the linkages between DFI and antitrust, particularly the more specific theories examined, will provide insights and trigger ideas for further research.

Notes

* The opinions expressed here are those of the authors and not the US Federal Trade Commission. We would like to thank Doug Dobson for his work on potential-competition theory, particularly the case citations he provided, and Scott Harvey for his insights into mutual forebearance theory.

1. See Maule (1969 and 1970) and Reuber (1970) for further discussion of the issues involved.

2. For a discussion of the antitrust laws of other countries, see Goldsweig (1981), Schlieder (1981), Hunter (1981), Uesugi (1981), Rowe (1981) and Andriessen (1981).

3. Antitrust laws are only part of a larger governmental regulatory environment. This point should be kept in mind when comparing the 'restrictiveness' of antitrust laws across countries. For example, to the extent that Japanese government is a direct participant in or close regulator of corporate decision-making, antitrust enforcement may not be as necessary as it is in a more *laissez-faire* economy.

4. This guide, US Department of Justice (1977), details joint-venture guidelines, and also discusses acquisitions of foreign companies.

5. In the *United States* v. *Ciba Corp* (SD, NY, 1970) case, two Swiss chemical companies consented to divest assets and licence patents because of overlaps in the United States.

6. *Pacific Seafarers Inc.* v. *Pacific Far East Line Inc.* (DC Circuit, 1968).

7. *United States* v. *Aluminium Co.* of America (Second Circuit, 1945). The case emphasised that the action must have both 'effects' and intend to cause such effects for there to be US jurisdiction.

8. *United States* v. *Watchmakers of Switzerland Information Center Inc.* (SD, NY, 1962). However, some have phrased this as any effect that is not both unsubstantial and indirect. See *Occidental Petroleum Co.* v. *Buttest Gas & Oil Co.* (CD, Cal, 1971).

9. The problems raised by foreign 'blocking statutes' that limit discovery by antitrust complaint counsel are not discussed here, but they can also limit enforcement efforts. Basically, these statutes prohibit foreign companies from responding to a US subpoena. Resolution of the conflict requires careful negotiation.

10. *Interamerican Refining Corp.* v. *Texaco Maracaibo Inc.* (D. Del., 1970). The plaintiff alleged that a refusal to supply its New Jersey refinery with Venezuelan oil was an illegal boycott, but the defendants successfully showed that the Venezuelan government had threatened to suspend their right to export oil. The key focus of the defence is on whether the acts were compelled.

11. See *International Association of Machinists* v. *OPEC* (Ninth Circuit, 1981). Here decisions about oil were thought to be the 'essence' of sovereignty to the OPEC nations.

12. See, for example, *Timberlane Lumber Co.* v. *Bank of America* (Ninth Circuit, 1976) and *Mannington Milles Inc.* v. *Congoleum Corp.* (Third Circuit, 1979). The Department of Justice cautiously endorsed the *Timberlane* approach in its 1977 *Antitrust Guide for International Operations* (pp. 6–7).

13. These ten points are from the *Congoleum* case. *Timberlane* produced a basis for this more detailed list.

14. Uranium Antitrust Litigation (Seventh Circuit, 1980).

15. In the early 1950s, about one-third of new affiliates were acquired. Today, roughly half of all affiliates established by US multinationals are acquired. For US inward DFI, just over 40 per cent of the roughly 1,600 businesses started by foreigners were acquired. However, this percentage rises dramatically to 95 per cent when percentages are calculated in terms of investment outlays.

16. The current minimum of $15 million was raised in November 1979 from $10 million.

17. Filing totals include transactions subsequently found to be non-reportable due to exemptions.

18. During 1981, 1,083 transactions were reported under the HSR programme. The smaller number, 762, reflects adjustments to eliminate the following types of transactions: (1) transactions involving certain financial businesses, (2) transactions involving two- (or more) step transactions between the same parties, (3) transactions found to be non-reportable due to size requirements, (4) incomplete transactions in which only one party to the transaction filed notification and (5) secondary acquisitions reported as a result of a reportable primary transaction. The number does include, however, competing offers and transactions involving two or more acquiring or acquired persons.

19. No transactions involved joint ventures outside the United States or joint ventures between only foreign firms.

20. In addition, the FTC sought eight preliminary injunctions to block the consummation of mergers or acquisitions. Six of the proposed acquisitions, including an acquisition of a US industrial equipment manufacturer by a West German firm (Mannesmann AG), were abandoned by the parties. The FTC was unsuccessful in seeking the preliminary injunction to block the remaining two transactions, but it subsequently challenged the acquisition in administrative complaints.

21. One of the complaints against a merger between two domestic firms had international implications. In fiscal 1980, the FTC issued an administrative complaint against Champion Spark Plug Co., alleging that Champion's acquisition of the Anderson Company lessened competition among replacement windshield-wiper producers. Champion's European subsidiaries produced such products at the time of the complaint, and consequently were viewed as likely potential entrants into the US market.

22. While the US Supreme Court has laid down guidelines for a challenge under the actual potential-competition doctrine, it has reserved approval of the doctrine. See *United States* v. *Marine Bancorporation*, (1974); *United States* v. *Falstaff Brewing Corp.* (1973); *rev'd United States* v. *Falstaff Brewing Corp.* (DRI, 1971). The perceived potential-competition doctrine was approved in *Falstaff.*

23. See, for example, *United States* v. *Marine Bancorporation* for the first three points and *United States* v. *Falstaff Brewing* for the fourth point. It is important to recognise that all entries are not equally significant. Some courts have taken this into account when studying potential entrants. See, for example,

FTC v. *Tenneco Inc.* (DDC, 1977).

24. *Brunswick Corp.* v. *FTC* (1979), affirmed, *Yamaha Motor Co. Ltd.* v. *FTC* (Eighth Circuit, 1981).

25. *Pennock* v. *Dialogue (Supreme Court, 1829).*

26. Section 3 of the Clayton Act specifically includes 'patented goods' as under its reach.

27. While this section focuses on activity in the United States to limit imports, it should be remembered that US antitrust laws may be able to reach foreign activity that limits imports, such as voluntary restraint agreements. See, for example, *Consumer Union of United States* v. *Rogers*, 353 F. Supp. 1319 (DCC, 1973), *affirmed in part, vacated in part*, 506 F.2d 136 (DC Circuit, 1974), *cert. denied* 421 US 1004 (1975) which challenged the 1972–4 steel voluntary restraints and led at least the District Court to recognise serious Sherman Act problems. The Trade Act of 1974, Section 607, gave antitrust immunity to the 1972–4 steel restraints.

28. Three advantages are apparent: (1) treble damage and lawyer fees may be paid for antitrust actions; (2) there are better discovery-provisions that will give access to foreign documents and impose costs on the importer whom one is trying to discourage; and (3) injunctive relief may be obtained.

29. Others have advanced similar theories. Aharoni (1966) discusses the 'bandwagon effect'. Vernon (1968) discusses risk-minimisation as a motive for responsive DFI. More recently, Flowers (1976) has used Knickerbocker's methodology to study clustering of European and Canadian DFI in the United States.

30. Foreign firms not only enter but they also exit. The phenomenon of direct foreign divestment (DFD) has received little attention. One question that suggests itself is: How do recent increases in DFD compare to the phenomenon of spin-offs by firms that are retrenching after conglomerate growth through mergers? For a brief review of DFD, see Boddewyn (1979). Note that an increase in DFD would be expected to follow an increase in DFI, to the extent that failures increase with the number of entry attempts.

31. Knickerbocker (1973, pp. 21–2) lists three reasons for responsive DFI: (1) entry by a rival may imperil the profits the firm was earning from the entered country before DFI; (2) profitable operation in the entered country may be key to the responding corporation's logistical network; and (3) the rival's entry may offer learning or scale advantages that advantage the rival if no parallel action is taken.

32. Knickerbocker (1973, pp. 50–2) points out that, in another Harvard dissertation, Stobaugh (1968) studied five-digit petrochemical industries and found no evidence of oligopolistic reaction.

33. The potential sources of bias are: (1) inherent collinearity between Knickerbocker's measure of clustering and concentration because of the way the clustering variable is calculated and (2) his finding of statistical significance might be sensitive to which of the SIC codes are excluded. Indeed, the bulk of Knickerbocker's sample appears to cluster around the eight-firm concentration level of 50 per cent, which is well below the 70 per cent critical concentration level of Bain (1956).

34. Coughlan (1982), in her study of DFIs in the semiconductor industry, found that ongoing marketing efforts were important to the decision to integrate into marketing in the foreign country. She concluded that firms' horizons were longer than the life of a single product.

35. Scholars have related the level of antitrust activity to market structure and performance with varying amounts of success. See, for example, Posner (1970), Long, Schramm and Tollison (1973), Asch (1975) and Siegfried (1975). Findings have generally indicated that industry size, concentration and profitability play a

role in determining where cases are brought.

36. An example of retaliatory mergers that led to increased concentration might have been the British response to the 1901 entry of American Tobacco, which entered Great Britain through the acquisition of Ogden Ltd. Within a month of American Tobacco's entry, 13 British producers combined to form Imperial Tobacco Company. A market sharing agreement was made in 1902 in which Ogden became part of Imperial Tobacco, which was given exclusive rights to British and Irish markets, while American Tobacco was given the US market.

37. See, for example, Feinberg (1981) who extends a simple duopoly model to include cross-market effects and finds that an expectation of retaliation can induce output restraint. Reynolds (1976) shows that in a duopoly, price cutting may be deterred by cross-market threats that are consistent with independent profit maximisation and thus are credible.

38. Statistical findings have been mixed. For example, Heggestad and Rhoades (1978) found that multi-market linkages between dominant banks do decrease the rivalry (as measured by share instability) within markets. Strickland (1977) found price-cost margins were lower in markets that were linked (according to the 1963 activities of 195 of the top 200 industrial firms) than those that were not. Given the difficulty of statistical analysis and data problems in testing this theory, perhaps one of the more hopeful efforts is experimental testing of the theories. For an early effort in this direction, see Feinberg and Sherman (1981). Their laboratory experiments produced preliminary statistically weak support for the view that 'meeting the same rivals in two markets may lessen competitiveness' (p. 14).

39. *United States* v. *Marine Bancorporation Inc. et al.* (S. Circuit, 1974) at 2832. See also *United States* v. *Connecticut National Bank* (S. Circuit, 1974) at 2793, where a similar theory led to a similar result.

* * *

COMMENT

Robert G. Hawkins

First, let me indicate in a positive vein that the chapter by Nelson and Silvia makes a contribution and is well worth reading. It is one of the few systematic linkings of US antitrust policy and how it may affect direct foreign investment (DFI), including intra-industry DFI (IDFI). I hasten to add, however, that the chapter leads to few, if any, conclusions about how existing antitrust policy affects DFI; or what the effects should be; or, given the structure of new DFI flows, what antitrust policy should involve. As a result, the chapter is a frustrating one.

Nelson and Silvia provide a thorough review of US antitrust policies and of the literature on their effects on inward and outward DFI. Unfortunately, much of the literature was not critically assessed, aside from a serious swipe at Knickerbocker's 'oligopolistic reaction — follow the leader' findings. I agree that those findings have little practical relevance for current antitrust policy.

The chapter then reverses things, asking how IDFI affects antitrust enforcement in the United States. It identifies four theories (or more appropriately, characteristics) about how IDFI affects (or should influence) the application of our received doctrine (precedent) on antitrust. One might quibble over whether these are the only linkages or theories, but most of the landscape is covered.

Overall, this is a useful study, but let me now indicate some of my views about IDFI in general and what the chapter might have done. First, the subject matters (or issues) addressed here are one of the two most important of this volume (the other deals with technology, R and D and IDFI). One of the shortcomings of the chapter, and its menu of possible effects (all non-quantified) of antitrust policy on DFI, and vice versa, is its failure to consider how IDFI influences the rate of technological progress and the distribution of the fruits of that progress. Certainly, antitrust or industrial policy more broadly defined affect both the rate of technological change and the division of the spoils, but how and by how much are not known. Related to this is the chapter's lack of consideration of the interrelationships between US antitrust policy and antitrust policies abroad. Yet the result of antitrust action in the United States will − with increasing frequency − depend upon related policies in the rest of the world.

The third shortcoming (and of most of the literature in the field) is the isolation of antitrust policy from the broader range of policies affecting IDFI: subsidies, taxation, securities-laws, etc. Again, this omission is extremely serious when viewed in the larger universe of policies implemented by foreign governments that affect their firms, and the incentives or restrictions on those firms for IDFI. Did US policy-makers or academic experts examine fully, and with what tools, the General Motors–Toyota joint venture, the joint venture of Renault and American Motors, and many other examples of technology-sharing by presumed competitors in the same industry? Is antitrust policy benignly irrelevant? Or, it is out of step with technological realities: the shrinking relative role of the United States in international production; the growing dependence of US firms on foreign markets; and, a world of asymmetrical policies on aids to industry, trade barriers, and government pre-emption of industry segments? I fear that we in the United States have not done this analysis, despite a number of piecemeal efforts by some government agencies and academic researchers. This is not to criticise the authors of this chapter for taking on this complex and burdensome analysis. Indeed, perhaps we do not have the analytical or conceptual tools to do so. But someone should try, because it is one of the more important unresolved economic-policy issues facing the United States.

Finally, the whole notion of *intra*-industry trade or of IDFI has never caught my fancy. The distinction between intra- and inter-industry trade or investment does not seem very important to me. In my view, intra-industry trade (or investment) has some simple explanations: markets are not perfect, products are not homogeneous, and there are *sunk* costs. What else do we need? While I do not oppose conceptualisation and theorising about IDFI, or the search for new data to describe it, it does not stimulate my juices. We need progress in finding how DFI affects real income, technological change, and income distribution world-wide; and, how antitrust and other government interventions affect those variables, jointly and separately. This covers both inter- and intra-industry DFI. This chapter stimulated me; it did not satisfy me.

* * *

COMMENT*

William W. Nye

The Nelson and Silvia chapter is divided into two main parts. The first part catalogues many of the ways in which antitrust enforcement might affect intra-industry direct foreign investment (IDFI). The second part discusses how IDFI might influence antitrust enforcement. I have learned much from this chapter. Various aspects of the relation between IDFI and antitrust enforcement have been discussed in the literature but never, to my knowledge, has the whole relation been surveyed as thoroughly. I am sure that future investigators in this area will often refer to this chapter.

I have two general comments to offer, one about the discussion of the effect of IDFI on the enforcement of US antitrust laws and the other about the effect of antitrust on IDFI. Nelson and Silvia review the literature on four possible ways in which IDFI could affect antitrust enforcement. The four alternatives are: (1) potential-entrant theory, (2) foreclosure theory, (3) infant-industry theory and (4) maverick/mutual forbearance theory. The literature on each of these topics can contribute to our understanding of the manner in which IDFI affects antitrust enforcement. It is not clear, however, why these literatures are any more relevant to the effect of *foreign* investment on antitrust than to the effect of domestic investment on antitrust. Consider the potential-entrant theory, for example. Antitrust officials should and do take into account the possibility of entry by foreign firms just as they should and do take into account the possibility of entry by domestic firms when considering mergers, joint ventures and other matters that come to their attention.

Suppose, for example, that a Canadian bottle manufacturer that does not currently sell in the United States acquires a New York bottle producer. This investment – which is classified as foreign because of the border – would he subject to much the same antitrust scrutiny as would the acquisition of the New York producer by a Californian bottle manufacturer. The new US Department of Justice (DOJ) Merger Guidelines would deal with these two hypothetical mergers similarly. First, the DOJ would attempt to ascertain whether the Californian or Canadian producer was in the same geographical market as the New York producer and hence was in direct competition with the latter. Next, even if they were not in the same market, the DOJ would ask whether either the Californian or Canadian producer would have been a potential entrant into the New York producer's geographical market.

Nelson and Silvia are correct in pointing out that the potential-entrant theory, the foreclosure theory, etc. can contribute to our understanding of the ways in which IDFI affects the enforcement of antitrust laws. These insights apply equally well, however, to the much larger class of domestic investments. The characteristics of DFI which give it a unique impact on antitrust enforcement are connected to the volatility of exchange rates, the possibility of trade barriers and the difficulties connected with the enforcement of US laws when foreign fims are involved.

My second comment concerns the impact of antitrust enforcement on IDFI. Nelson and Silvia classify the impact of antitrust enforcement into direct and indirect effects. Direct effects would occur either when specific DFIs were challenged on antitrust grounds or when specific DFIs were not undertaken because of the fear of antitrust action. Indirect effects occur largely through the impact of antitrust policy on market structure. For example, Nelson and Silvia suggest that if weak foreign antitrust enforcement leads some foreign firms to face higher prices for their factor inputs than those available in US factor markets, these firms could be encouraged to invest in the United

States in an attempt to take advantage of competitively supplied US inputs.

Nelson and Silvia have performed a useful service by cataloguing the large and sometimes contradictory literature about the many ways in which antitrust enforcement, through its impact on market structure, can affect DFI. It may be worth noting, however, that many of the possible lines of causation suggested by Nelson and Silvia do not deal specifically with *intra-industry* DFI as distinct from one-way DFI. Any regulatory policies which make business relatively more attractive in a particular location may affect the flow of DFI. IDFI, as a subset of total DFI, will necessarily also be affected. But to the extent that antitrust policy simply affects the costs and risks of doing business in a particular country, it is unclear why IDFI should be specifically affected.

The Knickerbocker theory of reactive oligopolists offers a possible hypothesis according to which antitrust enforcement could specifically affect IDFI. But as Nelson and Silvia point out, there are many difficulties with the Knickerbocker hypothesis, including the question of why oligopolists should be more sensitive to DFI opportunities than competitive firms. Moreover, even if most oligopolists did behave in the reactive manner suggested by Knickerbocker, it is not clear what role antitrust policy had in causing the resulting DFI activities with the exception of permitting the existence of the oligopolies that made the investments.

For IDFI to be specifically affected by antitrust policy, there may need to be differential (and probably non-optimal) enforcement of national antitrust laws by the antitrust authorities of some of the governments involved. Suppose, at the extreme, that there were no antitrust laws in a certain country. Such a policy might provide a powerful incentive for DFI that was specifically intra-industry in nature as firms attempted to make acquisitions that enabled them to exercise market power. It might be interesting, in this respect, to do a careful comparative survey of different national antitrust enforcement policies and to try to determine how economic markets are defined in each case. Such a survey might reveal the direction of an expected flow of IDFI. The IDFI might be difficult to detect statistically, of course, because of the volume of *inter-industry* DFI moving for the reasons suggested by Nelson and Silvia.

Note

* The opinions expressed here do not necessarily reflect the views of the US Department of Justice.

5 US DIRECT FOREIGN INVESTMENT AND TRADE: THEORIES, TRENDS AND PUBLIC POLICY ISSUES

Rachel McCulloch

Introduction

Until the 1970s, the phenomenon of direct foreign investment (DFI) was, from an empirical point of view, dominated by US outward DFI — so much so that Penrose (1971) could characterise the multinational enterprise (MNE) as a peculiarly American institution rather than as a global phenomenon. As long as US subsidiaries abroad comprised the major part of DFI globally, theorising about the nature of DFI and its consequences for economic efficiency and welfare focused almost exclusively on the single pattern of one-way DFI by 'home' country, that is, US firms in various 'host' countries. Likewise, the validity of competing theories was judged primarily on the basis of their ability to account for the specific characteristics of US outward DFI and its variation in importance across industrial and potential host countries.

A large but ultimately inconclusive body of research on the causes and consequences of DFI was addressed to major US policy concerns, specifically the relationship of US outward DFI with US domestic employment and the US balance of payments. Most of this research attempted to evaluate the degree of complementarity or substitution between US exports and host-country production by US subsidiaries and, to a lesser extent, between US production for domestic markets and imports from subsidiaries abroad (for example, Musgrave (1975), Dewald, Gilman, Grubert and Wipf (1978), Bergsten, Horst and Moran (1978, Chapters 3 and 4)). From a theoretical perspective, the answer depended on whether US outward DFIs were 'defensive', that is, required to secure overseas markets that would otherwise be lost to foreign rivals. Sympathetic observers like Vernon (1971) inferred from case studies that US outward DFIs were in fact largely defensive, but most US labour unions and as well as some academic researchers, for example, Frank and Freeman (1978), took a less optimistic view. Empirical testing was complicated by the product-cycle character of most US DFI abroad; the industries and firms with above-average

129

propensities to invest abroad were also those with above-average propensities to export.[1]

During the 1970s, the United States emerged rather suddenly as a leading *host* country, probably edging out Canada in this role by the end of the decade (Hawkins and Walter, 1980). However, while foreign investors and especially Europeans acquired a rapidly growing stake in US manufacturing, trade, financial services, natural resources and real estate, DFIs by US firms also continued to grow, albeit at a slower rate than in the 1950s and 1960s. As the new DFI patterns of the 1970s became evident in the statistics (still acknowledged even by the officials responsible for collecting them to be highly inadequate), the focus of both theorising and empirical testing began to shift to explanations of changing patterns of investment (for example, Dunning (1979), Kojima (1978), Lall and Siddharthan (1982)) and of cross-DFI and in particular intra-industry DFI (IDFI) (for example, Graham (1978), Erdilek (1982a)) – phenomena that had been of very limited practical interest as long as US investments abroad dominated the global aggregates.

The past decade has provided analysts of DFI with a wealth of new information that can be used to expand our knowledge of this important economic phenomenon. This is true especially in the case of IDFI, which may well be the 'typical' pattern of the future, just as one-way US outward DFI was typical in the 1950s and 1960s. In this chapter, established and newer theories of DFI, along with their implications for public policy, are evaluated in the light of recent trends in the DFI position of the United States. The chapter emphasises particularly the novel pattern of IDFI and its relationship to trade in goods and services.

The Eclectic Theory and Beyond

The central puzzle concerning DFI is, of course, why it takes place at all. Most analysts accepted the answer advanced by Hymer (1960) and expanded by Kindleberger (1969), Caves (1971, 1974b), and many others, that the investing firm must possess an 'advantage' in terms of product, process or management that is sufficient to outweigh its obvious disadvantages relative to actual or potential indigenous competitors in the host country. Furthermore, most analysts associated the required advantage with the existence of significant market-imperfections. This view accorded well with the facts of US outward

DFI, which was typically undertaken in markets characterised by oligopoly, product differentiation, barriers to trade or some combination of these.

Despite nearly unanimous agreement on this aspect of the underlying rationals for DFI (one notable dissenter was Aliber (1970)), further elaboration was required in order to generate empirically testable hypotheses concerning the distribution of DFI across industries within a given host country or across countries. Although the many authors who have contributed to the huge literature in this area have differed in their emphases, as noted in the recent surveys by Bergsten *et al.* (1978), Agarwal (1980), and McClain (1983), Dunning's synthesis in his proposed 'eclectic theory' provides a convenient means of classifying the major themes (Dunning, 1981c).

Dunning's approach identifies three broad categories among the determinants of DFI. First, as a necessary condition, there must be the *ownership* (O) advantage. In practice, this usually refers to a technological advantage. In most empirical studies an R and D or labour-skills variable has been used to measure ownership advantage. Without the ownership advantage, there is no source of benefits to the investing firm to offset the additional costs of operating abroad. Second, the host country must offer a *locational* (L) advantage in terms of costs of serving a particular market. These costs may reflect the traditional components of comparative advantage and transport costs, as well as policy-determined costs and benefits arising from tariffs and non-tariff barriers, labour legislation, pollution control policies, incentives to or restrictions on DFI and so on. In the absence of a locational advantage, exporting will be chosen over DFI as a way of exploiting the firm's ownership advantage.[2] Finally, even when the foreign location is advantageous, there must be an *internalisation* (I) advantage that causes the firm to opt for DFI over the alternative of licensing foreign production or other arm's-length (that is, external to the firm) modes. Dunning posits that the level and distribution of DFI will be determined by the relative strength of these three sets of factors, OLI for short.

Dunning's eclectic theory has been of great value to students of DFI in providing a unified framework for considering the multitude of hypotheses advanced to explain the phenomenon. Yet Dunning's extremely lucid exposition of his tripartite system gives rise to the observation that the three categories of determinants are not on equal footing. Only one of the three 'advantages' is decisive, and that one, contrary to the emphasis of Hymer, Kindleberger, Caves, and others, is internalisation. Indeed, DFI *is* precisely internalisation across national boundaries; firms engaging in DFI are by definition alone those that can benefit from internalisation across national boundaries.[3] A 'general' theory of DFI must therefore of necessity be a subset of the general theory of internalisation. Rugman (1980a) has made exactly this point, thereby drawing a polite but firm demurral from Dunning (1981c, p. 33). Rugman argues persuasively that the current stock of competing theories of DFI can be subsumed under the general theory of internalisation. However, Rugman's own version of this 'general' theory is itself insufficiently general, so that much of the potency of his thesis is lost.

Although Rugman cites the seminal work of Coase (1937) on the subject, there is little of Coase in Rugman's own version of internalisation theory. Rugman's discussion is heavily studded with the phrase 'market imperfection' and variants on it. This concept appears nowhere, either explicitly or in other language, in Coase's own classic treatment – indeed, one would be most surprised to find it in the work of a patriarch of the Chicago School. Rugman has evidently been influenced by the received wisdom of the older theories constructed to explain US outward DFI, especially that market imperfections (and particularly those produced by national policies) are the central motivating force behind DFI. Although valid as an empirical generalisation from DFI patterns of the 1950s and 1960s, the emphasis on 'imperfections' in a world where no market is 'perfect' draws attention away from other, potentially more interesting predictions of the internalisation hypothesis.

Internalisation and Direct Foreign Investment

It is instructive to return to Coase's own framework, in which the degree of internalisation of economic activity reflects the relative costs of carrying out a given business function through a market transaction or internally. Internally, at least for Coase, does *not* mean through an 'internal market', another of Rugman's frequently used phrases that suggests a very un-Coasian model of internalisation. Coase's view is that the firm is a voluntary command economy, in which entrepreneurs (managers, in the framework of the MNE) substitute their own judgement for a market process.

As noted earlier, the one thing that all DFI has in common is the choice of internalisation across national boundaries as a management strategy. Focusing on this one common element provides a useful reinterpretation of past empirical research on US outward DFI. Case histories of US-based MNEs reveal that investing firms have typically been those making above-average expenditures for R and D and for advertising — giving rise to the notion expanded by Vernon (1966, 1971) and others that 'product differentiation' provides the central impetus for DFI. However, Horst (1972b) showed that correction for industrial characteristics in a multiple-regression analysis left only one statistically significant determinant of multinationality, namely, firm-size. This is exactly what the (general Coasian) theory of internalisation would predict for US firms. Big firms are those which profit from internalisation, whether for firm-specific or industry-specific reasons. For a firm located in the large US market, it is natural to expect that the gains from domestic internalisation will be nearly exhausted before international expansion is undertaken, for precisely the reasons given in all standard treatments of DFI as disadvantages to the MNE in operating abroad. And the same type of domestic-versus international-expansion argument can be used to explain the often noted fact that the typical non-US-based MNE is smaller, so that the average size of MNEs has been declining in recent years. Likewise, this argument would explain the relatively large presence of smaller industrialised nations, for example, Switzerland and the Netherlands, as direct investors, as noted by McClain (1983).

To characterise internalisation as substitution of an internal for an external market is to imply, incorrectly, that its objectives are achieved primarily via decentralised managerial decisions carried out in semi-autonomous profit centres.[4] Although this is one possible way of managing a very large business, it is by no means the only one. In particular, a degree of centralisation (that is, command allocation) is essential to achieving the full advantages of internalisation, whether domestically or across national boundaries.[5] The cost of centralised control is obviously related to that of long-distance communication and travel. This provides an attractive rationale for the rapid expansion of DFI following the Second World War.

Coase emphasised the usefulness of internal transactions in cases of longer-term relationships entailing considerable uncertainty. This seems a fruitful point of departure in explaining the surge of US inward DFI in the 1970s, but it dovetails neatly also with the usual explanations of DFI by US manufacturing firms (uncertainty on the part of contractors makes arm's-length exploitation of new products and processes impractical) and coincides precisely with the standard explanation for vertical backward investments in sources of primary inputs.

Of the many 'differences' of the 1970s from earlier decades that might help to account for abruptly altered patterns of DFI, increased *uncertainty* seems by far the most conspicuous. The variability of every important economic indicator was greater in the 1970s than in the 1960s: unemployment, capacity utilisation, real and nominal interest rates, national inflation rates and exchange rates. It is thus plausible that risk-management motives tipped the balance for many firms in favour of internalisation across national boundaries, and especially DFI in the United States. However, international diversification of portfolio investment also increased markedly during the 1970s for basically similar reasons. In addition, some European DFIs, particularly in US real estate, have been retailed to diversification-minded European portfolio investors.

What is particularly significant about the function of internalisation in optimisation under uncertainty is that the investing firm's essential advantage arises from *being* multinational.[6] Thus, the notion that investments are located to best serve a particular market may be somewhat misleading. When diversification or, more generally, optimisation under uncertainty is a primary investment motive, the preferred distribution of a firm's assets will depend on locational considerations very different from those suggested by Dunning's OLI paradigm. In particular, the recent growth of DFI in the United States, and especially of IDFI, can be seen as representing at least in part a response by foreign firms to increased economic uncertainty rather than a shift in the locational attractions, as conventionally defined, of the United States as a production site. I do not mean to ignore, however, a less novel but, for the 1970s, extremely relevant consideration, namely, the effect of US trade-barriers. I discuss this in some detail later.

The Role of Exchange Rates

It is almost a commonplace that the overvalued dollar of the 1960s contributed to the rapid growth of US outward DFI. But why? In fact, the period in which most of the world's stock of DFI was built up can be divided neatly into three sub-periods according to the likely role of exchange rates. The period of the 1950s, in which the multinational expansion of large US firms first became conspicuous, was characterised by a 'dollar shortage' and less than full convertibility of most European currencies. (The Bretton Woods system did not become fully operational until 1959.) During this period, the dollar was basically undervalued at its official parity. Hence, the dollar shortage. But the widespread use of exchange controls acted as a broadly based barrier to imports from the United States. Like other types of protection discussed below, this shifted the OLI balance for US firms (and European firms) in favour of expanding production in Europe and thus favoured the substitution of US outward DFI for exporting.

During the 1960s, the dollar was considered to be increasingly overvalued at its official parity. A pervasive but somewhat misleading explanation of US DFI abroad in the 1960s is that an overvalued dollar made foreign assets, like foreign goods, bargains in the eyes of US purchasers. But if a foreign asset is seen as a claim to a future stream of foreign-currency-denominated profits, and if profits will be converted back into dollars at the same exchange rate that prevails at the time the asset is purchased, the level of the exchange rate does not affect the present discounted value (in dollars) of the investment. Thus, overvaluation is irrelevant; there is no reason to expect purely financial foreign assets to be perceived as bargains by US investors. Indeed, the actual net flow of portfolio investment in the 1960s was the reverse of what the 'bargain asset' view would predict.

A correct way to state the case is that the overvalued dollar made European *production* a bargain for US firms, thus reinforcing other OLI motives for investment abroad. European production yielded higher dollar-profits (lower dollar-costs) than those of exporting from the United States or domestic production for the US market. In this present-value calculation, the level of the exchange rate does not cancel out. The overvalued dollar acted like a uniform tax on all US exports and a subsidy to all US imports (at the rate of the percentage of dollar overvaluation). Put in more contemporary language, the overvalued dollar discouraged tradeables production in the United States and encouraged their production abroad both for foreign markets and for export back to the United States. In the former case, overvaluation promoted DFI as a substitute for US exports; in the latter, DFI plus importing (usually intra-firm) replaced domestic production.

Still, because the overvalued dollar merely favoured European production over US production, by itself it does not account for the ability of US subsidiaries rather than indigenous firms to capture the implied locational benefits. The overvalued dollar could only influence the preferred location of production. (This is the sense in which US outward DFIs during the period could be correctly characterised as defensive.) Advantages of internalisation would also be required to make control of foreign production a profitable strategy for US firms.

A possible second way that the overvalued dollar might have spurred US DFI abroad is through anticipation of an eventual parity change. Because the direction of the change was obvious but its size and date uncertain, real foreign assets became more attractive. However, if this speculative motive had been important for US firms, one would have anticipated a sell-off of these same assets after 1971 or 1973. This did not materialise, suggesting that the speculative motive was not an important independent determinant of US outward DFI in the 1960s.

For the 1970s, the foreign-exchange-rate levels explanation, probably appropriate for the 1960s, continues to be cited, particularly in the business press, but with less justification. However, the collapse of the Bretton Woods system may have influenced incentives for DFI in several distinct ways. First, the end of the Bretton Woods system brought about a significant reduction in the use of capital controls for balance-of-payments purposes. This not only facilitated new DFIs (except for those financed locally or through reinvestment of local earnings) but at the same time increased the attractiveness of investing abroad, by improving prospects for repatriation of future profits and royalties generated by foreign operations.

Second, under the regime of generalised floating, the main characteristic of exchange rates has been not their levels but their volatility, a pattern that is expected to persist for the indefinite future. While the run-up of DFIs by European firms in the United States has probably not been a response to the end of dollar overvaluation, it may in part reflect a desire to achieve diversification not conveniently available through other means (external markets) of many types of increased risk, that of exchange-rate changes just one among them.[7]

Finally, to the extent that volatility of exchange rates has increased pressure for new protection in the United States and other industrialised countries (Bergsten and Williamson, 1982; Aho and Bayard, 1982), this would increase the attractiveness of investments to serve markets through local production instead of exports, that is, substitution of IDFI for intra-industry trade.

The Role of Trade Barriers

No other incentive for DFI has been as much discussed and empirically tested as import barriers.[8] In fact, the presumed link is so strong that most writers addressing the normative consequences of protection or

DFI do not even question that a barrier to imports will attract DFI to the protected industry, but move on immediately to ask whether this is a good thing. Further complicating the issue is that many writers (and especially theorists) do not distinguish adequately between inflows of foreign 'capital' in the physical sense and DFI, which may involve no change at all in the capital stock of the protecting nation and possibly no flow of financial capital either, if DFI is financed through local borrowing. Yet as the earlier discussion of the OLI paradigm makes clear, protection alone cannot explain the existence of DFI.

Protection obviously favours local production in the sheltered industry but does not in itself determine that the local production will be undertaken by a subsidiary of an MNE rather than by an indigenous national firm (with or without a licensing arrangement with the foreign firm that under free trade would supply the market). Thus, the highly protected US apparel and footwear industries are virtually devoid of inward DFI. On the other hand, only a small fraction of the supply of US imports from developing countries in these industries is produced by US subsidiaries abroad (Balassa, 1981). For these low-technology industries, the ownership or the internalisation advantages needed to make DFI in either direction profitable are apparently absent.

Consistent with the trade-barriers hypothesis, the recent increase in actual and threatened protection in some industries — especially electronics and motor vehicles — has been accompanied by a highly publicised build-up of Japanese DFI in the corresponding sectors. Indeed, so large has been the ratio of publicity to increased domestic production capacity that one might suspect the existence of an element of oligopolistic strategy present, along with the obvious locational considerations. Japanese firms may have been wishing to demonstrate to their US rivals that efforts to defend established domestic market shares through protection from imports are doomed to failure. However, the planned US joint venture of General Motors and Toyota (of which Bhagwati (1972) offered a prescient discussion) suggests the shared desire of the leading domestic-producer and the leading import-producer for a mutually beneficial orderly transition to a new oligopolistic equilibrium. Other auto manufacturers with a significant stake in the US market for small cars have already indicated their opposition to the GM–Toyota plan.

The offshore-assembly provisions of the US tariff code are another case in which trade barriers or, more precisely, the structure of protection, may favour DFI. Items 806.30 and 807.00 of the US tariff code provide special treatment for goods assembled abroad using components produced in the United States. US imports of the assembled products are assessed the applicable tariff rate, but only on the value added in the foreign operation. The effect is to encourage offshore location of assembly activities while giving US firms a competitive edge over foreign producers of components. In this case also, whether the locational benefit offered by the offshore-assembly provisions is exploited through arm's-length-means or DFI (and intra-firm trade) appears to depend on the nature of the industry. Balassa (1981) notes that DFI by US firms for purposes of offshore-assembly is prevalent only in the industries such as electronics where technology is changing rapidly. These are also sectors in which protection-motivated DFI by Japanese firms in the United States has been important. Like their indigenous rivals, Japanese subsidiaries in the United States are able to benefit from the offshore-assembly provisions of the US tariff code. IDFI in these cases reflects the common technology-based ownership and internalisation advantages but somewhat different locational advantages as viewed by US firms investing abroad and foreign firms investing in the United States.

An interesting corollary to the theory that protection promotes DFI in the protected market is that selective protection, through voluntary export restraints and orderly marketing agreements, promotes DFI by the targeted exporter in locations where exports are not yet subject to similar control. US protection directed towards Japanese exports in a number of categories, particularly consumer electronics, may not have been the primary motive for the shift of production capacity through Japanese DFI to various Asian developing countries, but it must certainly have accelerated the process. In this case of third-country DFI in response to selective protection, the substitution is of imports from a restricted source by other imports, with no significant effect on domestic output in the protecting nation.[9]

For the United States, inward DFI motivated by protection is almost always IDFI, primarily because the same industry characteristics that have made US outward DFI abroad profitable tend to operate in favour of the establishment of foreign subsidiaries here. As in most import-substituting DFI (except in the presence of very stringent local-content requirements), foreign producers are likely to import a large share of intermediate inputs, so that the effect will be to substitute intra-firm trade in intermediate goods for trade in finished products.

A potentially important exception to this tendency arises in the case of significant plant scale-economies. The entailed loss of scale economies operates to discourage relocation of production in response to increased protection of a market previously served through exports. But if the incentive to invest is strong enough, the firm may choose to relocate a major part of its global production capacity and to serve other markets from the new subsidiary. Protection may thus result in a reversal of the previous pattern of trade. This is most likely to occur if, as in the case of the United States, the protected market is large and the production cost disadvantage relative to alternative sites is small. Local content, employment, or export requirements imposed by the host country also increase the likelihood of a reversal of previous trade-patterns for processes with significant economies of plant scale — although when this happens the requirements may not appear to impose binding constraints on the operations of subsidiaries. When protection tips the OLI balance in favour of DFI, the welfare implications are ambiguous and hinge in part on the underlying motive for protection. I return to this ambiguity later.

An Alternative Taxonomy

The OLI analysis suggested by Dunning has provided an immensely useful tool for relating within a single coherent theoretical framework the multitude of alternative theories of DFI proposed by various researchers. For purposes of analysing public-policy issues now facing the United States, however, the OLI classification is somewhat less useful. Obviously, it is possible to ask, for any given policy choice, how it affects the three components and thus is likely to tip the OLI balance towards or away from a decision to invest in a particular location. However, this is unsatisfactory for two reasons. First, it would be more helpful for this purpose to distinguish those stimuli reflecting considerations less amenable to change over a short period as a consequence of policy choices of home or host country governments. Furthermore, because the OLI paradigm stresses the choice of a specific location rather than the advantages of multinational over uninational operation, it applies less well to the motive of optimisation under uncertainty that is probably important in explaining the changes seen in patterns of DFI in the 1970s, and especially the emergence of IDFI in the United States.

Presented here is an alternative classification scheme that groups stimuli for DFI in a way that is helpful for a *normative* analysis, that is, one addressed primarily to public-policy concerns rather than the primarily positive approach represented by the OLI paradigm. (It needs to be stressed, however, that a normative approach can be no more useful than the positive analysis on which it rests; what we have here is largely a repackaging for analytical convenience of the fruits of past research on the causes of DFI.) In this scheme, stimuli are divided into five groups, reflecting primarily considerations of (1) comparative advantage, (2) product characteristics, (3) industry structure, (4) uncertainty and (5) public policy, representing a range from least to most amenable to rapid alteration through national-policy initiatives.

Comparative Advantage

These determinants of DFI are intrinsic to a host-nation's economy and typically change slowly or not at all – location considerations in the narrow sense. Into this category fall natural-resource-based DFIs as well as those motivated largely by relative production-costs (modified to take account of such considerations as transport costs and the need to be close to the market served). These DFIs are typically export-oriented rather than import-substituting, particularly if the local market is not a large one. That the exporting is undertaken by a foreign investor rather than an indigenous enterprise requires further explanation in terms of ownership or internalisation advantages. If one country has a comparative advantage in non-consecutive production stages, intra-industry trade in intermediate goods could occur, but there is no incentive for IDFI.

Because comparative advantage is the motivating force, such DFIs are likely to have favourable efficiency consequences for the world as a whole. Likewise, policies that tend to *offset* these locational advantages will typically do so at some efficiency cost, although perhaps in the interest of desirable 'non-economic' goals. However, where the focus of such policies is national rather than global welfare, the implied cost to other nations creates a natural environment for potential gains from policy co-ordination through bilateral or multilateral agreements.

Product Characteristics

DFIs are clustered in industries in which competing products are imperfect substitutes in the eyes of potential customers. Consequently, price cannot be viewed as a market-determined parameter unaffected by the individual firm's own actions. Where many firms produce competing although differentiated products, the theory of 'monopolistic competition' predicts that new entrants will force individual firms' profits towards zero. The welfare consequences of the resulting equilibrium are ambiguous. While the traditional Chamberlinian analysis stressed that inefficient proliferation of competing products results in the failure to exhaust scale economies at the firm level, modern versions, in which variety itself yields utility, allow the possibility of a Pareto-optimal outcome (Feenstra and Judd, 1982).

Monopolistic competition on the part of producers of differentiated products, along with scale economies in the production of any given variant, provides a satisfactory theoretical explanation of intra-industry trade among countries with similar cost conditions (Grubel, 1970; Krugman, 1981). However, although differentiated products are central to many DFI theories, product differentiation alone cannot account for DFI except to the minor extent required to facilitate exporting. The existence of differentiated products (an ownership advantage) will result in DFI rather than, or in addition to, intra-industry trade only when accompanied by the required advantages of foreign location of production and of internalisation.

The product-cycle scenario (Vernon, 1966) emphasised the dynamics of product innovation and specifically the typical change over time in comparative-advantage-based location resulting from standardisation of the product and its technology. In the early stages following the introduction of a new product, skilled labour is likely to be an important input; later on, relatively unskilled labour can be used more extensively. During the 1960s, this meant a gradual shift of production to Europe. In the 1970s, the cost-advantageous location was more likely to be one of the newly industrialising countries.

The required internalisation advantage could be provided in one of two ways. First, internalisation might be the most economical way of supplying the 'know-how' necessary to establish successful offshore production. In recent years management contracts have substituted to some extent for DFI, but this is at least partly a response to the desires of host-country governments. Know-how and 'learning-by-doing' may account also for a type of IDFI recently observed for some smaller industrialised countries and the more advanced developing countries. Here indigenous firms become experts at *adapting* new technologies to the needs of smaller markets or developing economies with very different factor proportions and infrastructure than those of the United States or other advanced nations. For the same reason that the new technologies were initially exploited in these nations through DFI, it is efficient for indigenous firms to make DFIs in other developing nations. Australia, India, Argentina, Brazil and Malaysia are examples for which this pattern has been observed.

A second and distinct motive for product-cycle DFI has been emphasised by Magee (1977). This rests on the plausible assumption that internal exploitation of a firm's unique technological advantage increases the period required before the advantage can be emulated successfully by potential rivals. Negotiation of arm's-length agreements with potential licensees would entail prior disclosure of many details of the product or process to be exploited, a risk that the innovating firm may well prefer to avoid.

Neither of the internalisation motives discussed above predicts a pattern of IDFI for the United States. While intra-industry trade would persist as long as innovation in the home country continues, with newer products exported and older products of the same industries (and often of the same firms) imported, a two-way flow of investment can be rationalised only by further assumptions, such as protection of the same industry on the part of two or more innovating countries.[10] Chemicals, pharmaceuticals, electronics and automobiles are examples.

Because it is stimulated mainly by the locational advantage of serving a protected market, the pattern of product-cycle IDFI signals a sacrifice of economic efficiency world-wide and probably net losses even for the major countries involved (United States, United Kingdom, Germany and France). Liberalisation of trade in the products of dynamic industries would encourage increased intra-industry trade in place of the present IDFI, allowing mutual gains with little likely cost of adjustment in the affected sectors.

Industry Structure

DFI has been a prominent feature of industries in which 'barriers to entry' (in most cases benefits to internalisation) are important and the market is dominated by a small number of firms. Much empirical research has focused on the role of barriers to entry in accounting for the observed distribution of DFI across industries (Bergsten *et al.*, 1978, Chapter 7). A somewhat different line of analysis has emphasised the behavioural implications of oligopoly. In oligopolistic industries, firms must take into account in their own managerial decisions the

effects of these decisions on the subsequent actions of other participants. Game theory is hence a natural tool for predicting possible
patterns of behaviour. However, theory offers little guidance concerning specific outcomes, except that stable equilibria are unlikely,
especially in a changing economic environment.

Knickerbocker (1973), Graham (1978) and others have explained
DFI patterns of the 1960s and 1970s as an oligopolistic or rivalistic
reaction to earlier DFIs of domestic or foreign competitors. While
Knickerbocker sought to explain in this way the clustering in time
and space of US outward DFIs, Graham posited a basically similar
explanation of European DFIs in the United States. Central to
Graham's thesis is that entry by US MNEs into European markets
upset established patterns of conduct within oligopolistic industries.
Furthermore, larger global (that is, US plus European) market shares
gave US firms a cost advantage over their foreign rivals. For European
firms with their own firm-specific advantages to exploit, entry into
the US market could restore a competitive balance and thus make a
mutually advantageous re-establishment of stable market-shares more
likely.

Although Graham does not distinguish in his treatment between
entry by exporting and entry by establishment of a foreign subsidiary,
it is obvious that the latter is more effective as a deterrent to aggressive
behaviour in Europe by US firms. Establishment of a US subsidiary
constitutes a large commitment of resources to maintaining a market
share, a 'credible threat' on the part of the European firm directed
towards its US-based rivals in Europe. As long as this advantage (the
implied signal of an intended commitment to maintaining a market
share) is sufficient to outweigh the relative disadvantages of going
abroad, the oligopolistic reaction or rivalry hypothesis predicts a
relatively long-lived pattern of IDFI that substitutes at least in part for
intra-industry trade in differentiated products. As an empirical matter,
one would expect to see this pattern in industries with multi-plant
rather than single-plant economies of scale and with relatively few firms
accounting for a large share of the market. Distribution of petroleum
products is one obvious example.

The efficiency implications of this type of IDFI are ambiguous.
As Caves (1971) has stressed, DFI typically represents entry by new
firms into a given market and can therefore enhance competitiveness.
This may be true even when the intent of the investors is, as the oligopolistic-rivalry hypothesis suggests, just the opposite. Furthermore, in
an industry producing differentiated products, each firm is likely to

attempt to maintain and increase its share of the market through accelerated introduction of new products, usually to the benefit of consumers. Thus, the central question is how effectively the rivals succeed in establishing or re-establishing stable patterns of tacit collusion. From a public-policy perspective, allowing free entry — including free entry of foreign firms through DFI — appears to promote the *national* interest, although at the likely expense of firms (indigenous or foreign) already established in the domestic market.

Optimisation Under Uncertainty

As noted above, Coase (1937) emphasised the role of internalisation as a means of dealing with uncertainty, especially over a long time horizon. The benefits from internalisation in this case do result from 'imperfect markets' in the technical sense of incomplete Arrow-Debreu markets for contingent claims (assets that provide future payments only in the event of a specific outcome). Perfect markets in the technical sense merely represent a (never observed) standard against which actual institutional arrangements for dealing with risk can be measured; deviations tend to reflect costs of information and enforcement rather than government restrictions (Hennart, 1982).

While the 1970s brought vastly increased 'risk' by almost any definition, this promoted the rapid development of new markets for arm's-length diversification. None the less, there is evidence that internal diversification of earnings streams — by currency, country and even industry — has become an increasingly important management objective for many firms (Rugman, 1977).

A perennial problem for economic theorists is why firms should care at all about the riskiness (variance) of their profits rather than only their expected value. Modern finance-theory views the firm as producing an earnings stream that can be characterised in terms of its mean and covariance. Financial markets allow the individual asset-holder to choose a diversified portfolio that provides the desired combinations of mean and variance. Why then should the managers of a steel or electronics firm attempt to take on the work of a specialised portfolio-manager?

The puzzle has two quite different solutions. The first has to do with the compensation of managers. In a world of costly information or satisficing behaviour, managers are evaluated on the basis of actual profits rather than the statistical expectation of profits. Accordingly, there is likely to be asymmetry between the treatment of managers showing losses and those showing profits. The alternative (or supplementary) explanation returns to the internalisation theme. Managers have access to proprietary information that can be used to produce 'better' income streams − that is, ones valued more highly by financial markets − internally rather than via arm's-length portfolio-transactions. Along with other activities profitably internalised by the MNE will be some degree of financial intermediation. The existence of policy-induced barriers to international portfolio-transactions reinforces the relative advantage of internal diversification but need not provide the main incentive.

As emphasised already, the opportunity for risk diversification through DFI represents primarily an advantage of being multinational rather than a motive for locating investments in any particular host country. As in choosing a portfolio of common stocks, diversification goals can be achieved through a wide range of alternative combinations. Yet US assets as a group may have been especially attractive to European and other investors in creating diversified earnings streams because of the relatively low covariance of their future earnings with those of otherwise comparable European assets (Rugman, 1977). This may help to explain the observed willingness of European direct investors to pay a premium for US companies over the going rate of 13 to 14 times earnings for domestic takeovers (*The Economist*, 25 October 1980, p. 20).

In the presence of admittedly well-developed financial markets for dealing in risk, why should firms find it profitable to choose an internal route to optimisation under uncertainty? In addition to policy-induced market-imperfections, there are basically two reasons. The first is the one stressed by Coase. It is one thing to recognise that a situation is inherently risky and quite another thing to specify that risk well enough to hedge through a contract. For example, if a German firm expects to receive a payment of a million dollars from a US customer next July 6, it is both simple and cheap to hedge that position, that is, ensure today the DM value of the dollar receipts, through a forward-market transaction. But if either the payment date or the amount is subject to some uncertainty, the simple hedge is no longer an available option. Often the actual payment in dollars is not independent of the future spot-rate; in this case a simple hedge could actually increase rather than reduce risk (Hekman, 1981). Vertical integration may offer a profitable solution. More broadly but for the same basic reasons, there are virtually no markets for insuring against the adverse effects of such important profit-influencing factors as weather, politics, strikes and business cycles. In some cases, problems of adverse selection and moral-hazard rule out an arm's-length alternative to internal diversification.

A second reason for internalisation to deal with risk is that *ex post* optimisation, with respect to at least some types of uncertainty, requires (centralised) managerial control rather than merely some small ownership-stake, for example, the ability to shift quickly some production from one location to another in the event of exchange rate movements, threatened union action, or new government policies. Thus, diversification in the narrow financial sense may only be a small part of the overall risk-managing benefit from being multinational rather than uninational (Kogut, 1983).

Because it reflects a benefit of being multinational rather than of operating in a specific location, risk-motivated DFI is likely to be IDFI and can be either vertical backward or horizontal. In the former case, IDFI would tend to be associated with increased intra-industry trade flows but reduced responsiveness to changed exchange rates and other factors that operate mainly to redistribute profits between home- and host-country operations or between two subsidiaries in different host countries. Horizontal risk-motivated IDFI could increase or substitute for intra-industry trade flows but tends to heighten the responsiveness of trade to changes in exchange rates or other cost factors.

The efficiency implications of IDFI motivated by risk are mixed. To the extent that reduction of overall uncertainty associated with a given type of activity means a lower required rate of return, the availability of this management strategy is in the interest of global welfare (Agmon and Lessard, 1976). On the other hand, the ability of multinationals to shift operations quickly between subsidiaries implies a weakened power of any given host country to influence the behaviour of firms operating within its boundaries – an implication of transnational internalisation stressed by Barnett and Muller (1974), Penrose (1971) and many others. Furthermore, to the extent that an environment of increased risk puts large firms that are able to pursue an internal diversification strategy at an advantage over smaller ones, the conflict between efficiencies of scale and market-power may be exacerbated. This is a quite different implication of increased economic uncertainty than the usual argument that exchange rate volatility tends to discourage international trade and DFI (McCulloch, 1983).

Public Policy

Virtually any type of government activity in the home country or potential host countries can influence significantly the OLI balance in favour of, or against, a decision to invest abroad. Even comparative-advantage motives will, over a relatively long period, be affected, through such policies as educational expenditures or incentives for capital formation. Similarly, government incentives for R and D are highly relevant for product-cycle investments, and, antitrust policy can influence industry structure. Macroeconomic policies may provide the stimulus for diversification through DFI, while differences in national tax systems offer tax-avoidance benefits.

But in all these cases, the likely effects on trade and DFI are at most a secondary motive for government action; for some, the presumed effects on trade and investment are so small or so distant in time that they are not considered or even anticipated. It seems sensible therefore to focus on those policies primarily motivated by their effects on trade (import restrictions and export incentives) or on DFI (investment incentives and performance requirements constraining the management of subsidiaries once established). Where the requisite ownership and internalisation advantages exist, these policies together determine the location of production facilities to serve any given market.

Through trade and DFI policies, countries in effect compete with one another for larger shares of the world market in a particular industry, or, more precisely, for larger shares in total world productive activity associated with that industry. Because the total level of world activity in a given industry is not likely to be affected by these efforts, such a competition nearly always represents a zero-sum or negative-sum games for the nation-players, beggar-your-neighbour solutions to the problems of macroeconomic stabilisation and sectoral adjustment to changing international competitiveness. But even the 'winner' may be disappointed by the outcome, depending on the underlying motives for policy intervention. Where protection results in significant DFI, domestic industry employment may be stabilised, but its composition by firm, and, more importantly, geographically, is likely to be altered. Thus, the problem of workers displaced by imports remains. Furthermore, since new entrants typically locate where unions are weak, the vested interests of industrial labour unions are threatened. Similarly, the entry of foreign producers via establishment of local subsidiaries is unlikely to preserve the market shares and associated rents of existing national firms. Thus, for industries in which ownership and internalisation advantages are important, 'protection' is likely to have little protective effect on national firms unless inward DFI is also restricted. On the other hand, an observed pattern of protection and IDFI is likely to mean that some (but not all) costs of protection have been avoided by bringing the qualities that made imports competitive into the domestic industry. This suggests that in some industries where IDFI has recently become important, a next step in the political pressure for protection from foreign competition will be demands from affected domestic firms and unions for restrictions on inward DFI. If successful, such restrictions would ensure that the United States bears the full cost of protection, rather than having some part of that cost dissipated by foreign competition brought home.

A more constructive approach would be to link negotiations on trade and DFI policies, with a view toward de-escalating the current competition to promote domestic production in favoured industries. Since the multilateral trade negotiations seem at least temporarily to have run out of steam, and because, at least for the industrialised nations, trade and DFI policies are basically two means of achieving (or attempting to achieve) the same proximate goal, linkage could provide more opportunities for mutually beneficial reductions in the resort to these policies. As noted above, the most obvious starting point is in the high-techology, product-cycle industries, where a variety of import barriers, export incentives, DFI incentives and disguised production subsidies currently offer ample grist for the negotiation mill. If successful, such negotiations could produce expanded intra-industry trade in newer products, while reduction of second-best IDFI would result in efficiency gains through fuller exploitation of plant scale-economies and lower costs of long-distance co-ordination.[11]

Some Implications for Research

The preceding discussion indicates that the welfare implications of IDFI in US industries depend critically on the primary stimulus, although in no case is there an unambiguous gain in world or national welfare. Likewise, the implications for policy depend critically on DFI motives. More information is therefore required on the primary motives underlying IDFI in specific industries. Available data are incomplete, especially where DFIs are financed through local borrowing. Also, by their nature these data lump together the results of very different types of business strategies, as well as some investments that are misclassified by the use of the mechanical 10 per cent ownership criterion for inclusion. This implies that the usual regressions of DFI penetration measures on industry and firm characteristics produce estimates of 'true' relationships that are biased towards zero and have large standard errors (low 't' statistics).

As the earlier sections of this chapter note, the central common element in all DFI and thus in IDFI is internalisation across national boundaries. Yet theorists have done little to explore this subject (Markusen (1984) is an exception). A better understanding at the microeconomic level of what functions MNEs choose to internalise, and why, seems essential to understanding the DFI process and to using (or refraining from using) available policy-tools. One promising avenue of research is to compare the spacial distribution within the United States of productive activity in a given industry with that internationally or at least in the United States plus Canada. A testable but heretical hypothesis is that the degree of US-controlled activity in the Canadian economy differs little from what would be observed in a fully integrated North American economy. Another testable hypothesis is that, contrary to the usual belief, DFI *increases* with 'psychic distance' (cultural and linguistic differences), at least relative to alternative arm's-length means of exploiting an ownership advantage. Yet another unanswered question concerns the differing extent of internalisation across product lines for a given firm.[12]

This chapter has emphasised that uncertainty fosters the growth of multinational activity in general and that increased economic uncertainty can account for a large part of the rapid increase of IDFI in the United States in the past decade. Although a number of researchers have begun to look at the MNE as a vehicle for financial diversification, this work has so far been quite narrow in its scope and has viewed internalisation of risk primarily as a second-best alternative to portfolio diversification. Yet, as suggested above, there are further internalisation advantages in risk management, with quite different implications for patterns of DFI and trade. More research on multinational strategies for optimising under uncertainty would be profitable.

Finally, in the area of the linkage between trade and IDFI, I have suggested that, depending on the primary incentive, either complementarity or substitution might be expected. These differences can provide the basis for empirically testable hypotheses concerning the relationship between US trade and IDFI. A particularly important question is whether IDFI as a risk-management strategy tends to increase rather than to reduce intra-industry trade.

Notes

1. In a recent contribution to this literature, Lipsey and Weiss (1981) related US exports and the level of activity of US manufacturing affiliates abroad not only to each other but also to the level of activity of foreign-owned subsidiaries in the same host countries. In addition to the expected positive relationship between US exports and DFI, their cross-section results provided some evidence of a negative relationship between US exports and DFI by other countries. This result supports the hypothesis that US outward DFI is largely defensive and that DFI by US firms is complementary with US export performance.

2. The firm's locational decision is usually described in a way that highlights the potential substitution between home and host country production, that is, between DFI and exports as alternative means of serving a given market. However, empirical studies, for example, Horst (1972a) suggest that a degree of complementarity is almost always present; in most instances successful exporting of manufactures apparently requires at least some minimum level of DFI in marketing and servicing facilities. In the case of service exports, this complementarity is even more important. The US insurance industry and other financial services sectors have experienced a significant increase in DFI from Europe (and thus of IDFI) during the past decade. For these industries, IDFI and intra-industry trade may be expected to grow together.

3. Commenting on an earlier version of this chapter, Dunning has pointed out that in this statement internalisation is taken as a dependent ('left-hand-side') variable. In other words, the motive for internalisation as a business strategy remains to be explained.

4. Despite his copious allusions to internal markets, Rugman himself has emphasised in several places the key role of centralised decision-making.

5. As a theoretical proposition, it is possible in many instances to assign internal prices so as to ensure that decentralised decision-making by autonomous-unit managers results in the desired outcome. But this will not typically be the most practical, that is, cheapest means of achieving management objectives, on account of the cost entailed in discovering the appropriate internal prices.

6. See especially Kogut (1983). However, being multinational offers advantages apart from those of risk-management. The most obvious is the flexibility to use transfer-prices as a means of minimising the effect of taxes on global profits.

7. See Rugman (1977) and Agmon and Lessard (1976) on DFI as a second-best alternative when international portfolio-diversification is restricted by government policies.

8. See Corden (1974, Chapter 10) and McCulloch and Owen (1983) for reviews of the arguments and literature.

9. This is just one of a host of possible unintended consequences resulting from selective protection from imports. Others include shift of production to as-yet uncontrolled commodities, for example, synthetics for cotton in the case of textiles, product-upgrading, and shift of import supply to the uncontrolled exporters through altered patterns of trade with other consuming nations.

10. In principle, the location advantage could be provided by high transportation-costs or the need to be close to the market served, rather than a trade-

distorting policy. In practice, these 'natural' barriers to trade appear to be unimportant in explaining IDFI in product-cycle industries.

11. For a full discussion of the benefits and costs of linking negotiations on trade and DFI, see McCulloch and Owen (1983).

12. Vernon and Davidson (1979), in their study of the overseas operations of US-based multinationals, offer a rich and thus far underutilised starting point for research on these topics.

* * *

COMMENT*

Bela Balassa

I welcome the opportunity provided by the reading of Rachel McCulloch's interesting chapter to examine the relevance of my ideas expressed in Balassa (1966) for recent trends in direct foreign investment (DFI). As McCulloch notes, during the 1970s, the United States emerged suddenly as a leading *host* country . . . [and] while foreign investors and especially Europeans acquired a rapidly growing stake in US manufacturing, trade, financial services, natural resources, and real estate, DFIs by US firms also continued to grow, albeit at a slower rate than in the 1950s and 1960s'. In the process, the dominant feature became '. . . cross direct foreign investment (CDFI) and in particular intra-industry direct foreign investment (IDFI) – phenomena that had been of very limited practical interest as long as US investments abroad dominated the global aggregates'.

McCulloch attempts to explain the emergence of IDFI by reference to the advantages of internalisation that might be the most economical way of supplying the know-how necessary to establish successful offshore production and of exploiting the firm's unique technological advantage while avoiding the risk of disclosure that may result under licensing arrangements. She suggests, however, that

> neither of the internalisation motives discussed above predicts a pattern of IDFI for the United States, [and] a two-way flow of investment can be rationalised only by further assumptions, such as protection of the same industry on the part of two or more innovating countries. Chemicals, pharmaceuticals, electronics and automobiles are examples.

Furthermore, in her view, '. . . although differentiated products are central to many DFI theories, product differentiation alone cannot account for DFI except to the minor extent required to facilitate exporting'. Thus, she submits that, '. . . the recent growth of DFI in the United States, and especially of IDFI, can be seen as representing at least in part a response by foreign firms to increased economic uncertainty rather than a shift in the locational attractions as conventionally defined of the United States as a production site'.

But even if uncertainty in economic conditions has increased over time – and there may be doubts on this count – this will not explain the change in the direction of DFI that has occurred. Uncertainty would have affected equally European DFI in the United States and US DFI in Western Europe and would not have resulted in the observed lop-sided pattern of expansion.

Nor can one explain the directional change in DFI by reference to increased protection. Protection has declined rather than increased as tariffs have been greatly reduced in a parallel fashion in the United States and in European countries in the framework of the Kennedy and Tokyo Rounds, and quantitative restrictions have not been imposed on their mutual trade in the products cited.

The causes for the recent changes in the pattern of DFI, and for the emergence of IDFI, then, would have to be found elsewhere. While McCulloch follows Coase (1937) in belittling the importance of oligopoly, the explanation can be found in oligopolistic market strategy. As suggested in Balassa (1966, p. 5):

> After having attained a more or less stable share in the home market, selling efforts aimed at increasing the firm's share in domestic sales are bound to meet with retaliation on the part of other enterprises, raising thereby the cost of expansion. On the other hand, although the cost of entry into foreign markets may be substantial, it will often be easier for the firm to carve out a new market for itself than to increase its domestic share – especially if the rate of growth of demand is greater and market structures are more fluid abroad.

At the same time,

> sales from domestic plants usually precede the establishment of plants in foreign countries. For one thing, the lack of familiarity with conditions abroad augments the risk of setting up foreign plants; for another, time may be needed to increase sales to the level where the establishment of a foreign plant is warranted. (Ibid)

What factors will, then, explain the shift from exporting to locating abroad? In Balassa (1966), I noted the impact of cost factors (production costs, transportation costs and tariffs) and non-price factors (the availability of funds, antitrust legislation and the servicing of foreign markets) on US DFI abroad. The same factors may be invoked to explain the changing pattern of DFI.

Until the end of the 1960s, cost factors favoured US DFI in Western Europe as wages were substantially lower there and the US dollar was overvalued. Subsequently, European wages rose rapidly and the US dollar was devalued. By the late 1970s, labour costs (inclusive of social charges) in Western Europe came to approach labour costs in the United States in terms of dollars while they were less than two-thirds of US labour costs ten years earlier.

There was, furthermore, an asset-motive associated with the overvaluation of the US dollar as US investments were undertaken in Western Europe in anticipation of a subsequent devaluation of the dollar. In turn, the devaluation removed the disincentive to purchase US assets that had been costly for would-be European investors beforehand. At the same time, it would be naïve to assume that productive assets, once purchased, would be sold again since a productive activity, once undertaken, will not be abandoned unless it becomes unprofitable.

While changes in relative wages and exchange rates contributed to the reverse flow of investments to the United States after 1970, changes in transportation costs have made little difference. For reasons mentioned above, changes in levels of protection do not provide an explanation either.

Nor did the establishment of the common external tariff of the European Economic Community (EEC) importantly contribute to US DFI in the earlier period; rather, this was related to the enlargement of national markets through economic integration (Balassa, 1966, pp. 8-11). The subsequent slowdown in the growth of markets in the EEC, in turn, made locating there less attractive, while the relatively rapid expansion of the US market in the second half of the 1970s enhanced its attractiveness for foreign investors. The increased rigidity of European market structures had a similar effect.

Among non-price factors, the availability of internal and external funds benefited US investors *vis-à-vis* their European counterparts during the period covered in Balassa (1966). The situation subsequently changed, however, with the increased profits of European firms, the development of domestic capital markets and, last but not least, the emergence of the Eurodollar market, thereby augmenting the financial capabilities of European firms to invest abroad.

Antitrust legislation in the EEC, too, may have favoured investment abroad, although this factor had been of much greater importance for the earlier expansion of US investments in Western Europe. Finally, as the European exports of manufactured goods to the United States grew, the advantages of servicing the US markets from local plants also increased. These advantages explain that 'as the sale of a given item in a foreign market reaches the level where the establishment of a plant is warranted, the question may not be whether the exporter should set up a plant or not but whether this firm *or* a competitor will establish a plant' (Balassa, 1966, p. 14).

While these considerations can be invoked to explain the shift from exports to locating abroad, and the directional change in DFI, the question still needs to be answered why domestic and foreign firms would co-exist in a particular industry in a particular market. The answer lies in product differentiation that involves the application of proprietary know-how on the part of the firm. This is not the case in industries manufacturing standardised products, such as steel, which fact may explain the lack of IDFI in these industries. Nor does one observe IDFI in competitive industries, such as textiles, clothing and footwear.

Thus the emergence of IDFI may be explained by oligopolistic market strategies in industries characterised by product differentiation. As I had earlier noted, 'foreign investment should be regarded as a part of the market strategy of the firm that aims at improving or, at least defending its position in domestic and in foreign markets' (Balassa, 1966, pp. 14–15). It is further apparent that oligopolistic firms responded to changes in costs and in non-price factors in effecting a directional change in foreign investment after 1970.

Note

* The author alone is responsible for the contents of this note, which should not be construed to reflect the views of the World Bank.

COMMENT*

Gene M. Grossman

Rachel McCulloch has provided a superb, integrative survey of the recent trends in and the literature on direct foreign investment (DFI), addressing both positive and normative issues of current theoretical and policy interest. She has taken what is, in my view, exactly the right approach to the subject, by treating DFI in the context of the theory of the firm, or more accurately, the theory of the multi-location firm. This approach leads one to focus on the ownership and control of certain economic units, rather than on the international migration of one or several factors of production. The central positive questions regarding DFI thus become:

1. Why does a firm choose to locate its operations in more than one location, and, in particular, in locations in more than one country?
2. What advantages does the multinational enterprise (MNE) have that allow it to overcome the inherent disadvantage it suffers in competing with indigenous entrepreneurs more familiar with local customs and market conditions?

McCulloch, like most of the literature which she surveys, deals exclusively with DFI in production activities. She does not attempt to develop a single explanation of when and why DFI will take place, and rightfully so. Instead she describes a host of industry-specific, firm-specific and policy-related circumstances which individually and together tend to favour DFI in a given situation over the MNE's alternatives of exporting or licensing on the one hand, and over production by a locally-owned firm on the other. Her prime candidates as factors favouring 'internalisation' are: comparative cost advantages (including those induced by overvalued currencies), production uncertainties, trade barriers and strategic competitive behaviour. To this list I would add bilateral-monopoly problems and information and reputation problems (partially subsumed in McCulloch's discussion of uncertainty).

A comparative-cost-based explanation of DFI requires, of course, that costs of production of various goods differ by location, but also that there exist significant 'economies of scope'. Such economies arise when a firm has a specific asset, such as technological know-how, managerial ability or a marketing network, that can serve as a shared input. The identifying attributes of such inputs are their public-good character, that is, the use of such an input in one plant or marketing campaign does not diminish significantly its productivity in additional usages. When such economies are prevalent, there are efficiency gains to be reaped by multi-product firms. Then, if some of the goods a firm chooses to supply can be produced most cheaply in one country, and others in another country, DFI is a potential outcome. It follows that DFI based on comparative-cost considerations should always be in (horizontally or vertically) differentiated products, and not in identical goods. Note further that DFI of this sort arises from industry-specific, rather than country-specific characteristics, and thus intra-industry DFI (IDFI) may well be observed.

Uncertainty can provide a motivation for DFI, since being multi-national by definition implies geographical diversification. Certain production risks, such as policy changes, exchange-rate movements, strikes and some cost increases are by their very nature country-specific. Location of plants in several countries allows the firm to pool these risks, and reduce overall income variability. Such diversification by the individual firm may be valued by stockholders even when opportunities for portfolio diversification are available, because the manager of a firm in a given industry may have superior information on how to hedge against particularly relevant risks, and because the specific insurance markets that investors might desire may be very imperfect or completely absent. This is especially true for investment in less developed countries, but McCulloch cites several examples of risks that would not be easily insurable even in a developed-country context. In addition, as McCulloch points out, firms may choose to diversify even when their shareholders would prefer risk-neutral behaviour, due to the way in which compensation schemes for managers must often be tailored when the manager's effort and ability are not directly observable.

A testable hypothesis that derives from the diversification motive for DFI is that these investments ought to involve as home and host locations, countries whose shocks are little or negatively correlated. Also, countries with underdeveloped capital markets should be involved in a disproportionately high share of such ventures. Finally, DFI that occurs for this reason may well involve production of the same good in several locations.

That tariffs and transport costs create incentives for a firm to engage in DFI rather than export to the protected market is well known. McCulloch points out that one must still explain in such cases why DFI occurs rather than production by indigenous firms. Here she notes that oligopolistic MNEs may invest abroad for strategic reasons, to serve notice to their competitors in a repeated-game setting that resort to lobbying for protection in one's home market is not likely to be a fruitful competitive strategy.

A related theme is that firms may invest abroad to commit themselves to a particular market, and thereby alter the nature of the oligopolistic competition that takes place with existing and potential firms deciding how much to sell in (or whether to enter into) that market. It should be noted, however, that DFI alone does not imply a commitment to any particular market, since exports *from* a foreign subsidiary are always an option for the firm. Thus, DFI as a strategic commitment requires the existence of trade barriers (tariffs or transport costs) that effectively cut off the host country from export markets. It is interesting to realise in this regard that tariff barriers in an MNE's home country or in unrelated third markets can contribute to an explanation of why a firm might invest in an *unprotected* market.

Both trade policies and strategic situations are market-specific phenomena. DFIs motivated by trade barriers will only be intra-industry if the same industries are protected in a number of countries. Similarly, IDFI emerges from the consideration of oligopolistic competition only when market conditions in an industry are similar in different countries. Finally, DFI that occurs for these reasons need not be associated with product differentiation, and is likely to be a substitute for international trade.

When production and sale require a number of distinct stages, a bilateral-monopoly problem can arise. These are most serious when components and downstream products are both highly differentiated, such that parts are specific to particular assembly operations and vice versa. Then vertical DFI, both upstream (into raw materials and intermediate products) and downstream (into marketing, packaging and servicing) may emerge to allow firms to avoid the costs and uncertainties of bargaining and contract-enforcement. Furthermore, there will often be efficiency gains associated with such vertical integration, since industry profits are maximised when inputs are priced at marginal cost.

Finally, firms may invest abroad for a multitude of reasons relating to imperfect information, difficulties in contract enforcement and the importance that attaches as a result of these to a firm's reputation for quality. The absence of a well developed international legal system causes DFI to substitute for some types of transactions that are observed intranationally. For example, a firm may wish to warranty its product, but may be unable to do so credibly if consumers cannot appeal to a local court in instances of dispute. A local presence by the firm (with the implication that the firm has locally attachable assets) may give warranties value in the eyes of consumers, when they would otherwise be viewed as worthless. As another example, firms such as McDonald's, which generally rely on franchising for domestic outlets, often engage in DFI so as to control foreign operations directly. One explanation is that the firm does not believe that the franchise agreement could be easily enforced if applied abroad. Similarly, vertical integration may occur in instances where a long-term contract with a supplier, if enforceable, would be preferred.

Some DFI takes place just to make a firm more visible to its consumers, allowing it to develop a reputation. In other cases, as McCulloch notes, information problems inhibit a firm in its efforts to sell or license its technology, since potential buyers cannot evaluate the worth of a new process or product until its details have been revealed. Finally, information gathering may be a motive for DFI, to the extent that there is validity in the notion from the product-cycle hypothesis, that product development is most cost-effective when it takes place in the market in which the product is primarily destined to be sold.

Many of the information-related market imperfections cited in the previous two paragraphs do not give cause for DFI in production activities *per se*. Indeed, a significant portion of the recent surge in DFI and in IDFI in particular, has not been for production, but rather for such functions as marketing, servicing and providing convenient replacement-part networks. These post-production activities account for a rising proportion of total cost in many industries, yet they have heretofore been largely neglected in the DFI literature.

McCulloch's excellent survey is suggestive of the extent to which formal model-building and hypothesis-testing on aspects of DFI have fallen behind more casual modes of theoretical and empirical analysis. And, since DFI is so often observed in circumstances of imperfectly competitive market structures, incomplete and asymmetric information, and inefficiently allocated risk, policy-makers will require much guidance in the formulation of sensible policy. Fortunately, recent advances in the field of industrial organisation and finance theory have provided us with a tool bag for addressing many of the interesting issues raised by the increased international mobility of firms.

Note

* I gratefully acknowledge support from the National Science Foundation under Grant No. SES 8207643.

6 NATIONAL AND INTERNATIONAL DATA PROBLEMS AND SOLUTIONS IN THE EMPIRICAL ANALYSIS OF INTRA-INDUSTRY DIRECT FOREIGN INVESTMENT*

Frank G. Vukmanic, Michael R. Czinkota and David A. Ricks

Introduction

Despite the importance of direct foreign investment (DFI) to a country's balance of payments and the implications for factors such as trade, employment and transfer of technology, national data on DFI are weak. Research on DFI issues are often hampered, if not precluded, by weakness in or a lack of the data.

The research experiences of Arpan and Ricks (1974) in the 1970s serve as an illustrative example of past research problems. Since basic facts regarding DFI in the US were not known, Arpan and Ricks decided to survey foreign-owned firms. However, it proved impossible to find a comprehensive listing of such firms. Their original research plan was to survey firms via a questionnaire. However, the major obstacle to this plan was that no one knew which firms were foreign-owned. Partial lists did exist, but no two were the same and none were complete or totally accurate. There was also a remarkable lack of overlap. For example, in 1972, the US Department of Commerce (DOC) had compiled a list of about 800 firms and Simon and Schuster had a list of over 1,400 firms. Upon closer inspection, it was discovered that these two lists had less than 50 per cent duplication. Further research revealed that many of the firms on these lists were either not foreign-owned or had gone out of business since the lists had been compiled.

There were several reasons for this somewhat surprising discovery:

(1) Firms were not required to report their foreign ties to the US Government.

(2) No agency of the US Government was formally charged with collecting these data.

(3) To be included in these data, the foreign-owned firm somehow

had to: (a) be identified by the Department of Commerce (DOC); (b) receive a questionnaire from the DOC's Bureau of Economic Analysis; (c) have made an investment of more than $2 million (due to this requirement, small firms were usually ignored); and (d) return the questionnaire.

(4) Reinvestment of profits was usually ignored.

Since the time these research problems were identified by Arpan and Ricks, substantial progress has been made in data collection, but as this chapter will show, there are still severe limitations associated with DFI data.

Attempts to conduct serious empirical research in the recently emerging area of intra-industry direct foreign investment (IDFI) are likely to confront the same, and perhaps even more severe, data problems. Effective analyses of IDFI would require even finer disaggregations of data by country and industry than more traditional analyses of DFI.

The purpose of this chapter is to examine the nature, availability and shortcomings of DFI data collected within the United States and internationally. The major portion of the chapter will be devoted to the former area. As a result of this examination, we will also offer possible approaches to help remedy some of the data problems.

International Data on Direct Foreign Investment

Attempts to examine DFI either globally or across countries are seriously handicapped by data problems. The combination of the lack of data collection in some countries and significant differences in data collection methodologies in those countries that do have collection systems makes it extremely difficult, if not impossible, to:

(a) develop a legitimate estimate of global DFI stocks and flows; and
(b) analyse inter-country and/or intra-industry DFI.

Various international institutions, such as the United Nations (1978), the OECD (1983) and the IMF (1977) have made efforts to remedy this problem. These efforts have met, however, with only limited success. Thus far they have resulted in the development of suggested guidelines and benchmarks for comparing different national data collection systems. For example, the OECD decided that, due to economic and political reasons, most countries would have considerable difficulty altering their definitions of DFI and their data collection methods. Therefore, it did not draw up a detailed definition for adoption by all member countries. Instead, it attempted to provide a 'detailed and more precise operational definition of direct investment against which each country can compare its present system' (OECD, 1983, p. 6).

Comparison of Selected National Data Bases

Analysts of DFI are not likely to be pleased with the OECD approach. However, the changes needed for developing a compatible data base, even among the OECD countries, whose data collection methods are relatively homogeneous, would be significant. This becomes evident if we look at the DFI data collected by various OECD nations (the United States, Canada, the United Kingdom, Japan, France, the Federal Republic of Germany, Sweden and Australia) in terms of the:

(a) definition of DFI;
(b) collection methodology;
(c) data coverage;
(d) type of data collected;
(e) periodicity of collection; and
(f) level of disaggregation (see Table 6.1).

While discrepancies between the data collection systems of these eight countries are quite severe, it should be kept in mind that they probably have much better data collection systems than many other countries. Comparisons of data bases of other countries may, therefore, be even more difficult.

Data Collection

Definition of Direct Foreign Investment. Most countries conform generally to the definition of DFI set out in the IMF/OECD Common Reporting System for Balance of Payments (BOP) Statistics. DFIs are those investments made to create or expand some kind of controlling interest in an enterprise (IMF, 1977, p. 135). As a basis for defining 'control', most countries have employed percentage levels of ownership. There has also been an increasing tendency for countries to adopt lower thresholds of ownership as a basis for collecting DFI data. It has been generally recognised that small, organised groups of stockholders may well control an enterprise, particularly if ownership is

Table 6.1: Comparison of Selected National Data Collection Systems

	United States	Canada	United Kingdom	Japan	France	Germany	Sweden	Australia
Definition	10% voting share or equivalent	10% voting share or equivalent	20% voting share or equivalent	25% voting share or equivalent	20% voting share or equivalent	25-50% voting share or equivalent	20-50% voting share or equivalent	25% voting share or equivalent
Methodology	company surveys	company surveys	cashflow & company surveys	cashflow & company surveys	cashflow	cashflow & company surveys (since 1976)	cashflow & company surveys	company surveys
Coverage	inward & outward stocks & flows	inward & outward stocks & flows	inward & outward stocks & flows	inward & outward selected stocks & flows	inward & outward flows	inward & outward stocks (since 1976) & flows	flows	inward & outward stocks & flows
Type of Data	BOP & financial & operating data	BOP (balance of payments)	BOP	BOP	BOP	BOP	BOP	BOP & financial & operating data
Periodicity	quarterly & annual	quarterly & annual	quarterly & annual	monthly & annual	monthly & annual	monthly & annual	quarterly & annual	quarterly & annual
Disaggregation	country & 3-digit SIC (133)		country & industry	country & industry (inward particularly)	selected countries & areas, 14 sectors	country & industry	country & industry	country & 22 sectors

Sources: Constantin, Ross and Robert V. Kennedy, *Survey of Direct Investment: Concepts and Compilation* (International Monetary Fund, Washington, DC, 1974); OECD, *Detailed Benchmark Definition of Foreign Direct Investment* (OECD, Paris, 1983); OECD, *Improvement of International Direct Investment Statistics* (OECD, Paris, 1982); OECD, *Recent International Direct Investment Trends* (OECD, Paris, 1981).

widely distributed (US Department of Commerce, 1976, pp. 5-6).

Despite this general tendency, there are significant differences in the thresholds employed by the OECD countries. In the United States, and Canada, the threshold is 10 per cent of voting shares or its equivalent; in the United Kingdom and France, 20 per cent; Australia and Japan, 25 per cent; the Federal Republic of Germany, 25-50 per cent; and Sweden, 20-50 per cent.

Purpose of Data Collection and Reporting System. The underlying purpose for collecting DFI data and method of collection also differ among these nations. DFI data are collected primarily to record balance of payments transactions or to fulfil exchange controls. Two methods are currently used by most countries for the collection of data: surveys of investing companies and reports of related cash-flows through the banking system. The United States, Canada, the United Kingdom and Australia rely on the company survey technique, while France, Japan, Sweden and the Federal Republic of Germany rely primarily on cash-flow data collected through the banking system. Some countries, such as Sweden and the Federal Republic of Germany supplement their cash-flow reporting system with company surveys.

Coverage. The scope and coverage of national statistics also differ substantially. Differences in reporting systems result in potentially significant differences in the composition of the DFI data. The company survey technique generally permits a more complete estimation of DFI than does cash-flow reporting. Forms of equity other than cash, such as reinvested earnings, company loans and local borrowing, which affect the net-worth or debt of foreign affiliates are often not covered by cash-flow systems. Hence there may be significant differences in the reported levels of DFI among countries using different reporting systems.

Most countries collect data on inward and outward DFI flows. However, DFI stock or position data, which measure the value of foreign-controlled assets abroad or domestically, are collected by only a small number of countries. They are Australia, the United Kingdom, the United States, the Federal Republic of Germany and Japan.

Differences also exist in the coverage of companies, based on whether they are publicly or privately held and whether they are branches or subsidiaries. Some countries also use cut-off points for reporting, based, for example, on the percentage of capitalisation

(Sweden) or the size of the transaction (Japan and the United States). Sectoral coverage also differs. While most OECD countries collect and publish data on all industrial sectors, there are exceptions. For example, the United Kingdom, for reasons of confidentiality, excludes from reporting the insurance and petroleum sectors, while French statistics cover only non-financial enterprises.

Data Availability

Periodicity. Countries collecting data on the basis of cash-flows through the banking system usually publish data monthly (Japan and Sweden) or quarterly (Canada, Germany and Australia). Survey data are collected at different intervals and usually are reported with a considerable time-lag. Annual surveys (the United States, Canada and the United Kingdom) may have a lag of up to a year. Benchmark surveys conducted by the United States (quinquennial) and the United Kingdom (triennial) may have reporting lags of up to three years.

Disaggregation. Most OECD countries publish statistics disaggregated by geographical area (country), sector and type of transaction. However, the levels of disaggregation employed across countries are diverse. Geographical disaggregation at the country level (for most important host and home countries) is present in most reporting systems. Sectoral disaggregation, however, varies widely. The United States collects data at the 3-digit US Enterprise Standard Industrial Classification (ESIC) level (133 categories), but publishes the data on a more aggregate level (20–59 countries, 11–13 sectors). Australia and France distinguish among 22 and 14 industrial sectors, respectively.

The types of transactions reported also vary substantially across countries. Most OECD countries group together loans and equity participation. The United States disaggregates data by net capital flows and reinvested earnings and for incorporated affiliates by inter-company accounts and equity investment. France disaggregates by new investments and liquidations and by equity capital and loans. Germany publishes data on new investment and liquidations and by shares, other equities and credits.

Potential Approaches

The quality of international data on DFI, as the previous section demonstrates, is extremely weak in many respects. Any empirical analysis of IDFI, which attempted to use data on a number of home and host countries, would face significant problems, for example, gaps in data and non-comparability of data (definition, periodicity, dis-aggregation, transactions, etc.). In addition, the fact that data are collected does not imply that they are available to researchers or governmental institutions (Erdilek, 1982b, p. 6).

International institutions, such as the OECD, have attempted to produce useful comparative national data series on DFI (OECD, 1981). However, the data are almost exclusively flows and are highly aggre-gated. Also, even in these highly aggregated data, there are differences in definition and coverage of transactions.

Unfortunately, as the OECD correctly notes, most countries are not likely, for both economic and political reasons, to change their systems in the near term to adhere to a standardised system. Installation of a standardised detailed data collection system is costly and, depending on the ultimate use of the data, the benefits that result may or may not be worth the cost. A shift to the standardised system is also likely to increase the burden on reporting institutions, which could have negative implications for DFI flows.

Analysts wishing to use publicly available data will be forced, at least for some time, to utilise a single, internally consistent national data source, or to rely on the highly aggregated and sometimes suspect data available from the UN, the OECD, and the World Bank. Requests should continue to be made, however, for a movement toward a stan-dardised system of reporting, akin to the system developed, but not yet adopted, by GATT members for reporting trade data.

Some researchers, such as Aharoni (1966), Dunning (1973), Erdilek (1982b), Frank (1981), Franko (1976) and Reuber *et al.* (1973), have attempted to overcome these data deficiencies by conducting narrowly focused surveys of DFI for certain sectors and/or countries. This approach, however, is costly and time-consuming and, therefore, out of the reach of many researchers. In addition, depending on the nature of the research, this approach, even when carried out with governmental resources, may not yield the hoped for results. For example, US multi-nationals surveyed by the US Government on their experiences with performance requirements imposed by host countries were unwilling to divulge information, fearing it would aid competitors or provoke retaliation by host-country governments.

Despite the potential problems, selective industry surveys that are confined to major home and host countries may be a method of collect-ing or supplementing existing data on IDFI. Certain sectors could be defined narrowly, for example, passenger automobiles, micro com-puters, and the number of countries could be limited so that the surveys would not be unwieldy and yet would cover relevant products and parties.

The development and publication of a comprehensive guide to DFI data would benefit researchers working in this area. The OECD has done extensive work in comparing national data on DFI and publication thereof for OECD countries. Similar work has been done by the UN Centre for Transnationals, the World Bank for data on developing countries, and the IMF for balance of payments data. However, there is no single source, of which we are aware, that gives a detailed guide to what data are available nationally and the publications, institutions, or agencies from which they can be acquired.

US Data on Direct Foreign Investment

Several US Government agencies collect data relating to DFI. They are the Federal Trade Commission, Internal Revenue Service (IRS), Securities and Exchange Commission (SEC), the Departments of Energy and Agriculture, the Federal Reserve Board, and the Department of Commerce's Bureau of Economic Analysis (BEA), Office of Trade and Investment Analysis and Census Bureau. The data collected by most of these agencies are limited to each individual agency's functional area of responsibility and are confined to US inward DFI. The exceptions are the Census Bureau, the IRS, the SEC and the BEA, which collect data on US outward DFI also.

The most comprehensive and important of these data collection systems for DFI is the company survey carried out periodically by the Bureau of Economic Analysis (BEA) of the Department of Commerce. The BEA was directed by the President, in accordance with his authority under the International Investment Survey Act of 1976, to secure information on capital flows and other information related to international investment.

The BEA was charged with collecting detailed data on US both inward and outward DFI for use:

(1) in computing and analysing the US balance of payments;
(2) in evaluating the employment and taxes of US parent and affiliate companies and the international investment position of the United States; and
(3) in conducting studies and surveys on specific aspects of international investment that could have significant implications for the

economic welfare and national security of the United States, as stated in the International Investment Survey Act of 1976 (USC 22 3 103 Sec. 4a).

Since the BEA is designated as and is the primary source of US data on DFI, a focus on the BEA collection system will be maintained in our analysis.

Data Collection

Definition of Direct Foreign Investment. The US Government, and the BEA, define DFI as 'ownership or control, directly or indirectly, by one US (foreign) person of 10 per cent or more of the voting securities of an incorporated foreign (US) business enterprise or an equivalent interest in an unincorporated foreign (US) business enterprise including a branch' (US Department of Commerce, 1976, Vol. 1, p. 5). Investments that result in less than 10 per cent ownership or control of a business enterprise are considered portfolio investments. Prior to 1974, the threshold level of ownership or control for DFI in the United States was 25 per cent; prior to 1966, the threshold for US DFI abroad was 25 per cent.

Purpose of Data Collection and Reporting System. The basic purpose of the BEA data collection system is to secure information for computing and analysing US balance of payments, employment and taxes of US parent and affiliate companies, and to determine implications of international investment for the United States. In order to meet these requirements, the BEA collects two basic types of data for both inward and outward DFI: balance of payments data and other financial and operating data.

Data related to balance of payments are collected primarily for inclusion in the US balance of payments accounts and for calculating the international investment position of the United States. For a given parent and affiliate, the major items collected are:

(1) parent's equity in the affiliate;
(2) inter-company loans between the parent and affiliate;
(3) the parent's share of the affiliate's income, dividends and re-invested earnings; and
(4) receipt and payments of fees and royalties between the parent and the affiliate.

Other financial and operating data cover the affiliate's transactions and position with all parties and generally include:

(1) balance sheets
(2) income statements
(3) external financial position
(4) employment and employee compensation
(5) destination of sales
(6) exports and imports
(7) changes in plant and equipment, and
(8) R and D expenditures.

The BEA collects these data via company surveys. Three types of surveys are employed: a (quinquennial) benchmark survey and annual and quarterly surveys. Not all the data listed above are collected in each survey (see Tables 6.2 and 6.3).

The balance of payments related data and other financial and operating data are collected in the benchmark surveys of US DFI abroad (Form BE-10) and DFI in the United States (Form BE-12). Both the inward and outward DFI benchmarks are considered universal surveys. However, for both there is a minimum exemption level to reduce reporting burdens for smaller firms and to conserve the BEA resources. Under the BE-10, foreign affiliates with $3 million or less in assets, sales, or net income, and indirectly-owned bank affiliates are exempt from detailed reporting. Indirectly-owned bank affiliates are required, however, to report detailed data to the Federal Reserve Board. For the BE-12, enterprises with assets, sales, or net income of $1 million or less, or 200 acres or less of land are exempt.

Exempt affiliates must, however, file an exemption claim and report several statistical items to the BEA. Thus, the BEA has some estimate of the importance of non-reporters. The BEA estimates that, on the basis of the percentage of total assets included in the benchmark survey, these exemptions result in an extremely small loss of coverage, between 1.4 per cent to 2.0 per cent of the total universe of inward and outward DFI. However, over 11,000 firms were affected by these exemptions in 1977, that is, more than 21 per cent of the universe.

Foreign banking affiliates are required to report less data than non-bank foreign affiliates on the benchmark survey of US DFI abroad (BE-10). Since banks must report extensively to other US Government agencies, they are exempted from additional extensive reporting.

The 1976 Investment Survey Act provided that benchmark surveys

Table 6.2: BEA Company Surveys of Direct Foreign Investment in the United States

	Benchmark BE-12	Annual Survey BE-15	Transactions of US Affiliates, Except Unincorporated Bank with Foreign Parent BE-605	Transactions of Banking Branch or Agency BE-606B	Initial Report BE-13	Report on Assistance with Investment or Entry into Joint Venture BE-14	Industry Classification Questionnaire BE-607
Type of Data	BOP & other financial & operating data	Other financial & operating data	Balance of payments	Balance of payments	Identification information, cost, ultimate owner, etc.	Identification information plus value of transaction	Dist. of sales by BEA industry code
Coverage	Universe	Sample	Sample	Sample	All new investments	Potentially all new investments	New affiliate's first report or if industry changes
Exemption level[a]	$1,000,000 or 200 acres[b]	$5,000,000 & 1,000 acres Only non-bank affiliates	$5,000,000	$5,000,000	$1,000,000 in assets or cost of investment or 200 acres	$1,000,000 in asset or capitalisation and loans or 200 acres	Depends on other reports required
Frequency of report	Every 5 years	Annual	Quarterly	Quarterly	Once – at time of investment	Once	Once

Notes: a. Exemption levels are normally stated in terms of an affiliate's total assets, sales, or gross operating revenues, excluding sales tax, and net income after income taxes, whether positive or negative. For a given report, if all three items are equal to or less than the exemption level, then that report is not required to be filed. If any of the three items exceeds the exemption level for a given report, and if the statistical data requested in the report are applicable to the entity involved, then a report must be filed.
b. Exemptions levels are for 1980.

Table 6.3: BEA Surveys of United States Direct Foreign Investment Abroad

	Benchmark BE-10 A&B[b]	Annual Survey[c] BE-11, A&B	Expenditures, Property, Property, Plant and Equipment BE-133, C&B	Direct Transactions BE-577	Industry Classification Questionnaire BE-507
Type of Data	BOP/other financial & operating data	Other financial & operating data	Actual and projected capital expenditures	Balance of payments	Distribution of sales by BEA industry code
Coverage	Universe	Sample	Sample	Sample	US parent or foreign affiliate at point of investment or if industry changes
Exemption level[a]	$3,000,000 Indirectly-owned bank affiliates	$10,000,000 Only majority-owned, non-bank affiliates	$8,000,000 Only majority-owned, non-bank affiliates	$10,000,000	Depends on other reports required
Frequency of report	Every 5 years	Annual	Semi-annual	Quarterly	Once

Notes: a. Exemption levels are normally stated in terms of an affiliate's total assets, sales, or gross operating revenues, excluding sales tax, and net income after income taxes, whether positive or negative. For a given report, if all three items are equal to or less than the exemption level, then that report is not required to be filed. If any of the three items exceeds the exemption level for a given report, and if the statistical data requested in the report are applicable to the entity involved, then a report must be filed.
b. BE-10A data on parents; BE-10B data on affiliates.
c. 1978 BE-11 Annual Survey has been proposed but its status is uncertain.

were to be conducted at least once every five years. The most recent outward survey covered 1977 and the next will cover 1982. However, the Survey Act was amended so that the next survey following 1982 will be conducted in not 1987 but 1989, with the five-year schedule resumed thereafter. The reason for this change is to allow for a shift in the inward DFI survey to coincide with the year of the Census Bureau's domestic economic census.

The most recent inward DFI survey covered 1980. Because of the amendment to the Act referred to above, the next inward DFI survey will be conducted in 1987, rather than 1985, with the five-year schedule adhered to after 1987. This change will allow the domestic economic census and the inward DFI survey to be linked and will permit comparison on a company-by-company basis of the enterprise data from the inward DFI benchmark and establishment data from the census.

The BEA conducts annual, semi-annual and quarterly surveys to supplement its benchmark surveys of US inward and outward DFI. All of these surveys are sample surveys that capture, on the basis of value of assets, over 85 per cent of the universe, according to the BEA. Just as the exemption levels for the benchmark surveys differ, the exemption levels of these sample surveys differ from the benchmark and each other. The annual and quarterly surveys of US inward DFI have a $5 million exemption level. In contrast, the annual survey of US outward DFI has an exemption level of $10 million and includes only majority-owned non-bank affiliates. The semi-annual survey of plant and equipment expenditures has an $8 million exemption, and again includes only majority-owned non-bank affiliates. The quarterly direct transactions survey has a $10 million exemption level.

Composition and Availability of the Data Generated by the Bureau of Economic Analysis

The BEA surveys generate a significant amount of data at a high level of disaggregation (see Tables 6.4 and 6.5). Both balance of payments and financial and operating data are collected by country and by 3-digit US Enterprise Standard Industrial Classification level, as modified by the BEA.

Problems with the Bureau of Economic Analysis Data

The DFI data collected by the BEA are extensive and generally considered much more complete than data collected by other countries. Despite their amount and quality, a number of criticisms have been raised regarding the BEA data.

Completeness. The BEA has come under significant criticism from the US Congress and private researchers regarding the completeness of its survey coverage (Committee on Government Operations, 1980; Arpan and Ricks, 1974). Both groups contend, on the basis of independent research, that a large number of DFIs in the United States escape or are missed by the BEA surveys and that the value of total DFI in the United States is substantially underestimated. Presumably this occurs because of non-compliance in reporting and/or the exemption levels employed by the BEA.

In the BEA's defence, it must be mentioned that reporting is required to qualify for an exemption. Civil and criminal penalties may be assessed for non-reporting or for fraudulent reporting. The BEA believes that, with the exception of small investments, compliance is reasonably good. The BEA typically mails its forms to twice as many potential respondents as there are actual respondents and devotes considerable resources to follow-up contacts to secure compliance (Bureau of Economic Analysis, 1982, p. 15). Critics contend, however, that these excess mailings only highlight the lack of universe-knowledge, and that the BEA should move beyond a news-clipping information base and use other US Government data bases, such as those of the IRS and Census Bureau, to check its coverage and ensure compliance (Committee on Government Operations, 1980, p. 28).

Gaps. The BEA has also been criticised for gaps in its data. These gaps may be caused by several factors. The data supplied by individual companies to the BEA are confidential. The BEA is, therefore, constrained from reporting data that would divulge the identity of the reporting company. Gaps are also created by the failure to conduct surveys for certain periods or by a discontinuance or non-inclusion of specific item(s) from the BEA surveys. It is unlikely, for example, that the BEA will conduct an annual outward DFI survey (BE-11) for 1978. (Although deliberations regarding this survey may seem quite dated, surveys of this nature are usually conducted several years after the fact because complete data are available to reporters only with some lag.) If this survey is not conducted, there will be, according to many users of the data, a significant gap in time-series financial and operating data for US DFI abroad. The shift from a five- to a seven-year period between benchmark surveys is also likely to create significant gaps unless annual surveys are conducted for each of the intervening years.

Criticism has also been levelled against the BEA for discontinuing

Table 6.4: Data on Direct Foreign Investment in the United States
Generated by the BEA Surveys

Balance of Payments Data[a]
    Direct foreign investment (DFI) position (year-end)
    Equity and inter-company account flows
    Reinvested earnings of incorporated affiliates
    Income
    Interest, dividends and earnings of unincorporated affiliates
    Fees and royalties

Financial and Operating Data of US Affiliates[b]
    Employment
    Employee compensation
    Balance sheet data
    Income statement data
    Composition of external financing
    Property, plant and equipment expenditures
    US merchandise exports and imports
    Sales
    R and D expenditures
    Gross book value of land and other property, plant and equipment
    Land and mineral rights owned
    Land and mineral rights leased
    Gross product (1974 only)

Other Selected Data[c]
    Number of investments
    Number of investors
    Investment outlays
    Sources of financing for investment outlays*
    Selected operating data of US enterprises acquired or established:
        — total assets
        — net plant and equipment*
        — plant and equiment expenditures*
        — exploration and development expenditures*
        — sales
        — net income
        — employee compensation*
        — employment
        — acres of land

Notes: a. Sample data are collected quarterly by country and the BEA 3-digit
industry classification. These sample data are expanded to universe levels
quarterly for the balance-of-payments flow items and annually for the DFI
position. In general, the universe estimates are made and published at more
aggregated levels than the level at which the sample data are collected. For 1974
to the present, annual estimates (except for fees and royalties) have generally
been published for industries cross-classified by 20 countries, excluding subtotals.
Quarterly estimates of the flow items for all years, annual estimates of all items
for years prior to 1974, and annual estimates of the components of some items
are published at even more aggregate country-industry levels.
b. Subject to the BEA's confidentiality requirements, data are available for 1974
and 1977–9, by country and the BEA 3-digit industry classification. 1974 data are

universe data from the benchmark survey. Data for 1977-9 are sample data from the annual survey. Hence, data for 1974 and for 1977-9 are not comparable. Financial and operating data are published at various levels of disaggregation by the BEA.

c. Subject to the BEA's confidentiality requirements, annual data are available for 1979-81, by country and the BEA 3-digit industry classification. Annual data for 1982 are now being processed. Some selected operating data, among them the (*) variables, are no longer collected.

Table 6.5: Data on US Direct Foreign Investment Abroad Generated by the BEA Surveys

---

Balance of Payments Data[a]
    US direct foreign investment position[1,2]
    Equity and inter-company account flows
    Reinvested earnings of incorporated affiliates
    Interest, dividends and earnings of unincorporated affiliates
    Income[1,2]
    Fees and royalties[1]

Financial and Operating Data of Foreign Affiliates[b]
    Employment
    Employee compensation
    Balance sheet data
    Income statement data
    Composition of external financing[c]
    Property, plant and equipment expenditures[d]
    US merchandise exports and imports
    Sales[e]
    R and D expenditures
    Gross book value of property, plant and equipment
    Gross product

Other
    Summary of financial and operating data of US parent companies[f]

---

1 every country; 2 every industry

Notes: a. Sample data are collected quarterly by country and the BEA 3-digit industry classification. These sample data are expanded to universe levels quarterly for the balance-of-payments flow items and annually for the DFI position. In general, the universe estimates are made and published at more aggregated levels than the level at which the sample data are collected. For 1977 to the present, annual estimates have generally been published for 13 industries cross-classified by 59 countries, excluding subtotals. Also from 1977 on, annual estimates of the DFI position, income and fees and royalties are available for all countries (but not cross-classified by industry) and annual estimates of the DFI positions and income are available. For 1950-76, annual estimates are published in the details shown in *Selected Data on US Direct Investment Abroad, 1950-76*. Quarterly estimates of the flow items for all years, annual estimates of all items for years prior to 1950, and annual estimates of the components of some items are published at even more aggregated country-industry levels.

b. Except as noted in notes c-e, these data are available only in benchmark survey years and cover the universe of foreign affiliates. Subject to the BEA confidentiality requirements, they are available by country and the 3-digit BEA industry classification.

c. Annual data on the composition of external financing (sources and uses of funds) of a sample of majority-owned foreign affiliates are available for 1966–76. Similar data are available for 1977 from the benchmark survey. For years after 1977, annual data are not available because the annual survey in which these data were collected was discontinued.

d. Universe-estimates of the actual and projected property, plant and equipment expenditures of majority-owned non-bank foreign affiliates are published semi-annually. From 1977 onward, they have been published for 12 industries, cross-classified by 59 countries, excluding subtotals. For 1966–76, they have been published for 13 industries by 41 countries.

e. Universe-estimates of sales of majority-owned foreign affiliates are available annually for 1966–76. Similar data are available for 1977 from the benchmark survey. In years after 1977, annual data are not available because the annual survey in which these data were collected was discontinued.

f. Data are collected in the benchmark surveys and are available, subject to the BEA confidentiality requirements, by the 3-digit BEA industry classification.

the collection of a number of financial and operating data items. Inward DFI data on sources of financing, net plant and equipment, plant and equipment expenditures, exploration and development expenditures, and employee compensation will not be collected for 1982 (see Table 6.4). Collection of data on sources and uses of funds and sales by majority-owned US affiliates was discontinued in 1976. Halting the collection of these data creates serious problems for researchers. A lack of data on sales of majority-owned US affiliates, for example, handicapped recent efforts to analyse the effects of DFI performance requirements applied by Brazil and Mexico on US automotive trade (Rousslang, 1982). Similarly, recent attempts to discern the level of government ownership in foreign-owned firms has been hampered by a severe lack of data.

Levels of Disaggregation. Another complaint that has been raised regarding the BEA data is that the level of disaggregation is not fine enough (Lipsey, 1978; Musgrave, 1978). Researchers examining production and trade patterns of multinational enterprises (MNEs) contend they need data akin to that reported by the Census Bureau at the 5- to 7-digit level. At the 3-digit level of aggregation, the industries represented may not be homogeneous groupings. It may be difficult, therefore, to get accurate data for certain industries or products, or even for major product categories. Moreover, it is difficult to validly specify or sort out the influence of certain factors (explanatory variables) on such aggregated categories. For example, SIC 371 (motor vehicles and equipment) includes complete passenger automobiles, commercial automobiles, buses and trucks, truck and bus bodies, motor vehicle parts and accessories including engines, except diesel.

The BEA is aware of the need for finer disaggregation and has suggested that it may be possible to have the Census Bureau amend its trade data collection to reflect whether trade is between affiliates or not. However, as the BEA notes, the Census Bureau could not obtain data on trade between an unaffiliated US person and a foreign affiliate or person, or trade by foreign affiliates with countries other than the United States. Also, for such disaggregated trade data to be useful, establishment-level production data would also be needed at an equivalent level of detail (Bureau of Economic Analysis, 1982, p. 16).

Comparability of Data Over Time and Between Surveys. The differences in the exemption levels of the benchmark and annual surveys (see Tables 6.4 and 6.5) raise questions regarding the comparability of annual BEA data on DFI. These differences are further exacerbated by large changes in the exemption levels over time and a failure to blow up annual sample surveys to the benchmark or universe data level. For example, while the exemption level for the reporting of some balance of payments data in the 1977 benchmark survey of US outward DFI was $500,000, the exemption level for this survey in 1982 was $3 million. Also, annual surveys of US inward DFI for 1977 through 1979 are not expanded to the universe or benchmark level of 1974.

Despite the BEA's claims that coverage of both the benchmark and annual sample surveys is quite complete (over 90 per cent for both the benchmark and annual surveys), it is difficult to believe that the data are consistent and thus comparable. Researchers should be aware of these characteristics when they are conducting time-series and comparative statistical analyses of DFI using the BEA data.

For policy-makers, it is also particularly disquieting to see that increases in the exemption levels may result in a lop-sided loss of data. Since smaller-sized investments are frequently correlated with the level of economic development of a country, for some countries, an increase in the exemption levels can result in either a reduction of the size of various data groups, to such an extent that more information categories fall under confidentiality restrictions, or the complete elimination of important information. Consequently, policy-makers may not be able to consider DFI needs and important repercussions in their decision-making.

Industry Codes and Cross-Series Compatibility. The BEA is concerned with the accuracy of its industry codes. Parents and affiliates of an enterprise are assigned an industry code by the BEA on the basis of the distribution of their sales. As the BEA notes, a code based on sales is not as desirable as a code based on value added. The BEA is also concerned that companies provide inaccurate data, due partly to their lack of understanding of how to report the data and partly to the unavailability of data (Bureau of Economic Analysis, 1982, p. 14).

The BEA would prefer to have the Census Bureau provide industry codes for US parents and US affiliates. Assignment of codes for foreign parents and foreign affiliates could not be provided by the Census Bureau. However, the BEA believes that it can assign codes for foreign entities more easily than the Census Bureau could.

The BEA notes that industry codes assigned by the Census Bureau for US parents and US affiliates would be more accurate and consistent with the codes assigned to companies by other US Government agencies. However, current statutes prohibit the Census Bureau from releasing individual-company data to the BEA and thus prevent it from performing this function.

Questions also arise with regard to the compatibility of the BEA data at the 3-digit ESIC level with other domestic data series. The BEA 3-digit breakdown, besides not being compatible with other data series, cannot be matched via a concordance or aggregations of finer series. As a result, researchers who wish to conduct analyses using the BEA data in conjunction with the data collected by the Census Bureau and the Federal Trade Commission (line of business data), or other agencies, will encounter difficulties in matching the different types of information.

Even if such matching of codes were successful, any analysis would be severely hampered by problems resulting from code-assignment procedures. The BEA assigns its overall ESICs based on the primary product of a firm, that is, the ESIC appropriate for the product category with the highest sales volume. This practice makes data interpretations difficult (particularly as far as policy decisions about specific product categories are concerned), since for each firm the largest volume ESIC will be overestimated and all other ESICs will be underestimated. The fact that the Census Bureau assigns its SICs on the basis of payroll information compounds the problem.

This problem is quite adequately described by Chung and Fouch (1981, pp. 40-1) who note for a reported real estate measurement that:

However, this [real estate] estimate does not represent the total value of US real estate owned by foreign parents. It includes only direct investment in US affiliates that are classified in the real estate industry. Direct investment in affiliates in other industries, which may also hold real estate, is classified in the industries of those affiliates. Furthermore, the position in real estate affiliates reflects only the portion of total real estate held by such affiliates that is financed with funds from foreign parents. That portion may be small relative to the total because real estate investments usually are highly leveraged – the ratio of loans (largely from unaffiliated sources) to investors' funds used for equity purchases normally is high.

Revisions and Adjustments. Another area of concern with the BEA data is the significant *ex post* revisions made to reported both stock and flow DFI data. For users of contemporary BEA data, these revisions can create havoc, since analyses are often dependent on recent estimates. Information needs of policy-makers are frequently based on current-decision problems, and the time-lag in updating data may bias the assumption base of decisions.

In addition, the discrepancy between the book and market values has been exacerbated by the rampant inflation of recent years. As a result, the DFI-stock values reported by the BEA have been criticised as providing an inadequate information base for policy-makers to evaluate options. This lack of information is particularly pronounced for policy-makers attempting to incorporate DFI information on Iran and, more recently, on Mexico, into their decision-making framework.

Cross-fertilisation of Data Sets. As noted earlier, DFI data are collected by a wide variety of US Government agencies. Unfortunately, this variety, instead of contributing to a synergistic whole, results in a disarray of information. Frequently, the different mandates of different agencies appear to shape very different perceptions of data needs. As a result, there is often duplication of effort, different bases for collection (establishment vs. company, flow vs. stock, planned vs. actual) and different data sets. Despite efforts by the Office of Federal Statistical Policy and Standards to co-ordinate these efforts, it is very difficult to compare the different data series. In addition, actual and perceived confidentiality requirements result in a less than free exchange of data between the agencies. Efforts to remedy at least some of these problems are readily visible. But while, for example, the stated desire to achieve a confluence of the Census Bureau and the BEA Benchmark in 1987 is encouraging, the total lack thus far of discussions of data co-ordination between the two is not.

Input into Data Collection Changes. The Office of Federal Statistical Policy and Standards, aided by inter-agency committees and the agencies concerned, is charged with co-ordinating changes in data collection. Judging by the disparities in the data sets enumerated above, and by the continuous clamours of data reporters and users, improvements in co-ordination are needed.

Changes in data collection are managed by the Office of Management and Budget (OMB), which acts as broker between reporters and government agencies. If changes are considered, a 'Notice of Renewal' is published in the Federal Register and comments can be made by concerned parties. At this stage, there is little comment from the academic community. Frequently, academicians either do not know about the contemplated changes or do not have sufficient resources, knowledge or stamina to comment on them. As a result, potentially valuable input is lost.

Data Accessability. The BEA does not publish (in the *Survey of Current Business*) all the disaggregated data it collects. The data are published at much more aggregated levels. The primary reasons for this lack of publication, according to the BEA, are space constraints and disclosure requirements, which protect the confidentiality of reporters. However, subject to its confidentiality constraints, the BEA will make available, for a fee, disaggregated survey data.

Similar restrictions on the publication of DFI data exist for other data collection agencies as well, due not to malevolence but financial expediency. While in most instances data is *de jure* accessible, such access is extremely limited in practice for several reasons. First, one has to know about the non-published data in order to request them. Second, specialised data runs are available only after long delays — reportedly, up to six months or more. Third, the fees charged for such data runs are high and out of reach for all but the most well-endowed researchers. As a result, much data are not being put to any use, even if there is a need. On a more mundane level, even published data are difficult to access, due to the flood of existing information and the frequent lack of awareness on the part of researchers as to their availability.

Potential Approaches

From a research perspective, it is tempting to recommend that the BEA and other agencies collect and publish or make readily available extremely detailed disaggregated DFI data. It is not clear, however, that much of the data collected, and in turn the research based on it, would be of sufficient benefit to research users to justify the expenditures. In the same context, it is questionable that additional budget would be allocated to such endeavours.

In addition, there is the question of burden to reporters and the possible consequences of that additional reporting burden on DFI flows. The intent of the US Congress in the Investment Survey Act was that information on DFI should be collected with a minimum burden on respondents. Also, nothing in the Act is intended to restrain either inward or outward DFI. Stronger requirements imposed by the BEA to acquire information on the ultimate beneficial ownership of DFI have been criticised on both counts (Langley, 1982).

It is more realistic and practical to recommend approaches that attempt to refine and combine the currently collected data and to improve the data analysis than to propose sweeping additions to and changes in the collection system. In that context, the following recommendations are made in the areas of data collection, data management, data planning and dissemination and data analysis.

Data Collection

Establish A Special Study Task Force. Since policy concerns go in cycles, and data for policy decisions often need to be sufficiently detailed to cover 'specific industries, parts of industries, groups of workers, or geographical areas' (Lipsey, 1977, p. 2), the two basic alternatives in data collection systems are either to collect as many data as possible in order to have them available when needed, or to collect all but the regularly essential data on an 'as needed' basis. We believe that reporting burdens and budgetary considerations point towards the latter approach. Policy-questions are rarely in need of endless time-series data in order to be answered. The main imperative is rapid data availability. For example, by maintaining detailed listings of basic company, product and ownership information, with a continuing publication of aggregate information, special short-term task forces could then easily extract the necessary information after providing companies with some lead-time to prepare the data. Such a SWAT-team approach could greatly reduce the ongoing data collection cost and burden, while still maintaining the possibility of providing needed data. (The problem of country elimination through exemption, for example, could be easily handled that way.) Imperative for the success of such an approach, however, is an arrangement with the OMB for the allocation of funds and authority earmarked for such special studies so that the elapse of time and budget-seepage could be contained.

Conduct More Sample Surveys. Rather than placing an all-out emphasis on universal data collection, more sample surveys or even case studies should be conducted with an in-depth focus on specific issues, for example, the patent and royalty tax implications of joint ventures. Often basic information or information about processes is more important than a wide array of data. However, care must be taken that such planned sample surveys do not suffer the fate of non-implementation of the previous efforts in similar directions.

Make Use of Industry Sources. The private sector already collects substantial amounts of data for its own information. Both researchers and policy-makers should consider making more use of these existing data sources in their work. Such a step could conserve scarce resources while not diminishing (and possibly even increasing) the availability of information.

Fund Data Work For Government Purposes. Proposals should be put forward to have the US Government allocate funds for research on the refinement of certain elements of national and international data. These proposals should be evaluated by a small inter-agency group, in order to ensure the focus on information needed by the government. Outside researchers whose proposals are selected could be brought in to work on specific tasks. Such an approach should also contribute to a greater awareness of data availability among researchers.

Fund Data Work For Academic Purposes Jointly. Though much academic research may lack obvious and immediate policy-applicability, it is in the interest of the government to encourage academic inquiry. Governmental funding could be allocated to match funds from interested universities, research institutes, etc. One possibility would be the allocation of in-kind funds to permit access to non-published data. Alternatively, personnel from research institutions could work directly for the BEA and other data collection agencies, with the government providing data and facilities and interested individuals supplying their manpower. Such an arrangement could be a particularly attractive option for academicians on sabbatical and could result in a beneficial cross-fertilisation of information. The recent establishment of the Center for Economic Studies by the Bureau of the Census raises hopes for this recommendation. To ensure that the resulting statistical analyses are meaningful, project proposals should be evaluated by the National Science Foundation through peer reviews.

Data Management

Share Data More Widely. Although current statutes prohibit data sharing by various agencies, the possibilities for working within statutes to combine their separate data series should be investigated. This could include formal proposals to amend current statutes to permit the sharing of data. Such an approach is only useful, however, if it is preceded by an assessment of data incompatibilities and followed by earnest efforts to increase the incomparability of data between these agencies, provide conversion tables, or flag instances in which apples and oranges would be compared.

Link Numbers With Names. While confidentiality is certainly important to the reporters, and often of little bother to users, the BEA should consider the benefits of giving faces to some of its numbers. A wide variety of current and potential users in the executive and legislative branches and in industry would find important use for such information and, therefore, for the BEA data. By using information from publicly available data already collected, for example, the news-clipping base, the BEA would not only make its services more valuable, but could also contribute to a cost-effective consolidation of information gathering activities.

Update Information More Quickly. While it is understandable that in the use of the company survey technique, late filings and follow-up questionnaires will produce changes in the original estimates, we would suggest that the BEA publish its revisions in a more timely manner. Revisions could, for example, be published in the quarterly flow-data, rather than being held until the end of the year and reported as revisions to the annual flow and stock estimates for previous years.

Data Planning and Dissemination

Facilitate Input Into Data-change Process. First, this requires better rapport between data collection agencies and reporters. Ongoing contact can improve the understanding on the part of government agencies of the burden associated with the fulfilment of reporting requirements, and also serve to explain the need for and use of the data collected, thus improving the understanding, willingness and accuracy of reporters. Second, input from academics should be facilitated by fostering greater awareness of planned data changes. Such a task can be accomplished by special 'alert' mailings to interested academicians and by conducting special conferences on DFI data collection aimed at researchers.

Facilitate Knowledge About Data. As recommended earlier regarding international data, it would be useful to develop a guide to US data on DFI, with a special section on industry-specific DFI. This guide would include not only a listing of the data collected by agencies and a brief discussion on data comparability issues, but also a listing of the data published, the data available from agencies (but not published) and ways to acquire data, with some estimate of the potential cost and lead-times involved.

Data Analysis

Focus More On Analysis. Perhaps we are reaching a point of diminishing returns from data collection activities. In these times of frequent information overload, funds should be allocated to improve both quantitative and *qualitative* analyses. Much of the available data, for example, the foreign-investment identifier of the Census Bureau, are never used in analysis. Besides, many questions regarding the impact cannot be answered even with perfect data. More work could be done regarding the purpose of data collection, namely the obtaining of a better understanding of the *meaning* of change, and finding better and more creative ways of interpretation and understanding.

Notes

* The views expressed in this paper are solely those of the authors and do not necessarily reflect the position of the organisations they are affiliated with.

* * *

COMMENT

Robert E. Lipsey

Conceptual and Classification Issues

One obstacle to analysing data problems and solutions for analysis of intra-industry direct foreign investment (IDFI) is that few solutions can be achieved in one country. The nature of the questions likely to arise is such that they can hardly be analysed at all from data collected by a single country, except to the extent that one can learn something by comparing investment abroad by a country with investment by foreigners in that country. Vukmanic, Czinkota and Ricks seem quite pessimistic about international comparability of data and, therefore, devote most of their attention to the quality of US data, but the issue of DFI gets a bit lost in that discussion.

At least for some of the questions one would like to ask about IDFI, the prospects may not be quite so hopeless. From the point of view of information collection, we should probably distinguish two kinds of issues. One is about how affiliates of multinational enterprises are established and what flows of funds take place between affiliates and their parents at that point and later. The other is about how these affiliates operate in comparison with locally-owned firms, or how those from one country operate in comparison with affiliates of multi-nationals from other countries. The distinction is not a perfectly clean one but it suggests some possibilities for developing useful data on IDFI.

Flows of funds, sources of financing of affiliates, and types of financing are important for balance of payments and monetary policy problems. There are a few, if any, issues regarding IDFI for which such data are vital. Data on these topics must be collected at frequent intervals, must be up to date, and should not have gaps in time series. This type of information is probably sensitive for many countries but it probably need not be published at fine levels of industry detail, since it is mainly of interest for macroeconomic policy and it may be suitable for collection via flow data. Thus, for IDFI, what the authors refer to as 'cash-flow' data can probably be written off and attention should be concentrated on data from surveys.

On the other hand, data on who multinational investors are and how they operate are important for the analysis of IDFI. They are only useful for this purpose if the degree of industry detail is substantial, and it would be better yet if company data were available. They certainly need not and cannot be collected monthly or quarterly and some of the data probably need not be collected annually because they involve long-run characteristics of firms.

Questions about the operations of affiliates might include the following:

(1) What do they produce? What are the distinctive characteristics of their products? Do they introduce new industries or new products or do they substitute for local firms?

(2) How do they produce? Do they use more capital-intensive methods than local firms or more skilled-labour? Are they technologically more advanced? Do they receive transfers of technology from their parents? How do their wage rates compare with those of other firms? What materials do they use?

(3) Do they export or import more than local firms in the same industry? Are they heavily dependent on parent firms for components or markets?

(4) Do they tend to monopolise host-country markets or do they introduce new competition?

Most of these are questions that host governments wish to know about all establishments in their countries. Some, but not all, are already asked in Censuses of Manufactures, for example. Such censuses tend to ask similar questions in different countries and to follow similar industrial classifications, because a great deal of work has gone into developing internationally comparable classification codes. Therefore, the key to learning more about the activities of multinationals' affiliates is to identify them in these censuses and to develop tabulations for them that are comparable to those for locally-owned firms and comparable across countries. That would require little extra reporting-burden on respondents beyond what they already have for local censuses, except for information on ownership. Yet it would give us data far beyond what we now have. This is already done to some extent in Canada and Sweden and perhaps in other countries.

Although the authors are pessimistic about the possibility of achieving international comparability of information, it is worth mentioning that the Swedish DFI surveys, conducted by a private research institution, the Industriens Utredningsinstitut (Industrial Institute for Economic and Social Research) of Stockholm, ask questions quite similar to those in the US surveys and were probably designed with the

US surveys as a model. Perhaps it would not be impossible to come to some agreement among at least a few of the major countries.

The degree of industry detail, a point mentioned by the authors, is particularly important. The empirical measurement of IDFI and intra-industry trade are affected by the statistical classification used. If an 'industry' is constructed in such a way as to be extremely hetero-geneous, it will give the appearance of having a large amount of 'intra-industry' trade and investment even if there really is none. A possible example of the influence of industry classification is the fact that in the chapter by Rugman in this volume, the 'industry' that ranks highest in percentage of IDFI is 'Other Manufacturing', a collection of unrelated industries. The apparent IDFI in 'Primary and Fabricated Metals' might involve the steel industry in one direction and the aluminium industry in another, and in 'Chemical and Allied Products' might be pharmaceuticals in one direction and petrochemicals in the other. In each case, since the components differ greatly in their characteristics, the force at work might as easily be factor abundance or labour cost as the elements underlying the true intra-industry trade or investment. The correlation between intra-industry investment and intra-industry trade measured so crudely may represent only the degree of hetero-geneity in the broad industry groups.

The point of this comment is that without a much more detailed breakdown of industries very little empirical study of IDFI can be performed. It will be difficult to do any serious analysis of this pheno-menon if our measures are nothing but quirks of the classification system.

Availability of Data

Table 6.1 in which national data collection systems are compared is potentially very useful but the reliance on a few official sources of data makes the compilation seriously incomplete. It would be helpful to distinguish data on inward DFI from those on outward DFI because the former are collected by more countries than the latter, the respon-dents may be more obligated to report, and the opportunities for improvement are different. It would also be useful to have a compila-tion that treated stock and flow data separately or even dropped the flow data altogether since they are almost useless for any analysis of IDFI.

The reporting of data availability in Table 6.1 is rather incomplete.

The United Kingdom has collected at least some financial and operating data from surveys. Canada has collected financial and operating data on inward DFI. France publishes stock data on inward DFI. Sweden, shown as having only DFI flow data, has collected inward and outward DFI stock data and actually matches or surpasses the United States in the quantity and quality of data available. There are also inward DFI data for Belgium, Brazil, Singapore and quite a few other countries not listed. Some of the best information has been collected in private surveys or as part of censuses and may for that reason be omitted from the OECD compilations. The OECD reports need to be supplemented by examining national sources.

Many of the authors' statements about reporting need amplification because the extent of disaggregation, for example, varies among surveys. The United States is described as publishing data for 11-13 sectors. But the 1977 survey of US outward DFI published quite a bit of information for over 50 sectors.

Recommendations

More Data Sharing

That would be a great help, of course, but both statutory limitations and inter-agency rivalries limit the chances for progress here. Perhaps the best hope would be to concentrate on a few very limited goals. It would be a great step forward, for example, if the various agencies could agree upon a common industry-classification for individual firms and it is hard to believe that such agreement would reveal any important secrets.

Funding of Data Work

What is needed more than anything else is a commitment to accessibility on the part of the agencies, particularly the Bureau of Economic Analysis (BEA). Perhaps there should be a concerted effort to convince the agencies that it makes no sense to spend large amounts of money to collect good data and to impose heavy costs on respondents for providing the data and then to have the most of the information unused because access is so difficult. The only solution to access problems is to have a person or unit in each agency with the primary responsibility for providing access to outsiders, including other government agencies. Greater access would be worth some sacrifice of currently collected but inaccessible data.

Special Studies

Special studies by emergency SWAT-teams are a useful idea for investigating particular topics on a one-time or occasional basis, but they need long preparation and advance notification of respondents so that they can organise their internal data collection. Hastily organised task forces might well be costly and produce nothing useful.

Company Names

Researchers would probably be grateful for an efficient system of running statistical analyses at the company or affiliate level within the agencies without revealing individual company names. Such a system would be more valuable if it could accept individual company information from the outside, combine it with the agency's data, and analyse the combined data.

* * *

COMMENT

Harvey E. Bale, Jr

The question of direct foreign investment (DFI) and related data, is, of course, an important subject for both analysts and policy-makers. Unfortunately, much of the available data also constitute a significant limitation on the activities of these two groups. Indeed, they are a weak element in the government's work on important policy-issues such as performance requirements, national treatment, and our bilateral investment treaty initiatives.

My remarks will dwell on some of the reasons for the data difficulties and my own pessimism about the likelihood of substantial improvements in the areas of difficulties cited by Vukmanic, Czinkota and Ricks. I disagree little with their chapter except for the nonchalant assumptions about resource availability in the final prescriptive section. However, I would also prefer a reversal of the order of importance placed by them on data vs. analysis. I would like to have seen early mention by the authors of the importance of the development of further analysis of DFI flows, and multinational enterprise (MNE) activities and government policies that influence them, rather than the brief note of this matter at the very end of the chapter.

If we have better agreement on models of determinants and effects

of DFI and its intra-industry variant (IDFI), accompanied by industry
— as well as aggregate-level studies utilising existing data, we will be
in a better position to:

(1) approach the US Government (including the budget-minded
Office of Management and Budget, and Congress) and foreign
governments with requests for the allocation of resources to the
collection of more DFI and related data; and
(2) work to improve the international comparability of such data.

Much DFI data are in search of models and are functionally redundant.
I doubt, for example, that any of you have used very much of the data
in the BE-10 survey that the authors discuss at some length. In some
part, this is because the data are four years out of date when published.
But the other point is that we might be able to get better and more
timely data if we become more selective and precise about our data
needs. On the US side, I would like to stress the missing element of
current or recent overseas sales and trade data of MNEs and their
affiliates that are keys for analysis of performance requirements and
benefits/costs of MNEs to host and home countries. Here, I am addressing mainly US data. On the international side, data are more difficult to
obtain; and, the data that are available are non-comparable, as the
authors point out.

The current state of DFI data is very unfortunate in view of the
growing internationalisation of business and the high level of attention
being given to DFI policy issues in the UN, the OECD, the World Bank
and even the GATT. In addition, for the first time, the United States
has launched a major initiative to negotiate bilateral investment treaties,
designed to affect DFI flows into developing countries.

There is considerable and growing interest in the US private sector
in DFI policy issues that goes beyond the traditional business and
labour interest in the tax-deferral issue. For example, the Labour-
Industry Coalition for International Trade (LICIT) has examined the
question of DFI-related performance requirements. The Business
Round-table will soon release a major statement on DFI policy issues,
including those of freedom of establishment, national treatment, performance requirements and patent protection. Also, the considerable
US interest in international trade in services is generated, to a major
degree, by DFI-type policy issues (for example, freedom of establishment) affecting the banking and insurance sectors.

The private sector's interest in the full range of DFI and implicitly

IDFI issues raises the possibility of seeking a greater contribution from it to support more analytical work in this area. I think of this possibility more in terms of support for research and analysis, utilising existing data. Multinationals are generally quite reluctant to provide information beyond that contained in current government-surveys and company annual reports (which, in the latter case, can provide a lot). I would think, on the other hand, that the private sector should be keenly interested in some of the recent work quite relevant to policymakers done by Lipsey, Lall and economists at the National University of Singapore, among others. I also would not in this regard fail to mention the fine chapters by McCulloch and Rugman in this volume on the trade/investment linkage. Indeed, McCulloch's remark that she is a 'trade economist' and not an 'investment economist' is puzzling, given the quality of her chapter and the increasing difficulty of ignoring investment considerations in examining trade and trade-policy issues, for example, those related to intra-industry trade.

As Vukmanic *et al.* explain, the best available data are not as good as we would like them to be. But the available data are not easily accessed by researchers, as Lipsey's experience has shown. They are not always readily available even to policy officials. I am also pessimistic about the possibility of major improvements in the available data for the following reasons:

(1) There are serious and foreseeable budget and manpower constraints on those governmental bodies that collect, massage and publish the raw information from surveys and samples.

(2) The current and recent US administrations have been in favour of reducing paperwork and regulatory burdens on the private sector. For this reason, the next BE-10 survey will be scaled back, not expanded in several respects.

(3) There are the constraints of business and state secrecy. It has been noted that Switzerland publishes no DFI data. You cannot obtain figures in the United States on portfolio investment from Saudi Arabia and some other OPEC countries. The US Commerce Department suppresses much country and product detail on DFI.

(4) There still prevails in the United States a general lack of real concern about knowing what are the various aspects of DFI flows that override the constraints mentioned above. Some believe that more complete and refined data on trade and investment only stimulate greater government interference in the economy. I should note that the call for better investment data (outside the academic community)

has tended to be directed towards more information on DFI in the United States. It comes mainly from those who want to regulate or limit, by federal legislation, inward DFI.

Therefore, it will be difficult to develop investment data in order to meet the same degree of analytical and policy needs for which trade data have been developed. Investment data carry a much lower level of concern and a higher degree of business and political sensitivity. This should not, however, prevent or discourage more research and analysis of DFI/IDFI issues and related policies. Much work is going on at the sectoral level along with the development of *ad hoc* information without the co-funded projects or SWAT-team approaches suggested by Vukmanic *et al.* In the current environment, I do not believe that their proposals are practical.

I would hope that the business and labour groups will take more of an interest in funding serious DFI research. The US executive branch research-budgets have been reduced quite substantially. I do not know how often the National Science Foundation can put on as fine a conference as the one that produced this volume. But further work in this area deserves to be supported, particularly by those who will be most affected by future US Government policy decisions.

REFERENCES

Agarwal, J.P. (1980) 'Determinants of Direct Foreign Investment: A Survey', *Weltwirtschaftliches Archiv, 116*, 739–73

Agmon, T. and D. Lessard (1976) 'The Multinational Firm as a Vehicle for International Diversification: Implications for Capital Importing Countries' (mimeo), MIT, Cambridge, MA

Aharoni, Y. (1966) *The Foreign Investment Decision Process*, Harvard University Graduate School of Business Administration, Boston

Aho, C.M. and T. Bayard (1982) 'The 1980s: Twilight of the Open Trading System', Office of Foreign Economic Research, US Department of Labor, Washington, DC

Aliber, R.Z. (1970) 'A Theory of Direct Foreign Investment' in C.P. Kindleberger (ed.), *The International Corporation*, MIT Press, Cambridge, MA

Aliber, R.Z. (1983) 'Money, Multinationals, and Sovereigns' in C.P. Kindleberger and D.B. Audretsch (eds), *The Multinational Corporation in the 1980s*, MIT Press, Cambridge, MA

Andriessen, F. (1981) 'Antitrust in the International Sphere: Antitrust – An Endangered Species?' in 'Surveys of Foreign Antitrust Laws', *Antitrust Law Journal, 50*, 741–7

Arpan, J.S. and D.A. Ricks (1974) 'Foreign Direct Investment in the United States and Some Attendant Research Problems', *Journal of International Business Studies, 5*, 1–7

Asch, P. (1975) 'The Determinants and Effects of Antitrust Activity', *Journal of Law and Economics, 18*, 575–81

Bain, J. (1956) *Barriers to New Competition*, Harvard University Press, Cambridge, MA

Balassa, B. (1966) 'American Direct Investments in the Common Market', *Banca Nazionale del Lavoro Quarterly Review, 77*, 1–26

Balassa, B. (1981) 'Shifting Patterns of World Trade and Competition' in *Growth and Entrepreneurship: Opportunities and Challenges in a Changing World*, International Chamber of Commerce, Paris

Baldwin, R.E. (1970) *Non-Tariff Distortions of International Trade*, Brookings Institution, Washington, DC

Baldwin, R.E. (1979) 'Determinants of Trade and Foreign Investments: Further Evidence', *Review of Economics and Statistics, 61*, 40–8

Barnett, R.J. and R.E. Mueller (1974) *Global Reach*, Simon and Schuster, New York

Behrman, J.N. (1969) *Some Patterns in the Rise of the Multinational Enterprise*, University of North Carolina Press, Chapel Hill, NC

Behrman, J.N. (1971) *National Interests and the Multinational Enterprise*, Prentice-Hall, Englewood Cliffs, NJ

Behrman, J.N. (1972) 'Industrial Integration and the Multinational Enterprise', *Annals of the American Academy of Political and Social Science, 403*, 46–57

Bergsten, C.F., T. Horst and T. Moran (1978) *American Multinationals and*

American Interests, Brookings Institution, Washington, DC

Bergsten, C.F. and J. Williamson (1982) 'Exchange Rates and Trade Policy', paper prepared for the Institute for International Economics Conference on Trade Policy in the Eighties, Washington, DC (June 23–25)

Bhagwati, J.N. (1972) 'Review of R. Vernon, *Sovereignty at Bay*', *Journal of International Economics, 2*, 455–62

Bhagwati, J.N. (1982) 'Shifting Advantage, Protectionist Demands, and Policy Response' in J.N. Bhagwati (ed.), *Import Competition and Response*, University of Chicago Press, Chicago

Billerbeck, K. and I.Y. Yasugi (1979) *Private Foreign Investment in Developing Countries*, World Bank Staff Working Paper No. 348, Washington, DC

Boddewyn, J. (1979) 'Foreign Divestment: Magnitude and Factors', *Journal of International Business Studies, 10*, 21–7

Bork, R. (1978) *The Antitrust Paradox*, Basic Books, New York

Borrus, M., J. Millstein and J. Zysman (1982) *International Competition in Advanced Sectors: Trade and Development in the Semiconductor Industry*, monograph prepared for the Joint Economic Committee of the US Congress, US Government Printing Office, Washington, DC

Boyer, M. and A. Jacquemin (1983) *Organisational and Industrial Actions for Effiency and Market Power: An Integrated Approach* (mimeo)

Brander, J.A. (1981) 'Intra-industry Trade in Identical Commodities', *Journal of International Economics, 11*, 1–15

Brewster, K. (1958) *Antitrust and American Business Abroad*, McGraw-Hill, New York

Buckley, P.J. and M.C. Casson (1976) *The Future of the Multinational Enterprise*, Macmillan, London

Bureau of Economic Analysis (1982) *Work on Direct Investment Pursuant to the International Investment Survey Act of 1976*, US Department of Commerce, Washington, DC

Calvet, A.L. and M. Naim (1981) 'The Multinational Firm in Less Developed Countries: A Market and Hierarchies Approach', *Proceedings of the European International Business Association and the Academy of International Business* (December)

Carlson, S. (1977) 'Company Policies for International Expansion: The Swedish Experience' in T. Agmon and C.P. Kindleberger (eds), *Multinationals from Small Countries*, MIT Press, Cambridge, MA

Casson, M.C. (1979) *Alternatives to the Multinational Enterprise*, Macmillan, London

Casson, M.C. (1982) 'Transaction Costs and the Theory of the Multinational Enterprise' in A.M. Rugman (ed.), *New Theories of the Multinational Enterprise*, Croom Helm, London and St Martin's Press, New York

Casson, M.C. and G. Norman (1983) 'Pricing and Sourcing Strategies in a Multinational Oligopoly' in M.C. Casson (ed.), *The Growth of International Business*, George Allen & Unwin, London

Caves, R.E. (1971) 'International Corporations: The Industrial Economics of Foreign Investment', *Economica, 38*, 1–27

Caves, R.E. (1974a) 'Causes of Direct Investment: Foreign Firms' Shares in Canadian and United Kingdom Manufacturing Industries', *Review of Economics and Statistics, 56*, 279–94

Caves, R.E. (1974b) 'International Trade, International Investment, and Imperfect Markets', *Special Papers in International Economics* No. 10, International Finance Section, Department of Economics, Princeton University, Princeton, NJ

Caves, R.E. (1980) 'Investment and Location Policies of Multinational Companies', *Schweizerische Zeitschrift fuer Volkswirtschaft und Statistik, 3*, 321–38

Caves, R.E. (1982) *Multinational Enterprise and Economic Analysis*, Cambridge University Press, Cambridge and New York

Chung, W.K. and G.G. Fouch (1981) 'Foreign Direct Investment in the United States in 1980', *Survey of Current Business, 61*, 40–1

Coase, R.H. (1937) 'The Nature of the Firm', *Economica*, N.S., *4*, 386–405

Committee on Government Operations (1980) *The Adequacy of the Federal Response to Foreign Direct Investment in the United States*, US House of Representatives Report No. 92–1216, US Government Printing Office, Washington, DC

Corden, W.M. (1974) *Trade Policy and Economic Welfare*, Clarendon Press, Oxford

Coughlan, A. (1982) 'Vertical Integration Incentives in Marketing Channel Choice: Theory and Application to the International Semiconductor Industry', Doctor of Business Administration thesis, Stanford University, Stanford, CA

Daniels, J. (1971) *Recent Foreign Direct Investment in the United States*, Praeger, New York

Dewald, W., H. Gilman, H. Grubert and L. Wipf (eds) (1978) *The Impact of International Trade and Investment on Employment*, US Department of Labor, Washington, DC

Domeratzky, L. (1928) *The International Cartel Movement*, Trade Information Bulletin No. 556, US Department of Commerce, Washington, DC

Dunning, J.H. (1958) *American Investment in British Manufacturing Industry*, George Allen & Unwin, London

Dunning, J.H. (1970) 'Technology, United States Investment, and European Economic Growth' in C.P. Kindleberger (ed.), *The International Corporation*, MIT Press, Cambridge, MA

Dunning, J.H. (1973) 'The Determinants of International Production', *Oxford Economic Papers, 25*, 289–336

Dunning, J.H. (1974) 'Multinational Enterprises, Market Structure, Economic Power, and Industrial Policy', *Journal of World Trade Law, 8*, 575–613

Dunning, J.H. (1977) 'Trade, Location of Economic Activity and the Multinational Enterprise: A Search for an Eclectic Approach' in B. Ohlin, P.O. Hesselborn and P.M. Wijkman (eds), *The International Allocation of Economic Activity*, Macmillan, London

Dunning, J.H. (1979) 'Explaining Changing Patterns of International Production: In Defence of the Eclectic Theory', *Oxford Bulletin of Economics and Statistics, 41*, 269–95

Dunning, J.H. (1980) 'Towards an Eclectic Theory of International Production: Some Empirical Tests', *Journal of International Business Studies, 11*, 9–31

Dunning, J.H. (1981a) *International Production and the Multinational Enterprise*, George Allen & Unwin, London

Dunning, J.H. (1981b) 'A Note on Intra-industry Foreign Direct Investment',

Banca Nazionale del Lavoro Quarterly Review, 139, 427–37

Dunning, J.H. (1981c) 'Explaining the International Direct Investment Position of Countries: Towards a Dynamic or Developmental Approach', *Weltwirtschaftliches Archiv, 117,* 30–64

Dunning, J.H. (1982) 'Market Power of the Firm and International Transfer of Technology: An Historical Excursion', University of Reading Discussion Paper in International Investment and Business Studies, No. 67, Reading

Dunning, J.H. (1983) 'Changes in the Level and Structure of International Production: The Last One Hundred Years' in M.C. Casson (ed.), *The Growth of International Business*, George Allen & Unwin, London

Dunning, J.H. and M. McQueen (1982) 'The Theory of the Multinational Enterprise and the International Hotel Industry' in A.M. Rugman (ed.), *New Theories of the Multinational Enterprise*, Croom Helm, London and St Martin's Press, New York

Dunning, J.H. and J. Stopford (1983) *Multinationals: Company Performance and Global Trends*, Byfleet, Macmillan, Globe Book Services, London

Edwards, C.D. (1944) *Economic and Political Aspects of International Cartels*, monograph prepared for the Committee on Military Affairs, US Senate, Washington, DC

Erdilek, A. (1976) 'Can the Multinational Corporation be Incorporated into the General Equilibrium Theory of International Trade and Investment?' *Social and Economic Studies, 25,* 280–90

Erdilek, A. (1982a) 'Intra-industry Cross Direct Foreign Investment – A Survey of the Trends, Literature, and Public-Policy Issues', (mimeo), National Science Foundation, Washington, DC

Erdilek, A. (1982b) *Direct Foreign Investment in Turkish Manufacturing: An Analysis of the Conflicting Objectives and Frustrated Expectations of a Host Country*, J.C.B. Mohr, Tuebingen

Erdilek, A. (1983) 'Intra-industry Direct Foreign Investment – Policy Options and Implications for the United States', (mimeo), National Science Foundation, Washington, DC

Faith, N. (1971) *The Infiltrators*, Hamish Hamilton, London

Feenstra, R.C. and K.L. Judd (1982) 'Tariffs, Technology Transfer, and Welfare', *Journal of Political Economy, 90,* 1142–65

Feinberg, R. (1981) 'Mutual Forebearance As an Extension of Oligopoly Theory', Department of Economics Working Paper No. 6-80-6, Pennsylvania State University, University Park, PA

Feinberg, R. and R. Sherman (1981) 'An Experimental Approach to Analyzing Mutual Forebearance Behavior', paper presented at the Western Economic Association Meeting, San Francisco (July)

Finger, J.M. (1975) 'Trade Overlap and Intra-industry Trade', *Economic Inquiry, 13,* 581–9

Flowers, E.B. (1976) 'Oligopolistic Reactions in European and Canadian Direct Investment in the United States', *Journal of International Business Studies, 7,* 43–55

Frank, I. (1981) *Foreign Investment in Developing Countries*, Johns Hopkins Press, Baltimore, MD

Frank, R.H. and R.T. Freeman (1978) 'The Distributional Consequences of DFI', in Dewald *et al.* (eds), *The Impact of International Trade and Investment on*

Employment, US Department of Labor, Washington, DC

Franko. L.G. (1976) *The European Multinationals: A Renewed Challenge to American and British Big Business*, Harper and Row, New York

Goldsweig, D. (1981) 'Introductory Remarks' in 'Surveys of Foreign Antitrust Laws', *Antitrust Law Journal, 50*, 645–6

Gordon, M. and D. Fowler (1981) *The Drug Industry: A Case Study of the Effect of Foreign Control in the Canadian Economy*, James Lorimer, Toronto

Graham, E.M. (1974) 'Oligopolistic Imitation and European Direct Investment in the United States', Doctor of Business Administration thesis, Harvard University, Cambridge, MA

Graham, E.M. (1978) 'Transatlantic Investment by Multinational Firms: A Rivalistic Phenomenon?', *Journal of Post Keynesian Economics, 1*, 82–99

Gray, H.P. (1982a) 'Macroeconomic Theories of Foreign Direct Investment' in A.M. Rugman (ed.), *New Theories of the Multinational Enterprise*, Croom Helm, London and St Martin's Press, New York

Gray, H.P. (1982b) 'Towards a Unified Theory of International Trade, International Production and Foreign Direct Investment' in J.H. Dunning and J. Black (eds), *International Capital Movements*, Macmillan, London

Grubel, H.G. (1970) 'The Theory of Intra-industry Trade' in I.A. McDougall and R.H. Snape (eds), *Studies in International Economics*, North-Holland, Amsterdam

Grubel, H.G. (1977) 'A Theory of Multinational Banking', *Banca Nazionale del Lavoro Quarterly Review, 123*, 349–63

Grubel, H.G. (1979) 'Towards a Theory of Two-way Trade in Capital Assets' in H. Giersch (ed.), *On the Economics of Intra-industry Trade*, J.C.B. Mohr, Tuebingen

Grubel, H.G. and P.J. Lloyd (1975) *Intra-industry Trade: The Theory and Measurement of International Trade in Differentiated Products*, Macmillan, London

Hawkins, R.G. and I. Walter (1980) 'Multinational Corporations: Current Trends and Future Prospects' in *The International Economy: US Role in a World Market*, Joint Economic Committee of the US Congress, Washington, DC

Hay, G.A. and D. Kelly (1974) 'An Empirical Study of Price-Fixing Conspiracies', *Journal of Law and Economics, 17*, 13–38

Heggestad, A. and S. Rhoades (1978) 'Multi-market Interdependence and Local Market Competition in Banking', *Review of Economics and Statistics, 60*, 523–32

Hekman, C.R. (1981) 'Foreign Exchange Risk: Relevance and Management', *Managerial and Decision Economics, 2*, 256–62

Helleiner, G.K. and R. Lavergne (1980) 'Intra-firm Trade and Industrial Exports to the United States', *Oxford Bulletin of Economics and Statistics, 41*, 297–319

Hennart, J.F. (1982) *A Theory of Multinational Enterprise*, University of Michigan Press, Ann Arbor, MI

Hennart, J.F. (1983) 'The Political Economy of Comparative Growth Rates: the Case of France' in D. Mueller (ed.), *The Political Economy of Growth*, Yale University Press, New Haven, CT

Hexner, E. (1945) *International Cartels*, University of North Carolina Press, Chapel Hill, NC

Hirsch, S. (1976) 'An International Trade and Investment Theory of the Firm', *Oxford Economic Press, 28*, 258–71

Horst, T. (1972a) 'The Industrial Composition of US Exports and Subsidiary Sales in Canadian Manufacturing Industries: Some Comments and Empirical Results', *American Economic Review, 62*, 37–45

Hout, T., M. Porter and E. Rudden (1982) 'How Global Companies Win Out', *Harvard Business Review, 60*, 98–108

Hunter, L. (1981) 'Survey of Canadian Antitrust Laws' in 'Surveys of Foreign Antitrust Laws', *Antitrust Law Journal, 50*, 699–707

Hymer, S. (1960) 'The International Operations of National Firms', PhD thesis, Department of Economics, MIT, Cambridge, MA

Hymer, S. (1970) 'The Efficiency (Contradictions) of Multinational Corporations', *American Economic Review, 60*, 441–53

Hymer, S. and R. Rowthorn (1970) 'Multinational Corporations and International Oligopoly: The Non-American Challenge' in C.P. Kindleberger (ed.), *The International Corporation*, MIT Press, Cambridge, MA

International Monetary Fund (1977) *Balance of Payments Manual*, 4th edn, IMF, Washington, DC

Jarrett, J.P. (1979) 'Offshore Assembly and Production and the Internalization of International Trade within the Multinational Corporation', PhD thesis, Department of Economics, Harvard University, Cambridge, MA

Johnson, H.G. (1970) 'The Efficiency and Welfare Implications of the International Corporation' in C.P. Kindleberger (ed.), *The International Corporation*, MIT Press, Cambridge, MA

Kamien, M.I. and N.L. Schwartz (1978) 'Potential Rivalry, Monopoly, Profits, and the Pace of Inventive Activity', *Review of Economic Studies, 45*, 547–57

Kindleberger, C.P. (1969) *American Business Abroad: Six Lectures on Direct Foreign Investment*, Yale University Press, New Haven, CT

Knickerbocker, F.T. (1973) *Oligopolistic Reaction and the Multinational Enterprise*, Harvard University Graduate School of Business Administration, Boston, MA

Knickerbocker, F.T. (1976) 'Market Structure and Market Power Consequences of Foreign Direct Investment by Multinational Corporations', Occasional Paper No. 8, Center for Multinational Studies, Washington, DC

Kogut, B. (1983) 'Foreign Direct Investment as a Sequential Process' in C.P. Kindleberger and D.B. Audretsch (eds), *The Multinational Corporation in the 1980s*, MIT Press, Cambridge, MA

Kojima, K. (1977) 'Direct Foreign Investment Between Advanced Industrialized Countries', *Hitotsubashi Journal of Economics, 18*, 1–18

Kojima, K. (1978) *Direct Foreign Investment: A Japanese Model of Multinational Business Operations*, Croom Helm, London

Kojima, K. (1982) 'Macroeconomic Versus International Business Approach to Direct Foreign Investment', *Hitotsubashi Journal of Economics, 23*, 1–19

Kravis, I.B. and R.E. Lipsey (1982) 'The Location of Overseas Production and Production for Export by US Multinational Firms', *Journal of International Economics, 12*, 201–23

Krueger, A.O. (1977) *Growth, Distortions, and Patterns of Trade Among Many*

Countries, Studies in International Finance, No. 40, International Finance Section, Department of Economics, Princeton University, Princeton, NJ

Krugman, P.R. (1981) 'Intra-industry Specialization and the Gains from Trade', *Journal of Political Economy, 89*, 959-74

Krugman, P.R. (1983) 'The New Theories of International Trade and the Multinational Enterprise' in C.P. Kindleberger and D.B. Audretsch (eds), *The Multinational Corporation in the 1980s*, MIT Press, Cambridge, MA

Lall, S. (1980) 'Vertical Linkages in LDCs: An Empirical Study', *Oxford Bulletin of Economics and Statistics, 42*, 203-27

Lall, S. and N.S. Siddharthan (1982) 'The Monopolistic Advantages of Multinationals: Lessons from Foreign Investment in the United States', *Economic Journal, 92*, 668-83

Langley, M. (1982) 'International Investment Survey Act: The High Cost of Knowledge', *Law and Policy In International Business, 14*, 481-504

Larson, D. (1970) 'An Economic Analysis of the Webb-Pomerene Act', *Journal of Law and Economics, 13*, 461-500

Lipsey, R.E. (1977) 'Report on Foreign Investment Surveys', Report Submitted to the Inter-agency Committee on Direct Foreign Investment Statistics, Washington, DC (June)

Lipsey, R.E. (1978) Submission to the Hearings Before the Subcommittee of the Committee on Government Operations, *The Operations of Federal Agencies in Monitoring, Reporting on and Analyzing Foreign Investment in the United States, 1*, US House of Representatives, US Government Printing Office, Washington, DC, 301-13

Lipsey, R.E. and I.B. Kravis (1982) 'US-Owned Affiliates and Host-Country Exports', National Bureau of Economic Research, Working Paper No. 1037, Cambridge, MA

Lipsey, R.E. and M.Y. Weiss (1981) 'Foreign Production and Exports in Manufacturing Industries', *Review of Economics and Statistics, 63*, 488-94

Long, W., R. Schramm and R. Tollison (1973) 'The Economic Determinants of Antitrust Activity', *Journal of Law and Economics, 16*, 351-64

Magee, S.P. (1977) 'Information and the Multinational Corporation: An Appropriability Theory of Direct Foreign Investment' in J.N. Bhagwati (ed.), *The New International Economic Order*, MIT Press, Cambridge, MA

Magee, S.P. (1981) 'The Appropriability Theory of the Multinational Enterprise', *Annals of the American Academy of Political and Social Science, 458*, 123-35

Mansfield, E. and A. Romeo (1980) 'Technology Transfer to Overseas Subsidiaries by US-based Firms', *Quarterly Journal of Economics, 92*, 737-50

Mansfield, E., A. Romeo and S. Wagner (1979) 'Foreign Trade and US Research and Development', *Review of Economics and Statistics, 61*, 49-57

Markusen, J.R. (1984) 'Multinationals, Multi-plant Economies and the Gains from Trade', *Journal of International Economies, 14* (forthcoming)

Maule, C.J. (1968) 'Antitrust and the Takeover Activity of American Firms in Canada', *Journal of Law and Economics, 11*, 423-32

Maule, C.J. (1969) 'Antitrust and the Takeover Activity of American Firms in Canada: A Rejoinder', *Journal of Law and Economics, 12*, 419-24

Maule, C.J. (1970) 'Antitrust and the Takeover Activity of American Firms in Canada: A Final Comment', *Journal of Law and Economics, 13*, 261

McCharles, D.C. (1983) 'Specialization, Intra-industry Trade and Canada's Changing

Industrial Structure', paper presented at a Symposium on Intra-industry Trade and Industrial Structural Adjustment Policies, Brussels (May 5–6)

McClain, D.S. (1974) 'Foreign Direct Investment in United States Manufacturing and the Theory of Direct Investment', PhD thesis, Department of Economics, MIT, Cambridge, MA

McClain, D.S. (1983) 'Foreign Direct Investment in the United States: Old Currents, "New Waves", and the Theory of Direct Investment' in C.P. Kindleberger and D.B. Audretsch (eds), *The Multinational Corporation in the 1980s*, MIT Press, Cambridge, MA

McCulloch, R. (1983) *Unexpected Real Consequences of Floating Exchange Rates*, Essays in International Finance, No. 153, International Finance Section, Department of Economics, Princeton University, Princeton, NJ

McCulloch, R. and R.F. Owen (1983) 'Linking Negotiations on Trade and Foreign Direct Investment' in C.P. Kindleberger and D.B. Audretsch (eds), *The Multinational Corporation in the 1980s*, MIT Press, Cambridge, MA

Mueller, C. (1973) 'Monopoly' in R. Nader (ed.), *The Consumer and Corporate Accountability*, Harcourt Brace Jovanovich, New York

Musgrave, P.B. (1975) *Direct Foreign Investment Abroad and the Multinationals: Effects on the United States Economy*, US Senate Foreign Relations Committee, Washington, DC

Musgrave, P.B. (1978) Submission to the Hearings Before the Subcommittee of the Committee on Government Operations, *The Operations of Federal Agencies in Monitoring, Reporting on and Analyzing Foreign Investments in the United States, 3*, US House of Representatives, Washington, DC, 691–3

Nelson, R.R. (1981) 'Competition, Innovation, Productivity Growth, and Public Policy', in H. Giersch (ed.), *Towards an Explanation of Economic Growth*, J.C.B. Mohr, Tuebingen

Newfarmer, R.S. (1979) 'Oligopolistic Tactics to Control Markets and the Growth of Transnational Corporations in Brazil's Electrical Industry', *Journal of Development Studies, 15*, 108–40

Norman, G. (1981) *Spatial Competition and Spatial Price Discrimination: An Extension*, University of Reading Discussion Papers in Urban and Regional Economics, No. 7, Reading

Norman, G. (1983) 'Spatial Pricing with Differentiated Products', *Quarterly Journal of Economics, 98*, 291–311

Olson, M. (1965) *The Logic of Collective Action*, Harvard University Press, Cambridge, MA

Olson, M. (1982) *The Rise and Decline of Nations*, Yale University Press, New Haven, CT

Organisation for Economic Cooperation and Development (1981) *Recent International Investment Trends*, OECD, Paris

Organisation for Economic Cooperation and Development (1983) *Detailed Benchmark Definition of Foreign Direct Investment*, OECD, Paris

Ozawa, T. (1979a) *Multinationalism, Japanese Style*, Princeton University Press, Princeton, NJ

Ozawa, T. (1979b) 'International Investment and Industrial Structure: New Theoretical Implications From the Japanese Experience', *Oxford Economic Papers, 31*, 72–92

Parry, T.G. (1979) 'Competition and Monopoly in Multinational Corporation

Relations with Host Countries' in R.G. Hawkins (ed.), *The Economic Effects of Multinational Corporations*, JAI Press, Greenwich, CT

Penrose, E. (1971) 'The State and Multinational Enterprises in Less-Developed Countries' in J.H. Dunning (ed.), *The Multinational Corporation*, George Allen & Unwin, London

Porter, M.G. (1980) *Competitive Strategy*, Free Press, New York

Posner, R. (1970) 'A Statistical Study of Antitrust Enforcement', *Journal of Law and Economics, 13*, 365–421

Pugel, T.A. (1978) *International Market Linkages and US Manufacturing: Prices, Profits, and Patterns*, Ballinger, Cambridge, MA

Reuber, G. (1969) 'Antitrust and the Takeover Activity of American Firms In Canada: A Further Analysis', *Journal of Law and Economics, 12*, 405–17

Reuber, G. (1970) 'Antitrust and the Takeover Activity of American Firms in Canada: A Reply', *Journal of Law and Economics, 13*, 257–9

Reuber, G., H. Crookell, M. Emerson and G. Gallias-Hammano (1973) *Private Foreign Investment in Development*, Development Centre of the OECD, Oxford

Reynolds, R. (1976) 'Intermarket Symmetry and Stable Collusion' (mimeo), Economic Planning Office, US Department of Justice, Washington, DC

Richardson, J.D. (1971) 'Theoretical Considerations in the Analysis of Foreign Direct Foreign Investment', *Western Economic Journal, 9*, 87–98

Robertson, D. (1971) 'The Multinational Enterprise: Trade Flows and Trade Policy' in J.H. Dunning (ed.), *The Multinational Corporation*, George Allen & Unwin, London

Rousslang, D.J. (1982) 'The Effects of Performance Requirements on US Auto Trade with Brazil and Mexico' (mimeo), US International Trade Commission, Washington, DC

Rowe, F. (1981) 'Commentary: Antitrust as Ideology' in 'Surveys of Foreign Antitrust Laws', *Antitrust Law Journal, 50*, 721–9

Rugman, A.M. (1977) 'Risk, Direct Foreign Investment, and International Diversification', *Weltwirtschaftliches Archiv, 113*, 487–500

Rugman, A.M. (1979) *International Diversification and the Multinational Enterprise*, D.C. Heath, Lexington, MA

Rugman, A.M. (1980a) 'Internalization as a General Theory of Foreign Direct Investment: A Re-Appraisal of the Literature', *Weltwirtschaftliches Archiv, 116*, 365–79

Rugman, A.M. (1980b) *Multinationals in Canada: Theory, Performance and Economic Impact*, Martinus Nijhoff, Boston

Rugman, A.M. (1981) *Inside the Multinationals: The Economics of Internal Markets*, Croom Helm, London and Columbia University Press, New York

Rugman, A.M. (ed.) (1982) *New Theories of the Multinational Enterprise*, Croom Helm, London and St Martin's Press, New York

Rugman, A.M. (ed.) (1983) *Multinationals and Technology Transfer: The Canadian Experience*, Praeger, New York

Rugman, A.M. and D.J. Lecraw (1985) *International Business*, McGraw-Hill, New York (forthcoming)

Schelling, T.C. (1960) *The Strategy of Conflict*, Harvard University Press, Cambridge, MA

Scherer, F.M. (1967) 'Research and Development Resource Allocation Under

Rivalry', *Quarterly Journal of Economics, 81*, 359–94

Scherer, F.M. (1980) *Industrial Market Structure and Economic Performance*, Rand McNally, Chicago

Schlieder, W. (1981) 'European Competition Policy' in 'Surveys of Foreign Antitrust Laws', *Antitrust Law Journal, 50*, 647–98

Schmalensee, R. (1982) 'Product Differentiation Advantage of Pioneering Brands', *American Economic Review, 72*, 349–65

Schumpeter, J.A. (1950) *Capitalism, Socialism and Democracy*, 3rd edn, Harper and Row, New York

Servan-Schrieber, J.J. (1967) *The American Challenge*, Hamish Hamilton, London

Siegfried, J. (1975) 'The Determinants of Antitrust Activity', *Journal of Law and Economics, 18*, 559–74

Stern, R.M. (1980) 'Changes in US Comparative Advantage: Issues for Research and Policy' in R.R. Piekarz, S. Okubo and A.I. Rapoport (eds), *International Economic Policy Research*, National Science Foundation, Washington, DC

Stewart, F. (1981) 'International Technology Transfer: Issues and Policy Options' in P. Streeten and R. Jolly (eds), *Recent Issues in World Development*, Pergamon Press, Oxford

Stobaugh, R. (1968) 'The Product Life Cycle, US Exports, and International Investment', Doctor of Business Administration thesis, Harvard University, Cambridge, MA

Stocking, G. and M. Watkins (1951) *Monopoly and Free Enterprise*, Twentieth Century Fund, New York

Strickland, A. (1977) 'Conglomerate Mergers, Mutual Forebearance Behavior and Price Competition' (mimeo), University of Delaware, Newark, DE

Teece, D.J. (1981) 'The Multinational Enterprise, Market Failure and Market Power Considerations', *Sloan Management Review, 22*, 3–17

Teece, D.J. (1982) 'A Transactions Cost Theory of the Multinational Enterprise', University of Reading Discussion Papers in International Investment and Business Studies, No. 66, Reading

Teece, D.J. (1983) 'Technology and Organisational Factors in the Theory of the Multinational Enterprise' in M.C. Casson (ed.), *The Growth of International Business*, George Allen & Unwin, London

Tharakan, P.K. (1982) 'The Economics of Intra-industry Trade: A Survey', Paper 82/57, Centre for Development Studies, University of Antwerp

Thurow, L.C. (1980) *The Zero-Sum Society*, Basic Books, New York

Tschoegl, A. (1982) 'Foreign Bank Entry into Japan and California' in A.M. Rugman (ed.), *New Theories of the Multinational Enterprise*, Croom Helm, London and St Martin's Press, New York

Uesugi, A. (1981) 'Japanese Antimonopoly Policy – Its Past and Future' in 'Surveys of Foreign Antitrust Laws', *Antitrust Law Journal, 50*, 709–19

United Nations (1978) *Transnational Corporations in World Development: A Re-examination*, UN, New York

United States Department of Commerce (1976) *Foreign Direct Investment in the United States, 1*, US Government Printing Office, Washington, DC

United States Department of Justice (1977) *Antitrust Guide for International Operations*, US Government Printing Office, Washington, DC

United States Federal Trade Commission (1967) *Webb-Pomerene Associations: A 50-Year Review*, US Government Printing Office, Washington, DC

Vernon, R. (1966) 'International Investment and International Trade in the Product Cycle', *Quarterly Journal of Economics, 80*, 190–207

Vernon, R. (1968) *Manager in the International Economy*, Prentice-Hall, Englewood Cliffs, NJ

Vernon, R. (1970) 'Foreign Enterprises and Developing Nations in Raw Materials Industries', *American Economic Review, 60*, 122–6

Vernon, R. (1971) *Sovereignty at Bay*, Basic Books, New York

Vernon, R. (1974) 'The Location of Economic Activity' in J.H. Dunning (ed.), *Economic Analysis and the Multinational Enterprise*, George Allen & Unwin, London

Vernon, R. (1974) 'Competition Policy Towards Multinational Corporations', *American Economic Review, 64*, 276–82

Vernon, R. (1977) *Storm Over the Multinationals*, Harvard University Press, Cambridge, MA

Vernon, R. (1981) 'Organizational and Institutional Responses to International Risk' (mimeo), Harvard University, Cambridge, MA

Vernon, R. and W.H. Davidson (1979) 'Foreign Production of Technology-Intensive Products by US-Based Multinational Enterprises', Harvard University Graduate School of Business Administration Working Paper 79–5, Cambridge, MA

Watson, C. (1982) 'Counter-Competition Abroad to Protect Home Markets', *Harvard Business Review, 60*, 40–2

Wells, L.T., Jr (1977) 'The Internationalization of Firms from Developing Countries' in T. Agmon and C. Kindleberger (eds), *Multinationals from Small Countries*, MIT Press, Cambridge, MA

Wilkins, M. (1970) *The Emergence of Multinational Enterprise*, Harvard University Press, Cambridge, MA

Wilkins, M. (1974) *The Maturing of Multinational Enterprise*, Harvard University Press, Cambridge, MA

Wilkins, M. (1977) 'Crosscurrents: American Investments in Europe, European Investments in the United States' in P. Uselding (ed.), *Business and Economic History, 6*, Bureau of Economic and Business Research, University of Illinois, Urbana, IL

Wilkins, M. (1983) 'History of Foreign Investments in the United States' (unpublished draft), Florida International University, Miami, FL

Williamson, O.E. (1975) *Markets and Hierarchies: Analysis and Antitrust Implications*, Free Press, New York

Williamson, O.E. (1981) 'The Modern Corporation: Origins, Evolution, Attributes', *Journal of Economic Literature, 19*, 1537–69

Willmore, L. (1979) 'The Industrial Economics of Intra-industry Trade and Specialisation' in H. Giersch (ed.), *On the Economics of Intra-industry Trade*, J.C.B. Mohr, Tuebingen

Yannopoulos, G. (1983) 'The Growth of Transnational Banking' in M.C. Casson (ed.), *The Growth of International Business*, George Allen & Unwin, London

CONTRIBUTORS

Bela Balassa
Johns Hopkins University
Baltimore, Maryland,
and the World Bank
Washington, DC

Harvey E. Bale, Jr
Office of the US Trade
Representative
Washington, DC

Michael R. Czinkota
Georgetown University
Washington, DC

John H. Dunning
University of Reading
Whiteknights, Reading

William F. Finan
US Department of Commerce
Washington, DC

Edward M. Graham
University of North Carolina
Chapel Hill, North Carolina

Gene M. Grossman
Princeton University
Princeton, New Jersey

Robert G. Hawkins
New York University
New York, New York

Jean-Francois Hennart
University of Pennsylvania
Philadelphia, Pennsylvania

Irving B. Kravis
University of Pennsylvania
Philadelphia, Pennsylvania

Paul R. Krugman
Massachusetts Institute of
Technology
Cambridge, Massachusetts

Robert E. Lipsey
Queens College of CUNY and the
National Bureau of Economic
Research, New York, New York

Rachel McCulloch
University of Wisconsin
Madison, Wisconsin

Philip Nelson
US Federal Trade Commission
Washington, DC

George Norman
University of Reading
Whiteknights, Reading

William W. Nye
US Department of Justice
Washington, DC

David A. Ricks
University of South Carolina
Columbia, South Carolina

Donald J. Rousslang
US International Trade Commission
Washington, DC

Alan M. Rugman
Dalhousie University
Halifax, Nova Scotia

Louis Silvia
US Federal Trade Commission
Washington, DC

Raymond Vernon
Harvard University
Cambridge, Massachusetts

Frank G. Vukmanic
US Department of the Treasury
Washington, DC

INDEX

205